THE TEEN INTERPRETER

ALSO BY TERRI APTER

Passing Judgment: Praise and Blame in Everyday Life

Difficult Mothers: Understanding and Overcoming Their Power

What Do You Want from Me?: Learning to Get Along with In-Laws

The Sister Knot: Why We Fight, Why We're Jealous, and Why We'll Love Each Other No Matter What

The Confident Child: Raising Children to Believe in Themselves

You Don't Really Know Me: Why Mothers and Daughters Fight and How Both Can Win

The Myth of Maturity: What Teenagers Need from Parents to Become Adults

Secret Paths: Women in the New Midlife

Working Women Don't Have Wives: Professional Success in the 1990s

Altered Loves: Mothers and Daughters during Adolescence

THE TEEN INTERPRETER

A GUIDE TO THE CHALLENGES AND JOYS OF RAISING ADOLESCENTS

TERRI APTER

W. W. NORTON & COMPANY
Independent Publishers Since 1923

The Teen Interpreter is a general information resource for parents. The names and identifying details of all study participants have been changed. This book is not a substitute for individualized professional advice. Standards of clinical practice and protocol change over time, and no technique or recommendation is guaranteed to be effective in all circumstances. If your teen is talking about suicide or is committing acts of self-harm, seek professional advice and support as soon as possible. If your teen has an eating disorder or is experiencing panic attacks, or for other case-specific questions and guidance, you also should seek professional advice and support.

Printed in the United States of America
First Edition

For information about permission to reproduce selections from this book, write to
Permissions, W. W. Norton & Company, Inc., 500 Fifth Avenue, New York, NY 10110

For information about special discounts for bulk purchases, please contact
W. W. Norton Special Sales at specialsales@wwnorton.com or 800-233-4830

Manufacturing by Lakeside Book Company
Production manager: Devon Zahn

Library of Congress Cataloging-in-Publication Data

Names: Apter, T. E., author.
Title: The teen interpreter : a guide to the challenges and joys of raising adolescents / Terri Apter.
Description: First edition. | New York, NY : W. W. Norton & Company, [2022] | Includes bibliographical references and index.
Identifiers: LCCN 2021052465 | ISBN 9781324006510 (hardcover) | ISBN 9781324006527 (epub)
Subjects: LCSH: Parent and teenager. | Adolescent psychology. | Teenagers. | Parenting.
Classification: LCC HQ799.15 .A6784 2022 | DDC 306.874—dc23/eng/20211108
LC record available at https://lccn.loc.gov/2021052465

W. W. Norton & Company, Inc., 500 Fifth Avenue, New York, N.Y. 10110
www.wwnorton.com

W. W. Norton & Company Ltd., 15 Carlisle Street, London W1D 3BS

1 2 3 4 5 6 7 8 9 0

To Miranda and Julia

who introduced me to the joys and challenges of parenting teens

CONTENTS

THE TEEN INTERPRETER

INTRODUCTION

JUDY SITS in her kitchen relishing the morning's rare quiet moments. Today she doesn't have to be at work until noon, so there is no frantic clock watching. Noises coming from the bathroom assure her that her fourteen-year-old daughter Kirsty is awake. Today, at least, she will not have to shout, "Time to get up." Today she will not be "that parent who is always on her case" as Kirsty says, nor endure the sound of her own stressed-out voice as she tells her daughter to "get going."

Hearing the shuffle of Kirsty's oversize slippers, Judy looks up from her phone. Her daughter's tousled hair and sleepy face fill her with tenderness and joy. There is a distinctive adolescent edge, particularly in the sideways glance and grunt of greeting, but the adorable, adoring child is retained in the familiar features and luminous skin, delectable and kissable. A low chuckle emerges from her throat. Kirsty blinks twice, as though her mother's pleasure pains her.

Judy glances back to her phone. Her lips press together and she breathes in and out, deep and slow, resetting her positive mood. "Breakfast?" she suggests brightly. "How 'bout some porridge today? Or toast?"

Kirsty sighs, and for a moment, with a rucked forehead and tightening lips, she looks as though she might cry. "Toast?" she repeats. "What a stupid . . . what a stupid suggestion."

Judy blanches and looks back at her phone. She concentrates on her messages. Kirsty turns away and mutters, soft but still audible, "You are *really* stupid." For a moment there is silence, and for a moment both are still. Then Judy stands up briskly and says, "Get your own breakfast."

"I always get my own breakfast," Kirsty retorts. Her tears fall now, but she slaps them away with the palm of her hand, and then reaches for a paper towel. "I want to get my own breakfast," she says as she blows her nose. This is almost an explanation, inching toward apology. "And I never eat toast." After a beat she repeats, "You know I never eat toast."

"Fine," Judy retorts. Her light mood has been extinguished. She is hurt, angry, and fed up with this impossible teen.

"You know I don't like talking when I just get up. I'm not really awake." Kirsty is pleading with her mother to understand. But Judy does not hear this plea. She sees insult and rejection only. "Fine," she repeats, unrelenting.

"Fine," Kirsty mimics. The conciliatory voice is gone. She, too, feels rejected, and insulted.

"You are impossible! There's no point talking to you. Is there?" Judy demands.

"*You're* impossible! And there's no point talking to you!" Kirsty leans against the counter, her arms crossed against her chest. The tears still come, but there are no sobs. "All you want—," she begins but pauses to gain control of her breath, "all you want is some sweet little kid." As Judy, face frozen, walks away, Kirsty calls out, "You drive me nuts." As her mother leaves the room, Kirsty kicks a chair.

It is easy to respond to this scene (one of many I witnessed in the course of three decades' observing teens and parents in their homes) with a familiar scoff, "*Teenagers!*" We know they are impossible, don't we? We know they are unreasonable. Today we even have evidence from neuroscience that teens' brains are immature, with self-control and foresight lagging way behind their physical maturity. Teens are impulsive and reckless yet long to be free from the parental control they (on some level) know they need. So what else can parents expect beyond senseless outbursts, rudeness, and rebellion?

The aim of this book is to shift parents' expectations of teens by presenting a new perspective—the perspective of teens themselves. All too often adolescence is considered a phase parents must weather by standing firmly on their higher ground, resisting rather than sharing the teen's perspective. Books on teens generally offer advice to parents about boundaries and control, along with analysis that reduces teens to hormonally driven neurotics. Adolescents' forthright observations, their exquisite sensibilities, their joys and terrors in self-discovery are belittled, marginalized, ignored. The subsequent loss of focus and respect for teens' inner world takes a heavy toll on teens and parents alike.

THE TEEN/PARENT DISRUPTION

Working with teens and parents as I have done over the past three decades is like watching a complicated interplay of passion, connection, and rejection. While filled with love, this dynamic sometimes feels very, very uncomfortable.

Many parents and teens experience a disruption in the rhythms of parent/child engagement. These rhythms begin in infancy with moment-by-moment interactions—looks, expressions, sounds, and gestures that last only seconds but are packed with meaning. These interactions may seem inconsequential, yet they are intricate, nuanced, and mutually coordinated. Each partner in this dynamic—parent and child—changes the other's inner world, adding to it, supporting it, challenging it, revising it, monitoring and validating it.

For the infant and then the child, a parent's view of the world is the trusted one. The parent is the authority on what things mean, what actions are right, and what people are expected to feel. The parent contains and manages the infant's own difficult emotions. Fear and frustration in a young child quickly reach storm levels. Screams and tantrums ensue, and a parent, often enough, calms these with soothing words and gestures, versions of "There, there, it's okay." A parent shows the child that he or she can survive emotional upheavals. There will be times, many times, when the parent's own frustrations and anger are triggered by the child's, and both explode, but as long as a parent shows her power to contain the child's difficult emotions about 30 percent of the time, she offers a model of *emotional regulation*—the ability to manage intense emotions by learning that these go as well as come, and that the child can call on others for help in weathering life's squalls.

In adolescence the microresponsiveness between parent and child is disrupted. A shift occurs away from the child's willingness to trust the parent either as a source of wisdom or as helpmate in emotional regulation. Many parents experience this shift as rejection; they tell me, "My teen now thinks I'm useless," and "My teen doesn't care what I think," and even "My teen hates me. There's no love there anymore." These parents are in effect traumatized by the loss of a bond they value. That parental attunement—the special alert parents have to signs and signals in their children—goes awry. Feeling threatened by loss of love, and by fear that they are unable to control their teen—control the teen badly needs—parents can become rigid and defensive. They are alert to signs of rejection and danger, but ignore signals of love and need.

We can see this in Judy's response to Kirsty.[1] I am not saying that the fourteen-year-old's behavior here is acceptable. It's not. Any parent of a child of any age would be frustrated, possibly infuriated, by Kirsty's rudeness. My focus, however, is not on whether parent or teen is doing something "right" or "wrong." It is on how parent and teen form a dyad, a close partnership in which together they build up or tear apart their relationship.

Rather than focusing on what, exactly, is unacceptable in this particular moment, Judy complains about Kirsty's overall character, not just her current behavior. "You are impossible" and "There's no point talking to you" signal a rupture in their relationship. Judy leaps to these extreme statements because she herself is hurt.

Yet if Judy took a closer look, if she could be the calm containing parent (as she would be if Kirsty's outburst came from a four-year-old, rather than a fourteen-year-old), she would see something else. She would see Kirsty's explanation that, in her view, her mother is "babying her." Perhaps, if Judy listened further, she might understand why her affectionate offer to get breakfast strikes her fourteen-year-old daughter as patronizing. She might even come to understand that Kirsty asks for recognition of her new individuality. Kirsty is frustrated, for example, that her mother hasn't kept up with her (new) dislike of toast.

In a calmer frame of mind, Judy would catch the apology Kirsty is offering when she says, "And you know I don't like talking when I just wake up. I'm not really awake." If she were aware of the teen's distinctive body clock, Judy would understand how the teen's moodiness might be informed by the physiological discomfort Kirsty experiences in the early morning. While parents describe teens as lazy, and blame their morning lethargy on their refusal to "go to bed on time," teens' bodies are set with a different biological timer, filled with sleep hormones in the morning and stoked by their absence in the evening.[2]

If she could interpret her teen's behavior, or see through her teen's eyes, the fear that her daughter is rejecting her would disappear. Instead, Judy would notice Kirsty's profound distress at her mother's frozen face and cold voice. She might feel empathy for her teen's irritability and impatience that combine two protests: "Why is my mother arguing with me?" and "Why am I being so awful?" Understanding her teen's perspective would transform her own responses. Instead of quarreling, parent and teen would connect.

WHY THIS BOOK?

In large part my own profession is to blame for blindness to the meanings of teens' behavior and for the relational missteps that subsequently arise. Throughout much of the last century parents were told that teens were trying to "divorce" them,[3] that adolescence was a time of separation and rebellion during which teens struggled against their childhood love and tried to depose the parent as a trusted source of knowledge. While more up-to-date research shows that teens remain closely bound to parents, intent on gaining recognition and approval, the model of adolescence as rebellion and rejection remains fixed in popular culture and in the minds of many parents.

My aim in this book is to take a new look at teens, presenting (as clearly as any adult can) the world through teenagers' eyes. I want to provide teens with an ally in self-expression and self-understanding. I want to guide parents toward new engagement with teens' struggles as they learn to name powerful emotions and make use of their emerging skills in self-reflection. I want to reintroduce parents to their teens, and teens to their parents, by highlighting the positives in this often-turbulent relationship. But no one can understand the vital and positive elements in this relationship without acknowledging its difficulties.

Not knowing how people we love see the world is profoundly disquieting. The lives of teens have changed enormously in recent decades, and parents cannot keep up. The change most commonly cited by parents is social media, which absorbs teens' attention and shapes their identity and relationships. But the texture of teens' society has changed in many other ways, too. Teens stand in the shadow of uncertain futures. They worry about their opportunities, about the environment, about their livelihood. Parents, sharing these pressures and uncertainties, want to protect their teen, but feel ill equipped to do so.

Scientific understanding of teenagers has also undergone enormous change over the past two decades. With the remarkable technology of magnetic resonance imaging, scientists now use powerful but harmless magnetic fields and radio waves to produce detailed images of the brain in living humans. Such close inspection of brains in action was not possible until the end of the last century. Now the mysteries of the distinctive teen brain, with structures and behavior different from that of either a child or adult, are gradually being revealed.

With functional magnetic resonance imaging, or fMRI, scientists detect the brain in action by tracing blood flow and oxygen levels. These indicate which brain areas are at work when decisions are being made, when we talk to someone, or when we are afraid, or in love, or bored. Through fMRI scientists can see how certain brain systems—particularly those that deal with emotions and social activity—follow distinctive routes in the teen brain.

The fascinating new discoveries of teen brain development should bring us closer to our teen, but do they? Sometimes these discoveries widen the chasm between teen and parent as teens are seen to be strange, alien, and unreachable. Presented by adults for adults, the new findings in neuroscience are often seen as deficits and immaturities. But the distinctive teen brain is highly adaptive, quick to learn, curious, and courageous. The willingness to take risks, the penchant for excitement, and the longing for adventure gear the teen up for exploration and innovation. Since the human environment is constantly changing, each generation needs new knowledge and new skills to manage its special challenges. The adolescent brain's high level of plasticity—or ability to change—allows teens to build a brain equipped to navigate the particular challenges of their world.

At the same time, teens, like their parents, want to maintain their primary and fundamental relationships. Nothing damages a relationship as much as failure to understand. Teens, like grown-ups, crave respect. Calling their feelings "crazy" and their brain "immature" insults them. It is time for the new science of adolescence to be joined to the experiences of teens in ways that do justice to their aims and intelligence and dignity.

The case histories presented in this book are based on a series of studies on teens and families I have done over the past thirty-five years, including transcripts of interviews and video footage and the diaries teens and their parents shared with me. Over sixty families from two countries—the UK and the US—from diverse backgrounds, ethnicity, and culture participated in this work. Their experiences reveal parenting as a complex dynamic that is sensitive to teens' changing lives. Many themes in the parent/teen dynamic—connection, trust, safety, growth—endure across generations, but as teens' education, communication, and leisure change, as their social and political and financial environments change, keeping up with change is a formidable task. Yet this is also an important and rewarding task, for as parents learn to interpret their teen, they become positive collaborators in the teen's mind's growth.

Parenting is not a closed system in which a line can be drawn from a parent's behavior to a teen's response. Therefore, I do not draw a blueprint for "what a parent should do" because each individual parent and each individual teen construct their own relationship, with its rhythms and meanings, embedded in a particular family and culture. Instead, I present a series of patterns showing how different actors in the parent/teen drama constantly influence one another's behavior depending on how each interprets what the other says and does.

Any parenting advice should be checked alongside the question: "Does it pass the Copernican revolution test?" This was, initially, the paradigm shift from a model of a stationary world circled by the sun, and then eventually to a far more complex and counterintuitive model of the earth not only circling the sun but following an orbit also influenced by the mass and movement of other planets.[4] In the realm of child and parent, the comparable paradigm shift moves away from a model that puts either parent or child at the stationary center around which one orbits solely in response to the other.

According to the outdated paradigm, when a child goes off course it is because of what the parent does. Or, with the child at the stationary center, genes or character are fixed, and a parent has to accept "that's who the child is." In the new paradigm, however, influences are multidirectional, and many different forces shape both the child's and the parent's pathway.

Parent and teen are a dynamic team, and the responses, assumptions, and associations of each influence the other. A teen's actions evoke responses in a parent, through hope, memory and fear, and these parental responses in turn shape teens' behavior. A parent's influence, however, is mediated through teens' environment—both the social environment in which friends' and contemporary norms are increasingly important and the teens' neurobiological environment with its fast-moving brain and body development. Interpreting teen behavior—often apparently irrational or chaotic—as goal-directed, purposeful, and intelligent helps parents understand and make the best use of their powerful bond.

1

"You don't know who I am (but I don't either)."

Teens' Alien Self

I WAS TAUGHT to fear adolescence long before I myself became a teen. Leaning against my mother as she read to me, I felt encompassed by her deep breathing and soft body. She read with a self-conscious actor's voice that distracted me from the story. I watched her mouth uttering the staged sounds, and was transfixed by the downy hairs above her upper lip. Coated with makeup, they glistened in the light of the heavy lamp on the table beside her. She was knitting as she read and the movement of her arms lifted and lowered my seven-year-old body in a gentle rocking motion. "Will you always read to me?" I asked suddenly, not waiting for a break in the story. "Even when I'm older?"

At this interruption she turned her attention from the book to the knitting. She was nearsighted and leaned forward so that her eyes were only inches from the needles. She counted the stitches in twos, sounding out the numbers in a breathy whisper. Satisfied with her stitch count, she settled into the back of the sofa and declared, "By the time you're a teenager, you won't want me to read to you. You won't listen to anything I say."

I looked around the room and tried to fix it in my mind. I wanted to preserve this memory, to anchor myself here and find protection from the stranger who was waiting to take my place. The assurance I had sought—of continuity and permanence—was shattered. Adolescence lay ahead and, whether I liked it or not, it would transform me into a stranger.

For many years I assumed this was my mother's peculiar take on who I would be as a teen. It was only two and a half decades later, when I began research on adolescence, that I learned my mother's view was a common one. "She was such a happy child. What has made her so moody?" parents ask. "He was such an open and confiding child. Why won't he talk to me now?" parents ask. Often, too, I hear, "I don't know who she is. It's as though my sweet child has been overtaken by an alien."

THE STRANGER WITHIN

The idea that in adolescence an alien invades one's lovely child marks the cultural image of a teen—a loved one turned stranger, bent on destroying the good child buried deep within. The embedded belief that adolescence disrupts their core identity does not go unnoticed by teens. A teen's sense of self is in a state of flux; this can be exciting, but a parent's misinterpretation of these changes can generate teens' confusion and fear about who they are.

My approach to adolescence is layered across generations. It includes my mother's forebodings of me as a teen. It includes my own visceral memories of what it felt like to be a teen—irritable, angry, and full of longing. It includes the tussles with my own teenage daughters, when I was stunned by their annoyance, and gripped by the dread of losing the close bond between us. Now it includes my daughter's anxiety about what her children will be like as teens. The defiance of her four-year-old fills her with as much pride as exasperation, but presents a dark image of the future: "I hate to think what a nightmare she'll be as a teenager," she sighs. And though on some level I know better, I too reflect on the openness, trust, and delight of the small child, and worry that will all be lost in adolescence.

As a psychologist, however, every time I hear a parent say, "My teen is a stranger," or, "It seems like an alien has taken over my sweet child," I want to reach out to both the parent and the teen to show that the apparent stranger is still the familiar kin and the teen still longs to be the parent's beloved child, even as she wants to establish her individual, independent identity.

This tension between continued need and longing for independence generates an ambivalence that is as confusing to the teen as it is to the parent. Teens say both "I want you to be here for me" and "I want you to leave me alone." They complain, "You don't understand me" while insisting, "Why don't you keep out of my life?" There is part of a teen that resents a parent's presence, and a part of the teen that is deeply grateful to a parent for "being there." Part of the teen wants to be left alone, and part of the teen wants to shake a parent into a new mode of attentive listening. One part shows indifference or contempt for a parent's views, and another constantly thinks about and longs for a parent's approval.

When parents complain about their "impossible" or "alien" teen, they overlook the huge part of the teen that wants to make itself known, and in seeing the teen as an alien, a parent magnifies the teen's own unease at the stranger lurking inside.

THE STRANGER IN THE MIRROR

"My how you've grown!" are words a child is delighted to hear. Getting bigger and older is a source of pride. It imbues a child with the promise of doing more, and being more. But for many teens, getting bigger and getting older are also accompanied by a sense of loss for the familiar, taken-for-granted child's body.

The teen's physical growth is rapid. I first meet Keira as a lithe eleven-year-old, filled with enthusiasm for gymnastics and animals. She showed me her newly honed double somersault. ("Do you want to see it?" she asks earnestly. "I'll show you if you want." After her routine, she glows with triumph.)

When I see her again two and a half years later, her face and welcoming smile are immediately recognizable. What strikes me is not how much she's changed—the increased height and filling out of breast and thighs are what I expected—but how her relationship with her body has changed. She sits on the sofa with legs crossed and shoulders forward. She wears an oversized sweater and bends forward, pulling the hem over her knees. As we talk, her gaze rests on me momentarily before swerving away. When I ask about gymnastics, she bites her lower lip and rubs her fingers along the sleeves of her sweater. "I don't know. It's not . . ."

I wait, and eventually she continues. "I still do it. Every

day. It's still good. Well, practice is still good. The meets—I used to like them, I guess?"

I nod, reminding her that I know, that I remember how excited she was, the proud, natural performer.

"I really really don't like them now. All those eyes towards me. Coach says, 'They're your friends. They're rooting for you.' But they're looking at you, they're not friends. They're the worst kind of judges. Even my parents. I can feel their embarrassment ready to pop out if I mess up. And they're on edge, because they expect me to mess up. That's the same with everyone. All those eyes. It's mortifying."

"Mortifying" is a word that chills. It comes from *mortis*, which in Latin means "dead." Mortification suggests a wish to disappear, to play dead in order to avoid humiliation.

"How extreme," I think, though it takes me no longer than two seconds to quash my initial response. Embarrassment is one of the strongest feelings in teens' emotional repertoires. Brain imagery shows that physical danger, for teens, arouses less fear than self-consciousness.[1] Awareness that others are looking at them, possibly in a critical way, can be excruciating. Yet I am one breath away from minimizing Keira's experience ("Everyone finds it hard to step in front of a crowd. It's just something we have to get used to") before her words resonate with what other teens have told me.

"I walk into a room, and it is as though people's eyes are boring into me." Liba, at thirteen years, said that her "breasts sprouted overnight. One day my clothes were easy, sort of like familiar? Maybe even my friends? The next day I had to suss out every one of my tops. Most of them just didn't work. They were too tight. Too revealing. I don't know how I should look anymore." As she looks in the mirror, her reflection becomes a puzzle. How do other people see her? How should she dress, how should she walk, how should she sit to tame the prying eyes? "It isn't that everyone is rude or anything. And I can sort of see they don't want to stare. They sort of try to look away. And I feel bad for them. But I feel really bad for me."

Teens are keen observers of others' responses, and Liba is aware that other people—parents, teachers, friends—are taken aback by her rapid development. She internalizes an observer's perspective, an observer who sees her as unfamiliar. She also registers their unease and wonders, "Who am I now?"

For Jonas, age fifteen, it is his voice—what he hears when he speaks and what he thinks others hear—that triggers self-consciousness. He tells me, "Talking to people used to be easy. Now whenever there's more than two people, even if they're friends, or people I know really well, I hear my own voice like it's funny, you know, not right. I have this great idea in my mind, and I start to talk—like every time I forget how useless it's going to sound. I remember as soon as I start to talk, but it's too late. I have to finish, you know, I finish a sentence and I hear this awful squeak as though my voice is suddenly mocking me." His dark skin flushes and his hand shakes as he gestures, as though giving shape to his words. He looks at me, and the flush in his cheeks deepens further. His discomfort is palpable. But he bravely continues, and I know he is fighting his own cruel inner eye, when he explains how much he misses the unselfconscious absorption of childhood. Now, he says, he feels exposed because "everyone is looking at me."

Teens develop a "looking-glass self"[2] that arises from the newly urgent question, "How do other people see me?" and the belief that "people are always watching and judging." This imaginary audience[3] shifts from applause to boos with bewildering ease. Their social media platforms—Snapchat and Instagram and TikTok and (though decreasingly for teens) Facebook—present additional fodder for preoccupation with how others see them. Teens are always "out there," displaying first one and then another version of themselves, glowing when they are "liked" and burning with shame when they are mocked or ignored.

The closest grown-ups are likely to get to the teen's day-to-day self-consciousness is in "nakedness dreams." We are at work, or performing a public duty, or being presented to dignitaries and suddenly realize (in our dream) that we are undressed. We try to escape or put on clothes, but our arms or legs won't move, and everything we do to hide just makes things worse—until we wake with a jolt and fill with relief as we realize "It was only a dream." This is what the teen feels on a daily basis—completely exposed yet unprepared to be seen. Except for teens, this is real life, not a dream.

The rapid changes—in voice, in physique, in feeling, and in thinking—are exciting, but they are also perplexing and destabilizing. Novelists are more adept than psychologists in expressing this, and Carson McCullers gives a wonderful account of teen unease through the eyes of Frankie in *The Member of the Wedding*. Frankie, like many adolescents, stands in front of a mirror and studies her new body. "In the past year she had grown four inches . . . and unless she could somehow stop herself, she would grow to be over nine feet tall. . . . She would be a freak."[4] After all, how does Frankie know that this growth spurt is not a trend? She knows she cannot control it and she knows her future self is unknown. This realization forms what she calls "the summer of fear"—the summer in which she confronts the onset of adolescence.

Teens feel pride as well as shame in their changing bodies, and excitement as well as confusion in their new powers of understanding. Wrested from the familiarity of their child's body, their task is to invent a new persona, one that will be shaped by family and friends, by what they read and watch, by how they are taught in school, by their media icons and models, and by their own emerging desires and interests. But along the way, they check and recheck the progress of their inner self with reference to how others see them.

SELF-CONSCIOUSNESS: HIS AND HERS AND THEIRS

In the caldron of physical change we see a significant divergence between the paths our girls and our boys take through the teen years. Physical growth in a teenage boy has a far more positive social impact than physical development in a teenage girl. Gender norms have broadened and flexed over the past decades, and many parents say they treat daughters and sons "just the same" but, still, a boy's physical maturity is likely to signal, "I'm okay/You don't have to constrain me." While his sister's development leads to new constraints, his suggests greater competence and often results in greater freedom.

This is the context of Liba's raw self-consciousness. Why is she suddenly told she has to put on a bathrobe before she comes down to breakfast? What is she to make of her mother's warning that she should no longer sit on her granddad's lap and cuddle him? What is she to make of her father's disapproval of the physical tussles—sometimes friendly, sometimes hostile, but always fun—she and her brother routinely enjoyed throughout childhood? How can she make sense of her father's carefully evasive gaze as she leaves the bathroom? And why does her mother utter new warnings about appropriate behavior and dress outside the home?

The gender differences that arise in the teen years are not inborn or hardwired. They arise within a culture that is permeated with ideas of what a woman should or should not be, and what a man should or should not be. In childhood, gender is usually allowed some flexibility. Girls can roughhouse and boys can cuddle. Girls can construct model cars and boys can play with dolls and dress up. It is boys who, in childhood, lose this freedom more quickly. "Man up" and "Don't be such a sissy" are still said today by parents who would be shocked if their daughter were told, "It's your job to be pretty" or "You don't need to be smart." While many parents are comfortable when their girls play with toys that in the past were seen as toys for boys, or dress in ways that once would have been seen as "like a tomboy," they still feel uneasy when a boy dons "girly" clothes or fastens ribbons to his hair. Parents often tell me that they themselves do not disapprove, but they want to protect their son from the taunts that others would hurl at him.

In early adolescence gender flexibility, for both girls and boys, vanishes. Friends and teachers and TV soaps and social media trends trumpet what it means to be female. Ideals of beauty and body skew teen girls' self-esteem, not only because they believe they fall short of these ideals, but also because how they look and whether they please others takes on a new importance. Liba's changing body changes her relationship with her grandfather and brother and father, and her mother issues new directives about what her clothes and hair and makeup signal to others. In the name of love, the people around her induct her into what they see as the realities of being a physically mature woman. In so doing, they create her as an alien both to herself and to them.

Timing of physical development—relative to friends or siblings—also affects the level of a teen's self-consciousness. Liba's physical development is early and rapid. Her parents did not expect it just yet. Her older sister, Jessica, at age fifteen, is taller than Liba but retains the thin thighs and narrow chest of childhood. As the oldest child, Jessica has calibrated her parents' expectations, and the younger daughter's physical, sexual maturity alarms them.

Jonas's discomfort, on the other hand, arises from his still-high-pitched child's voice, whereas the boys around him, particularly at the new high school he has just joined, speak with deeper tones. They move with greater ease, confident they are meeting "manly" requirements. The male norms that pop up from time to time in childhood now tighten around him like a vise. The "guy code" is activated with a single word of criticism or look of contempt—not necessarily towards Jonas himself, but towards someone like him, cuing him to the social danger of failing to comply with male norms.

Adolescence changes boys' relationships, too. Just when a son would find special benefits in being close to his mother, being called "Mama's boy" is shaming. Just when boys would benefit greatly from frank and open and intimate friendships, boy-to-boy closeness comes under the scrutiny of the gender police. As teenage boys try to convey their dependence on a close friend, they are halted with the jeer, "You sound like a homo."[5] Needing other people is, according to the guy code, a sign of weakness, or "unmanly" affections.

For teens who feel that they are not in the right body and view their emerging sexual characteristics—whether male or female—as inconsistent with who they really are, physical development feels like a betrayal, forcing them into a gender category that feels alien to them. Matt, fourteen years old, explains, "It was okay being a kid. That sense that I was really a girl didn't matter. It was kind of my special secret. Now everyone talks about me being so handsome, and they come out with all these guy words. They're talking to me, and I want to say, 'This body is wrong. This isn't me. What you see is a stranger.' But they're treating me like that stranger. Everyone, even with my Mom. She laughs at me. She thinks it's cute 'cause I'm embarrassed. But I'm just trapped in this alien body."

Parents often feel helpless as they witness the teen's self-consciousness but underestimate their power either to ease or exacerbate the teen's disrupted self, in part because they don't understand its roots.

THE TEEN'S DISRUPTED SELF

In all known cultures, in all recorded times, humans are born into relationships of care and love. From birth we engage intimately with those who care for us, and these people are most commonly our parents. Parent and baby lock together in a mutual gaze, each looking back at the other. This early, prolonged eye contact is so important to both parent and child that it is not left to chance; a brain stem reflex ensures that the baby turns to the face of the person who holds him and soon also follows the voice of that same person.

My fascination with the emerging bonds between infant and parents was awakened when, as a junior assistant, I was tasked with recording mother/baby interactions in a neonatal unit. I spent hours noting how a newborn's jerky limbs and spidery play of the hand and searching movements of the head and mouth captured a mother's gaze and triggered a responsive tension in her arm. Even when a mother chatted with a friend or watched TV, her voice and gaze reacted to the baby's small movements. A private, barely audible conversation was constantly in progress.

Three months on, in the second phase of the study, I visited the mother and baby at home. That conversation now had a clear purpose. The infant was as curious about the parent as the parent was about the infant. Parent and baby, both absorbed in this getting-to-know-you process, took turns in an exquisitely choreographed exchange. The infant would make a bid for a parent's attention if her or his gaze wandered, with cooing sounds or an intensified gaze, often accompanied with a small kick or stiffening body. A parent then responded to this invitation, often by imitating, with a slight exaggeration, the sound the baby makes, or the expression on the baby's face.

An infant's despair at failing to secure such responsive attention from a parent is overwhelming. A nonresponsive parent, with a still or "frozen" face, sets a baby on a descent into despair. Within a short, two-minute period,[6] we can hear the primitive wails that signal terror, as though of abandonment and danger, even when the infant remains safe in a parent's presence.

Through responsive interactions with an adult, the infant learns that someone is curious about her, understands her, is able to meet her needs, and cares what she feels. When the parent shows indifference, loses curiosity, and fails to engage, the baby feels a loss of anchor, very much like a loss of self. When the parent shows interest and engagement, the infant or child enjoys what the psychologist and psychoanalyst Peter Fonagy calls an "epistemic match"—that satisfying "click" of feeling understood, connected, and accepted.[7]

The interpersonal "match"—the sense that someone is working hard to know you and wants to know you as you are—is never perfect. Many missteps occur along the way in both infancy and childhood, as parent and child negotiate one another's needs and demands. In the teen years, however, the number of missteps escalates. Teens grow impatient with interactions they enjoyed in childhood. The parent's familiar gestures and words of encouragement and comfort are rejected as "lame" or "useless" or "stupid." The once taken-for-granted "epistemic trust"—the belief that the other is basically good, and that each has a profound interest in and desire to understand the other's needs—falters, and is often replaced by fear and anxiety.

What undermines the foundations so painstakingly constructed in infancy and childhood? More than anything it is parents' failure to grasp the teen's new inner world, with its emotional upheaval, self-consciousness, and self-doubt. The teen is now building and imagining a new personal identity, and in the process their thoughts and feelings seem more opaque than ever. Yet in place of the curiosity parents showed to a child, there is facile labeling. "You are a teenager, so you are confused/immature/hormonal/rebellious." But none of these terms is quite right. None fits the teen's experience of her inner life. Teens, still deeply attached to a parent, still dependent on a parent to "read" their internal world, feel let down by parents who see the teen as alien. When a parent says, "An alien has taken over my child," teens, if unsupported by a parent's understanding, feel alien to themselves.[8]

It is not only teens who experience an alien self. We make a mistake, and a punitive inner voice sneers, "How could you be so stupid?" and "You always mess up." An alien self—one that deserves to be attacked and punished—comes to the fore. But as grown-ups, we are more likely to then switch to our familiar self, one that sometimes makes mistakes but generally does the best she can. Teens, however, remain caught up in negative reflections. Each social misstep, every sign of awkwardness, is magnified. Self-critical and self-conscious, they often see themselves through faults they fear others see.[9] When parents express exasperation and complain, "I can't understand you!" they unwittingly reinforce their teen's alien self. "How," the teen ponders, "can I be good or worthwhile if my parent no longer understands me?"

GENERATIONAL DIVIDES

Many parents insist that teens today are more alien than previous teen generations because they are growing up in an alien world, shaped by new technologies and global influences. Yet belief in a generational divide stretches across history. In the fourth century BC the philosopher Aristotle complained that young people "think they know everything," while lacking the real wisdom of their parents. Today's teens, like those in the fourth century, also think they know better, and fault their parents' generation with endangering, through greed and carelessness, their future well-being. The parents of today's teens, much like parents in the fourth century, think teens' wisdom is compromised by inexperience. The difference is that today's teens really do engage with new technologies that magnify the historical generational divide.

A private network nestles in plain sight, but, to parents, it seems unknowable. Teens "follow" and engage with celebrities and "influencers" their parents know nothing about. This is more, parents insist, than a complaint about "kids these days."[10] When I suggest that their fears are simply an updated version of the 1950s alarm over television—which was then seen as a danger to youth, damaging their eyes, their attention spans, and their brains—I am told, "No. This is different."

Today's screen time is indeed different from the television screen of the 1950s. It is interactive, more compelling, and highly immersive. The teen's phone is often as tattered, worn, and filthy as a toddler's teddy. Like the child's favorite toy, it remains close at all times, day and night. "What would it mean to you to lose your phone, or have it taken away?" I ask teens. "My life is on it. It would be losing everything," Arjun, fifteen, says. Losing her digital devices, eighteen-year-old Kayla told another researcher, would be "like losing a baby."[11]

Teens' engagement with social media comes in many forms, and will be discussed in many different contexts in this book, including friendships, isolation, anxiety, self-harm, and self-image. I start here, however, by showing how parent/teen tension about social media and digital devices offers a clear example of how parental anxiety about the generational divide—how different kids are, these days—can lead to a relational rift.

Teens believe that parents are "hysterical" or "stupid" or "clueless" about smartphones and their dangers. "My mom hears something on the news, like 'oh wow, there's porn on the Internet.' Right away, it's like, 'Oh you have to be careful,' or, 'Let me see what you're looking at. Show me!' It makes me so mad. I'll be looking at some joke or something, or posts of people, something she can't get her head around."

Arjun's mother, Saema, stares at the screen on her son's phone and, though she is relieved that it is not porn, she cannot fathom what it is that so absorbs her son's attention. "How can so little be so entertaining?" she asks. And there are other concerns she shares with many parents: "How can I tell if my child is exposed to sexual predators, or suffers from cyber bullying, or is enticed into pornography or gambling, while sitting apparently 'safe and secure' at home?" Alongside these acute concerns are more general worries: "How much time is she wasting?" and "Shouldn't he be getting more exercise?"

Parents report that while they are strict with children and ensure there are parental controls on children's Internet access, they allow their teens more freedom. But this is not how teens see it. Teens complain about the eye-rolling ignorance of their parents, their high-handed authoritarian approach ("It's all about 'You do it my way, or I'm going to take that phone away' " or 'Turn that thing off! Is it off? Let me see if it's off!' "), and their "constant worry over nothing."

Each day parents tackle micro decisions involving a teen's phone use. They want to monitor the time and content, but also want to "show I basically trust her." Some teens, in an effort to waylay a parent's anxiety, decide, "It's easier to lie. I say I'm talking to [a friend my mother knows], instead of explaining what I'm really doing. Or I say I'm looking up something for school, when I'm just scrolling through makeup sites." Some teens bide their time until a parent's attention focuses elsewhere. "I just sort of nod, 'Yeah, I'm careful. Yeah, it's fine.' Eventually they're distracted by something else."

Another far more successful teen strategy is to take on the role of teacher. Luis, sixteen, showed his parents what he was doing—how he found interesting news items, how he could connect with famous people by sending them comments. He offered to help his parents with any technical questions they had in using their phones. This approach diffused his parents' anxiety, gave him more freedom, and provided the opportunity for new closeness. As we'll see over and over again, when parents are persuaded to learn from their teen, they are more likely to avoid conflict and foster closeness.

A NORMAL CRISIS FOR BOTH TEENS AND PARENTS

Here, then, are some of the markers of the teen's world: changing bodies that generate baffling behavior in others; minds that are newly sensitive to others' perspective; thrilling new emotions that undergo unpredictable upheaval and reversal. These familiar markers of adolescence are today exacerbated by parents' anxiety about new digital influences they do not understand.

It is not surprising that adolescence has been called a period of *normal crisis*—that is, a period of acute tension, with a sense of change, uncertainty, and even danger, but also normal, and a necessary phase of development.[12] It feels extreme, even abnormal, but it is healthy.

In a crisis we feel that something basic in our life can no longer be managed in the usual way. For teens, it may be their own feelings or their relationships with friends or parents that seem unmanageable. Or maybe their identity—their sense of who they are—loses shape and coherence. When someone we love undergoes a crisis, we do too, because we no longer know how to respond or communicate or support that person. The ways parents have dealt with a child's problems in the past—simple praise to offer encouragement, the pressure on an arm to reassure, the sharp word to end bad behavior—no longer work. When parents discover that their usual approaches to a son or daughter go awry, they ask, "Where are the signposts?" and "Who am I as a parent?" They, too, feel threatened with the loss of a basic element in their lives. Both parent and teen lose the rhythm of their daily love. The relationship itself seems alien.

A common response to our own inability to deal with a problem is to blame someone else. "You are impossible!" we say (or think)—and with this exasperation signal that a teen is "beyond understanding" or "makes no sense." Parent and teen are placed in opposite camps, one intelligible, the other beyond reason. This division threatens the bond between them.

To preserve this profoundly important relationship, and to be there for our teen, we have to find a way to transform what seems impossible into something possible. The first step is the most difficult: it is to see our own role in our teen's particular crisis. Are we demonstrating curiosity about a teen's thoughts and feelings? Do we show this in a positive way, so that we listen and learn and work towards understanding?

As we identify the parts of the relationship that need mending, it is equally important to see which parts still work well. Influenced by embedded theories of adolescence, parents often believe that some parts that still work well are the parts that are broken, and try to make the broken—or changed—parts keep working in the same familiar way.

For example, some parents think the love and closeness they had with a child is inevitably lost during the teen years. They believe that they should "let go" as the teen (so they believe) tries to "separate" from them. This misconception about what teens need from parents was set down by Anna Freud, who—in spite of her stunning work in child development—saw adolescence as the psychological version of divorce between teen and parent.[13] The long reach of this distorted theory has left its mark, even though recent research shows that teens continue to love and need their parents, and benefit from their closeness throughout adolescence.

Unfortunately, many parents think that a difficult teen requires less understanding and greater control. Lynn says, "I have to shout, otherwise he won't hear me." But in fact, a parent's voice, to the teen's ear, is amplified. Every remark has a loud and lasting echo. While a parent believes the teen "thinks s/he knows best," teens feel bewildered by their own shifting feelings and thoughts. While parents despair when they think their teen is disorganized, "all over the place," or "a complete mess and completely oblivious," teens know their minds are hectic, messy places, enthralling but also daunting. And rarely do teens know how to convey—especially to their parents—their ambivalent feelings and their continuing love.

Parents of teens therefore need to reawaken the warm, respectful curiosity they had as a parent of a young child, asking, "Who are you?" and "What do you need?" This curiosity, as I shall show, needs to be responsive to the teen's signals, "This is what I am feeling" and "This is what I want from you." Subsequent chapters provide a guide towards developing and using that essential curiosity.

OVERVIEW AND EXERCISES

Teens want to understand themselves and shape who they'll become, but along the way, they want their parents beside them, cheering them on and offering a hand when they trip up. They do not want, when they engage with a parent, to see a reflection of the tormented alien within.

There is no official road map or instruction book for parenting your teen. The best that can be offered is a series of exercises, setting out things to try, with reminders of what you are aiming for. As the revolutionary model of teen and parent suggests, it is not so much the teen who needs changing as the teen/parent relationship. This relationship can only thrive when parents show genuine curiosity about the teen's evolving identity.[14] Parents need to be attuned to the teen's inner world, just as they were when they mirrored the infant's gestures, sounds, and facial expressions.

Since their teens are changing rapidly, parents' responses and "mirroring" must change too. Parents need to adapt to new information, not only the information a teen reports but also information a teen expresses. Without this, parents forgo the opportunity to collaborate with their teens on self-understanding and growth. Throughout the book practical guidelines are offered to help parents partner their teen's development. Below are some starting points:

> Look out for opportunities for the teen to take a lead and be the teacher. Spend time doing things together, things your teen likes to do, so it isn't all about you telling them what's what or you teaching them. Let teens introduce you to things. Ask them to recommend books or TV shows or people to follow on social media.

> Ask questions to get a clearer view. Even when you think you understand your teen, it is useful to check that you grasp the teen's meaning. This is sometimes a challenge, particularly when your teen seems unwilling to engage with you. When "How was your day?" doesn't get a satisfactory answer, don't give up. Ask more specific questions. "Did you see your friend?" and, "How

was he?" Or "Were your new boots comfortable?" and "How was the journey from school?" Small, specific topics can be a starting point for broader issues. Encourage a back-and-forth conversation. By showing interest and curiosity, you become a collaborator as your teen engages in self-reflection.

Make sure that conversations focused on the parent's agenda—about what the teen should do and how the teen should behave—do not outnumber conversations in which you seek understanding from the teen.

Your teen is still very sensitive to your responses, and quick to channel your emotions. When a teen says something extreme ("Everyone thinks I'm ugly/awkward/a loser"), you may be upset, but try not to amplify the teen's fears by showing your anxiety. Instead, remain as calm as possible and show interest in the teen's feelings. Ask questions about the situation, or ask for details. Think of your task as lookout for any window the teen is willing to open. Your teen is likely to interpret your interested patience as a show of respect—and respect is what they crave.

As you engage with your teen, keep in mind the teen's looking-glass self, and how it magnifies and distorts other people's perspective. Some conversations will help teens moderate their own social anxiety. "Are you sure people thought that?" "Why?" "What else might they be thinking?" "How bad would it be if someone thought that?" "Is it likely that everyone thought the same thing?"

Parents cannot get this right all the time. They are busy. They have their own distractions and can sometimes be overwhelmed by their own problems. But your teen does not need you to get things right every time. Your teen simply needs you to have a feel of what getting it right means, and be willing to work at it.

As a psychologist, mother, grandmother, and one-time teenager, I hope to bridge the chasm between teen and parent. This bridge will close the mutual bafflement between a parent who is terrified by a teen's chaotic development and a teen who is confounded by a parent who seems unable and even unwilling to know her.

2

"I feel like my mind is exploding."

The Astonishing Teenage Brain

THE CHANGES and challenges in teen behavior are often put down to "raging hormones." Teens are awash with new hormones that trigger puberty and are marked by the outward signs of sexual maturity—body hair, increase in height and body fat, and voice changes in boys and breast development in girls. But adolescence is far more than a period of biological development. It is also a unique period of psychological and social growth during which the brain itself is undergoing intensive remodeling. This developmental window presents an opportunity for individual teens to acquire skills and absorb knowledge that will serve them well as adults, but this hectic process also poses risks. In probing the secrets of the teen brain, parents will be able to guide and protect its growth.

EXUBERANT BRAIN GROWTH

The period from birth to the age of three years is sometimes referred to as a period of exuberant mental growth. The infant's new world is a constant adventure. Every experience stimulates the brain and presents opportunities to form or test a new belief about how this world works, and every second thousands of new connections form in the brain. But there is a second, less widely recognized phase of exuberant brain growth—adolescence.

Until recently, it was thought that adolescence—as opposed to puberty—was not a true developmental phase. Unlike infancy and childhood, adolescence was said to be an artificial phase imposed by modern societies. After all, most teens reach adult height in mid-adolescence and are sexually mature—capable of human reproduction—long before adolescence ends. The brain, too, reaches adult *size* by the age of ten years (or so), and many teens have the intellectual acumen, when it comes to dealing with abstract thoughts and reasoning, of an adult.

It therefore seemed reasonable to conclude that teens were, in objective, biological terms, grown up, and that it was only society that delayed their entry into adulthood. But during the past twenty years scientists have gained previously undreamt-of access to the brains of living humans.[1] Their discoveries have delivered shock waves to the understanding of adolescence.

Before the development of advanced brain-imaging technology, scientists overlooked the second period of exuberant brain growth because in adolescence the brain actually decreases in size by about 1.5 percent each year. But brain mass is a crude indicator of brain growth; in fact, this decrease in mass is actually a refinement of the brain, and it is accompanied by a different kind of growth—a growth in brain networks.

The brain is made of two materials—gray matter and white matter. The cells, with their branches and antennae, form the gray matter. These cells grow rapidly in late childhood, and by the teen years they form a dense and tangled mass. Messages from the executive control center (which manages the "thinking ahead" part of the brain) to the reward center (which seeks out pleasure and excitement) sometimes travel via inefficient routes. Messages containing "This is too much of a risk" and "You are too excited, calm down" and "Have some patience" navigate zigzag routes through weak neural fibers that will not attain adult robustness until the age of twenty-four years.

We can now understand the lament of the Shepherd in Shakespeare's *The Winter's Tale*, who said, "I would there were no age between ten and three and twenty, or that youth would sleep out the rest: for there is nothing (in the between), but getting wenches with child, wronging the Ancientry, stealing, fighting."[2] Here Shakespeare was way ahead of his time in pinning down the long stretch of adolescence—from late childhood to young adulthood, longer than the teen years with which it is usually associated.

But what Shakespeare's Shepherd did not know when he wished there were no age between ten and twenty-three is that the adolescent brain presents enormous opportunity and undergoes essential work. Through the dense gray matter an endless number of pathways can, potentially, be mapped. This mapping is what the teen is doing in everyday life, in moment-to-moment interactions—discovering and marking pathways that eventually will become strong and streamlined.[3]

This streamlining process is referred to as synaptic pruning. The brain circuits that are not useful—or not used—are pared away, while those that are used become stronger. The decline in the teen brain's gray matter leads to a more efficient brain. While gray matter decreases, the brain's white matter, or myelin, increases. Myelin is the white fatty substance that covers the stem-like protrusions (axons) of brain cells and, just like the plastic layer over wires, protects them. With more of this fatty white coating, a brain cell becomes more efficient. Impulses traveling through a coated circuit are one hundred times faster than those traveling through an uncoated one.

Every time we activate a specific brain circuit, we provide it with more myelin, and the connection strengthens. The more we study something, the more likely we are to remember it. The more we practice that piano piece, the more easily we can access our memory of it. This is the science behind the saying "Practice makes perfect." In our daily lives we feel the effects of myelination even if we do not know the science behind it.

The pruning, shaping, and strengthening of brain circuits are done by teens themselves, by what they do, feel, and think, over and over again. Their own needs, interests, experiences, and passions oversee the process of forming new connections. And so it is that the teen's brain is remodeled, custom designed for—and by—each individual teen.

This is why teens can be such fast learners. This is why memories formed in the teen years are so vivid, and have such sticking power throughout our lives. This is why the music we love as teens, the books we read, the films we watch, and the friendships we form have lasting resonance throughout our adult lives. They constitute experiences that have shaped our brains. When parents understand this process, they are better equipped to manage their frustration with their teen, and, at the same time, to appreciate how adolescence, which poses many challenges to parents, is also an amazing age of opportunity.[4]

THE LURE OF RISK TAKING

Appreciating the excitement and potential of adolescence, however, has to be balanced with the attraction teens have for risks that would be unacceptable to either a child or an adult. Many parents tell me stories about teen recklessness that leaves them anxious, confused, and very angry. Below is an account of one teen and one parent in an all-too-familiar scenario.

Fifteen-year-old Luanne had been housebound for sixty hours. A Chicago winter storm beat down, covering the steps, sidewalk, and streets. Cars were left stranded in the heavy snow, and emergency rooms were filled with people who had fallen on ice. "You're not leaving the house," Pete, Luanne's father, barked. "It's too dangerous out there." In reply, she grimaced and slammed her bedroom door.

Two days later, the storm eased. The city's army of snow plows was clearing the streets. One by one the vehicles abandoned in snowdrifts were being driven or towed away. Luanne, phone against her ear, peered through the bedroom window as she commiserated with her friend Marsha. "This sucks. Presidents' weekend, and the most boring ever. And my Dad says I can't go out." But after ten minutes' conversation, she and her friend had a plan.

Luanne knew better than to sneak out. Her father, still working at home, sat at the kitchen table, papers spread out around him. "It's stopped snowing now. I'll be careful. I won't stay out for long. I need to go out. I need to walk around. I'll explode if I stay here for one more minute."

Pete uttered his perfectly honed scoff. That was his daughter, all right, quick to argue her case and charm him at the same time. "One hour—," seeing her face freeze, he relents, "Okay, an hour and a half. And take your phone. Your *charged* phone. And be careful."

Luanne checked the battery on her phone. "Got it, Daddy!" she assured him, and slipped into the welcome freeze of the outside air.

Six and half hours later Luanne was sobbing on the sofa. Her father was standing before her shouting, "How could you be so stupid! You know *never* to walk on the ice by the lake. What part of 'be careful' did you not understand? What is wrong with you?"

Pete was furious, and he was also terrified. Luanne, with two friends, had climbed the mountains of ice that form along the shoreline of Lake Michigan where, every winter, people are warned to stay away, and where, most winters, people have to be rescued, as Luanne and her friends were, by Chicago's Fire Department. In spite of the freezing temperature, the snow boulders were unstable. Luanne's friend Marsha had run ahead of the others, squealing with delight. Suddenly, the ice cracked and broke away. Marsha balanced on an ice floe that wobbled as it moved farther away from the others. The friends cried out, initially with sheer joy of adventure. When they saw the danger, they froze.

From the window of a fifteenth-floor apartment nearby, someone saw Marsha's bright coat on the ice floe, and her clumsy jump towards Luanne. She called the Fire Department, but not before Marsha fell in the numbing waters of the lake. The girls were taken to the emergency room, and Marsha was admitted to the hospital, while Luanne was dragged home by her father to answer his unending questions: "How could you be so stupid?" and "What part of 'be careful' didn't you understand?" and "What got into you?"

As Pete fires these questions at his daughter, he is genuinely trying to understand. He trusts—or did trust—his daughter. She is—or was—a responsible child. She would walk her little brother to school. She would get her homework in on time. She was a good student; the few times she struggled in a subject, she would alert him. How did she suddenly become so reckless? He felt let down, his trust betrayed. "Who is this teenage girl?" Pete wonders. "What kind of person has she become?"

When I speak to Luanne later the next morning, the neighborhood is eerily quiet, not yet geared up to post-storm normality; but the sidewalks are clear and the steps to the front door are scraped of ice. Luanne, however, is grounded. She broods over her father's scolding. "He wants me to 'talk.' He won't let go of his fixed idea that if I understand my motives then I'll be suitably ashamed of myself. He wants me to 'think about my actions.' I've said 'I'm sorry' a hundred times, but he says he doesn't care about my being sorry. He wants me to tell him what was going through my mind. I tell him it just happened. It was fun. Okay? We were bored out of our minds. And when Marsha started floating away we were worried, sort of, but we also knew she would be okay.

"Now," she continued, "he won't stop badgering me to 'explain myself.' I wish he'd just ground me or take away my phone or dock my allowance until I've paid this stupid medical bill he's waving in my face. And then he complains that I 'refuse to talk to him.' He keeps finding more and more crimes in what happened."

Before I leave, Pete pleads with me, "As a professional, do you know what was going through her mind? Marsha could have died. They both could have died. My lovely, smart daughter could have died."

I see he is close to tears, and I see, also, that his daughter is a maddening puzzle. But Luanne's explanation is clear as day: "It was fun," and "We didn't think anything really bad would happen."

Luanne, in other words, was thinking and acting like a teen. To understand her, Pete does not need to probe her thoughts; he needs to understand her teenage brain.

PLEASURE AND FEAR IN THE TEENAGE BRAIN

An important difference between the teen and adult brains lies in experiences of pleasure located in areas referred to as the "reward center." On a brain-imaging scan, these areas glow when a person feels or anticipates pleasure.

Our brain functions by sending and receiving messages from other cells via neurotransmitters—chemicals that are constantly released in sync with what we are doing and thinking and feeling. The experience or anticipation of pleasure releases a neurotransmitter called dopamine. This is the chemical associated with that gratifying buzz from delicious food, from sex, from laughter, or from exercise. Dopamine is the pleasure chemical in both teen and adult brains, but the reward centers in each are very differently configured.

Pete's thirty-nine-year-old brain enjoys small comforts during the blizzard lockdown. Catching up on sleep, watching several episodes of a favorite television series, and avoiding his daily commute offer sufficient pleasure to sustain a comfortable mood. Luanne's teen brain, on the other hand, barely registers small familiar pleasures. It requires novelty and excitement.[5]

Without novel stimulation, teens can be overwhelmed by boredom. So while Pete enjoys the quiet time during which he can rest, think, and catch up with nonurgent tasks, his teenage daughter's reward center flatlines, and she feels like she is "going crazy."

Another difference in the adolescent brain is that its baseline, or everyday dopamine level, is lower than an adult's. This means that there are fewer moderate "Oh, this is nice" feelings throughout the teen's day. On the other hand, when novelty and excitement release dopamine—the pleasure hormone—the kick is greater. Conversely, the letdown when the dopamine jolt wears off is sharper. As Luanne walked with her friends along the lake's ice boulders, the thrill of movement and danger elevated her dopamine levels. Why focus on negative possibilities, her brain "reasoned," when you feel so utterly alive?

The allure of risk and thrill is particularly strong when a teen is with friends. Often parents believe that this or that friend is a "bad influence" on their normally sensible and responsible teen. In all likelihood, the issue is not the friend, but how the teen brain behaves in the company of friends when sensitivity to risk seems to switch off. (The influence of friends on the teen brain is discussed in more detail in Chapters Four and Five.)

One way to understand this is to recall the impact on Liba, Jonas, and Keira of "being seen" by others. Liba feels a kind of pain when (she thinks that) other people are looking at her critically. Jonas suffers excruciating discomfort when he knows that his voice is somehow "not right." Keira is "mortified"—as though losing her life—when unkind eyes watch her performance. Teens' exquisitely sensitive looking-glass self gives ultimate priority to how others see them.

When a teen is with friends, the danger that looms larger than any other is the danger of not looking "okay" or fitting in. Other dangers, such as physical harm or the consequences of a criminal charge or parental punishment, have less force in a teen's mind than the danger of being ridiculed ("Pussy!" "Buzz kill!") or being the odd one out.

The company of friends also gives teens enormous pleasure. They experience an irresistible "high" that promises excitement and delight. Adventure takes priority over safety as they explore unstable ice or drive fast or vandalize property or take drugs.[6] The teen brain craves new experiences and seeks adventure, and this means it is primed to embrace risk.

MENTALIZING IN THE TEENAGE BRAIN

At the same time teens seem at the mercy of their brain's reward system, their rapidly developing mental abilities have the potential to manage those impulses. Self-management is closely linked to understanding ourselves and understanding others.

Intrigued by other people's perspective, teens ask themselves, "What are other people thinking?" and "How do they see me?" and "What does this face, or voice, or gesture, signify?" The area of the brain known as the medial prefrontal cortex—the region involved in processing and responding to other people—springs to new life in adolescence. As we shall see, this bolsters the regulatory system that is crucial to self-control.

Mentalizing involves a feat of amazing imagination wherein we see others' behavior on par with our own. We enter an interpersonal world where people's feelings have an impact on our own, and where being understood makes difficult feelings bearable. This ability to make sense of people's actions (including one's own) in terms of thoughts, motives, and feelings is a skill with a long learning curve. It begins in infancy, in our close relationships with others. When people we love and trust respond to us, are curious about us, they help us see both our inner world and the meaning our words and actions have for others.

Mentalizing is more complex than either empathy—sharing others' feelings—or mindfulness—sometimes used to describe awareness of our own mental states. It has similarities to emotional intelligence—the skill in grasping what others are feeling—though mentalizing does not involve getting everything right about other people's inner lives, or our own. Mentalizing precedes emotional intelligence and often involves initial misunderstanding. In fact, grasping that you have misunderstood someone and then correcting your interpretation are crucial to learning about the complexity of others.

As teens reflect on their new, more sophisticated inner world, they also realize that the inner life of others is difficult to decipher. What they see on a person's face and what a person says reveal only part of the story. For teens, the pressing question posed by their looking-glass self—*how does this person see me?*—joins up with new awareness that other people's minds are often opaque. This awareness generates considerable social anxiety.

When scientists examine brain activity in the areas associated with social processing, they see, in any interpersonal situation, far more blood and oxygen flow in the teen brain than in either a child's or an adult's brain. Accompanying the teen's active brainwork are other signals of uneasy excitement, such as increased perspiration and heart rate.[7] And when teens focus on social emotions (such as embarrassment or, more positively, approval) they cannot think about anything else. The looking-glass self and "imaginary audience"[8] soak up all mental energy.[9] Teens feel self-conscious, and they will do just about anything to avoid social censure. Teens, as we have seen, are far more motivated to protect their image than their life, but the sensitivity to others' minds that puts them at risk can also, with a parent's engagement, reduce that risk.

RELATIONSHIPS STRENGTHEN THE TEEN BRAIN

Psychologists sometimes talk about the "three Rs" of adolescence—the reward system (which in a teen is more sensitive to medium-size and large stimuli and less sensitive to small stimuli), the regulatory system (which manages impulses, desires, and difficult emotions), and the relationship system—the ability to trust and feel close to others.[10] By seeing how the relationship system is linked to the regulatory system, we can begin to answer that parental conundrum: "How do I remain open to the opportunities of adolescence while providing parental protection?" The answer can be found in the dynamic of teen/parent love.

The first exuberant growth of brain connections in an infant is supported by parental love, a love characterized by *attunement*—responsive attention to a baby's feelings, observations, and needs. One function of this attunement is to soothe the baby, because, initially, a newborn's brain cannot do that work. Those primitive emotions—panic, distress, terror—erupt like lava from a volcano, filling the entire body. We can see, from the infant's heaving chest, rigid or kicking legs, and tense tummy, that there is nothing in his world other than distress. There is as yet no developed prefrontal cortex to message "Shhh . . . it's okay" to calm those emotions. The parent takes on that role, as a kind of outsourced brain regulator. In providing the infant with the experience of moving from distress to comfort, a caregiver is modeling what will eventually become the work of the baby's own regulatory system.

None of us is born with the ability to manage our emotions. We acquire it, and our teachers are those who love and care for us in infancy. When a parent soothes us, holds us, and speaks softly to us, we experience a significant shift—the shift from terror to security. When a parent shows us that she wants to learn about our feelings and our needs, she introduces us to the positive stimulation of relationships. When we have good enough experiences[11] as infants, our brain has a model for controlling the emotional floodgates. Even though it will take many years before a child can reliably (more or less) adhere to that model, we can think of this as phase one of self-regulation.

Phase two is in adolescence, during the second period of exuberant brain growth. Now teens are fascinated by their own mind and by the minds of others. Their thoughts and their feelings become more complex and volatile. Like much younger children, teens need outside help to manage their more unsettling and passionate feelings. As we have seen, parents manage an infant's and young child's feelings by showing curiosity, attentiveness, and understanding. Many psychologists describe this experience of being attended to and understood and loved as "held in mind." The importance of being "held in mind" is widely acknowledged for children, and widely ignored for teens. It is, however, crucial if we want them to learn to regulate those distinctive teen impulses.

Experiencing someone as trying to understand them and see the world from their perspective protects teens from both hyperarousal (when, as a result of too much stimulation, the teen responds with the urge to flee, or to fight, or to freeze) and hypoarousal (when, as a result of too little stimulation, the teen suffers an internal collapse). Being held in the mind of another inducts them into a more comfortable state (sometimes called "optimal arousal") whereby difficult feelings can be managed. Being held in mind assures teens that they matter to someone, that their feelings are important, and that they are not alone.

But how can parents do this? Teens lack the infant's skill in proclaiming their needs with piercing cries and expressive limbs. Teens' internal worlds are less easily read than a young child's, and teens' desire for parents to understand them is not always communicated helpfully, positively, or clearly. Teens want to take ownership of their own feelings, yet they need a partner, a co-regulator, to help them feel safe with their inner turbulence.

When a child becomes a teen, parents require new interpretation skills. What level of intimacy is this teen now comfortable with? How well does the teen know himself? How clear is this teen, today, about her goals and desires? What sparks the teen's interest? Where do the teen's greatest fears lie? How can a teen be offered assurance and a place of safety? What fills the teen with joy, and what leads her to despair?

As parents demonstrate their willingness to engage with the teen's mind, they encourage positive growth of the teen's brain. Such warm and engaged parenting, maintained even in the midst of inevitable conflict, has a unique influence on teen brain development. The amygdala—almond-shaped collections of nuclei deep in the brain's temporal lobe that play crucial roles in primitive impulse and emotion—becomes less easily aroused and more responsive to messages from the control center.[12] Remarkably, relationships that offer understanding and encourage self-reflection, and repair quickly after conflict and misunderstanding, yield brain effects associated with increased emotional management and more reasonable behavior in teens.

Until recently, *everyone's* ignorance about the teen brain hampered parents' ability to meet these challenges. What is not named cannot be seen, and so adolescent behavior was explained in a variety of unhelpful ways, leading to woefully inappropriate interpretations of teens' behavior. Teens are said to be driven by raging hormones, self-centeredness, tunnel vision, recklessness, and thoughtlessness. A teen who is viewed in this way is "defined" and "complained about" but not seen, not explored, and certainly not understood. Such teens are then deprived of the brain-strengthening love that parents offer when they can see through their teen's eyes.

THE TEEN BODY CLOCK

When I first started giving lectures on the teenage brain, I was uneasy about my audience's responses. Many in the lecture hall were still adolescents, even though they were, at between eighteen and twenty-one years of age, legally adults. I was telling them that their brains were not functioning as adult brains. Would they find this patronizing, yet another grown-up belittling them, amused by their quirks and curiosities?

To my surprise, they were intrigued, delighted, and relieved. "So that's why I feel like my brain's exploding!" one eighteen-year-old said. Some thought the "rapid growth" I described was "too tame" and should contain words such as "zooming" or "wild" or "erupting." They were delighted to hear about the details of circuits and synapses and pruning and myelination, which is why I spent some time explaining the processes earlier in this chapter. They quickly grasped the message that synaptic pruning was influenced by what they did. They were learning not about a process that was as passive as, for example, body changes in puberty, but about an intricate reshaping of a brain that was responsive to their interests and activities. But a discovery they particularly welcomed was of the teen's distinctive body clock.

The teen's body clock is out of sync with both the child's and the adult's. It is as though teens inhabit a different time zone, and the activities expected of them are out of step with what their body wants to do.

Each of us has an internal body clock set to "circadian rhythms." This comes from "circa" that means "around," and "diem" which means "day." These are the internal, biological mechanisms that shift over a twenty-four-hour period, making us feel awake at some hours and sleepy at others. During the phase when we are naturally awake, we are better at solving puzzles and quicker, generally, in thinking things through. We are also less clumsy, more careful, and our mood is more likely to be stable.

Key to waking and sleeping phases is sunlight. Light stimulates the eye's retina, and in the retina is a nerve with a pathway to another part of the brain called the hypothalamus. From there, at the very center of the hypothalamus, signals are carried to other parts of the brain that control body temperature, blood pressure, as well as other hormones that influence the body clock.

From this it would seem that teens cannot possibly be different from children and grown-ups. Teens, like children and adults, live within the cycle of daylight and darkness; they, too, have light-sensitive eyes with nerve pathways to different parts of the brain. So when a teen is groggy, grumpy, and lethargic in the morning, surely, most parents argue, the teen is lazy, or is blamed for "stupidly stayed up too late doing God knows what," as Caleb says of his daughter Mercy. Caleb's response was widely shared until psychologists, observing teens' struggle with the morning wake-up call and their inability to comply with directives to "get to bed at a reasonable hour," decided to investigate further.

Levels of the hormone melatonin are key to whether we feel awake or sleepy. When we travel from one time zone to another, the local bedtime might be our usual supper or even lunch time, when we have low levels of melatonin. We have trouble getting to sleep and, equally, we have trouble waking up at the new local time, not only because we are tired, but because our melatonin levels are high. It is morning, when we are usually alert and eager to start the day, but now, instead of the cortisol peak we usually feel at 9 a.m., our body is telling us that it is time to sleep.

In teens, melatonin—the chemical that makes us feel sleepy—is not produced until late in the evening. "I'm not tired!" teens insist, and are indeed unlikely to feel tired until well after 11 p.m. In the morning, as they are prodded to get up, however, their body is awash with high levels of melatonin, and they are primed for sleep. Their circadian rhythms leave teens with a long-term version of jet lag.[13] As a result, not only are they slow and groggy in the morning, they are also negative, irritable, and angry.

Many psychologists and educators, on the back of this research, lobby for a later start to teens' school day. They argue that the natural waking time for teens is late morning, and a later start would be more in keeping with teens' body clock. Teens would then be more receptive to teaching, more alert, and less bored. Teens, when truly rested, would also be less irritable and anxious.

When we are awake and alert, it is easier to focus on and manage what is happening around us. But when we are tired, reasoning slows down. The more primitive part of the brain—the amygdala—responds with unchecked alarm to possible threats,[14] whether it is a facial expression, a sudden movement, a difficult task, or an uneasy conversation. In such an aroused state we lose the ability to distinguish what is safe and what is threatening. Neutral faces seem angry or hostile, any loud noise suggests danger, and any interpersonal tension is exaggerated. Negative emotions, particularly anxiety, fear, and anger, are more intense. Fatigue speeds up negative reactions to reminders to do homework, or clean up, or get the next morning's clothes ready. Combine the teen's physiological jet lag with teen emotions that are quick to rise and slow to resolve, and you have a perfect storm for teen distress, when teens both appeal to and dump on the people who matter to them most—their parents.

CONVERSATION AND DISCIPLINE

Teens begin to explore deeper meanings within themselves, their relationships, and the rest of the world around them.

Music has wider resonance as teens make connections between the thoughts expressed in a song and their own experiences. They look at their parents more objectively, often seeing elements in the family that parents themselves do not see.

Teens' intellect can handle complex and abstract concepts, but their brains are ill equipped to put safety before excitement. Throughout adolescence, teens are very likely to show poor judgment from time to time. They need to be monitored, and sometimes they need to be disciplined.

Discipline—particularly any discipline that involves punishment—is a minefield for three reasons. First, any kind of physical punishment has a greater negative impact on a teen even than on a child. Corporal punishment stokes anger and humiliation. Instead of "bringing them to heel," it is likely to harden their resistance.

Second, a display of anger, such as shouting, is counterproductive. Teens are so sensitive to heated emotions that these block out everything else. When teens hear a parent yelling, they can focus only on the anger. The message contained in the heated words ("That's not safe" or "That's not acceptable") doesn't register. It's always difficult, for anyone of any age, to focus on a reasonable argument that a person is making if that person is shouting at us. For a teen, it is impossible.

Third, punishments such as grounding—which was Pete's initial gambit with Luanne—when a teen is only allowed out for school or other structured activities, or prohibitions on using the Internet or accessing a phone, are less effective than offering a reward after good behavior. Teens are less concerned than either children or adults by the prospect of loss, but are more excited by rewards.

This feature of the teen brain can be used to make discipline more effective.[15] The prospect of a phone upgrade or a promise to extend teens' freedom (on condition that they demonstrate responsibility/apply themselves to schoolwork/comply with parental rules) has a higher success rate. When punishment does seem necessary—when a teen damages a car or is careless with important or costly things, or when carelessness leads to financial costs—the punishment should relate to the consequences of the teen's action and should offer the opportunity for the teen to demonstrate that he or she is learning to do better.

Far more effective than punishment is conversation. First, articulate the problem posed by a teen's impulsive or thoughtless behavior. Pete did this when he said, "Marsha could have died/You could have died." Another problem he touched on was, "How can I trust you ever again to stay safe?" But Pete did not really ask Luanne this. He tells his daughter that she has created difficult problems for herself. A more effective second step would be to invite the teen to participate in proposed solutions to the problem.

How might this collaborative process be achieved?

Remember, Pete took a long time to absorb the shock of Luanne's reckless behavior. He "can't get over" how his teen daughter could be "so stupid," and he demands that she explain herself. But if he could take a step back and moderate his own emotional state (something that parents are better at than teens, though this is often derailed when dealing with teens), then he would realize that insisting "Explain yourself!" is a coercive move unlikely to elicit a reflective answer. Instead of opening a dialogue, it lays the groundwork for opposition.

Armed with knowledge of the teen brain, however, he

would know that Luanne is unable to explain herself in terms that would satisfy him. She did what was rewarding and most important to her at the moment, even though she knows, intellectually, it wasn't sensible.

Therefore, the way to avert a downward spiral in which parental anger generates teen frustration and fury is to look forward. The issue, moving ahead, is "What can Luanne learn about this?" and "How will any lesson increase responsibility?" and "How can Pete track Luanne's level of responsibility?"

Some parents and teens find it useful to draw up contracts of good behavior. Generally, the contract is along the lines of "When you demonstrate responsibility in the following ways, you can earn more independence."

A contract requires an agreement between both parties, with the teen assured that there will be some reward for compliance, but that every breach of the contract will also have consequences. For a contract to work, the terms have to be as clear as possible. They should be written down, and neither parent nor teen can modify them by adding or taking away conditions without the other's agreement. The benefits are that you can set clear conditions: "You can go if your schoolwork/project is done/if you help clean up every day this week/if there's no screen time after 9 p.m."

The downside of a contract is that it risks legalistic debate about whether or not the teen has complied, or, if the contract was breached, whether this was the teen's "fault," or whether it was unavoidable, or justifiable.

There is no surefire way to ensure that the teen is never again thoughtless, reckless, or irresponsible. The best parents can do is support and encourage those impulse-controlling brain networks. In a less heated moment, Luanne could be tasked with writing a story, or talking through the events of that winter's day as she saw them. At what point might she have made a better decision? At what point did she wish she had stepped away from danger?

Though Luanne is likely to see any such task as some kind of punishment, the exercise will encourage reflection on key questions, such as "What was my role in this incident?" and "How did I contribute to the consequences?" As Pete engages with his daughter's effort to take a somewhat wider view, both the parent/teen relationship and the teen's brain will take a step forward.

When teens learn about the exuberant growth of the adolescent brain, they feel vindicated. This knowledge equips them to say, "See, I'm not bad/useless/good-for-nothing/careless—I am a teen remodeling my brain." But this also equips parents to say, "I'm interested in this developing brain, and my input is necessary."

3

"You don't have any idea what I feel."

The Teen's New Language of Emotions

IN TEENS, as we have seen, the neural tracks on which emotions travel are slick and speedy, while brain circuits that manage and calm emotions are slow and inefficient. Anger, fear, sadness, and joy flare up quickly but are slow to resolve. In the previous chapter we saw how the teen brain is not yet equipped to manage these emotions without someone—ideally a parent—as part-time collaborator. Here we take a different perspective and explore how hard teens themselves are working to understand themselves and establish a new language for the complex and fascinating feelings that are shaping their identity.[1]

EMOTIONAL GRANULARITY

Young children use emotion words interchangeably. For a four-year-old, the word "sad" might be used to describe fear or anger as well as unhappiness. Children display what psychologists call "low granularity," which means that their descriptions are not finely focused on a specific emotion. They don't distinguish among very different feelings that may have some elements in common.

Teens, on the other hand, spend a lot of time focusing on the fine detail of their feelings, and the contexts in which their emotions occur. They talk about their feelings with their friends, and they fume if a parent attributes a feeling to them that does not seem right. "Why are you so angry all the time?" Todd's mother demands, while Todd retorts heatedly, "I'm not angry!" His mother smirks; his harsh protest proves her point. But for fifteen-year-old Todd, "anger" does not describe his rush of feeling.

"She doesn't get it," he tells me. "It's more like, sort of frustration." After a pause he adds, "And if I am what she says, well, it isn't anger, it's rage." This fifteen-year-old is grappling with subtle differences between one emotion and another. He is aiming for high granularity, and searches for the precise word to describe the specific emotion.[2]

Teens are also learning that emotions are complicated. When they feel sad, for example, they may also feel lonely or ashamed or isolated or neglected. When they are joyful, they may feel excited, powerful, proud, full of energy and longing. When they are afraid, they might feel weak, anxious, helpless, confused, and rejected. When they feel angry, they might also feel pain and resentment. When they are humiliated, they might feel helpless, but also vindictive.

As teens refine their concepts of emotion, they are often bewildered by the speed at which emotions can change according to their situation or mood. Ira is angry when his mother tells him he has to put his phone away and clean his room. He is frustrated because he cannot keep looking through a thread of news media that excited him. Scrolling through the related posts, he felt optimistic and eager and energized. His mother's orders disrupt the flow of concentration and remind him that he is still a boy expected to obey his parents. His own needs, he believes, are being ignored. All these thoughts are bundled into "what he feels."

When his mother then thanks him for responding to her request, "Even though I know you didn't want to," his anger eases, but when she starts to add to the list of "things that need doing now," such as taking the dog for a walk and folding the laundry, frustration melds into sadness, then anger, as he feels trapped "in this stupid awful family."

Children accept the transience of emotions as part of the human landscape. They move from what looks like utter despair—the tears, the cries, the rapid breathing, the tense limbs—to joy in the blink of an eye. But teens are flustered by the rapid shifts in emotion that seesaw from high to low. One night they get into bed feeling euphoric, powerful, and optimistic, yet the next morning they feel empty, rejected, anxious.

To some teens, these different emotional states suggest different identities. "There are three of me," a fourteen-year-old girl told Trudie Rossouw in a therapy session.[3] "One is angry, anxious, does not want to eat, wants to punish me and hates me. . . . The other me is happy, confident . . . and feels good about myself. . . . Then there is the one in the middle, feeling confused between the two poles."

Shifting emotions add to the teen's confusion about her identity. "Who am I?" Rossouw's client wonders, when different feelings rock her inner world. Teens ask themselves, "How can I process information about myself and other people when my feelings are so layered, and the different planes on which different emotions lie do not meet?" As Dan Siegel notes, "From inside these changes can become overwhelming. [Teens] may feel life is too much. [They] | get lost" but a parent's understanding can help them find their way.[4]

HOW THE BRAIN AND THE BODY MAKE EMOTIONS

Emotions do not come to us fully formed, ready-made, clearly bound. We construct emotions, in part, from our thoughts and from cultural prototypes—how they are presented in the books we read, the films we enjoy, and the way other people speak. We also construct emotions from our bodies. We build emotions in large part by interpreting our "gut sensations."

Some people think that gut feelings provide a reliable route to truth, and some argue that gut feelings are devoid of useful meaning and should always give way to reflection and reason. Neurologists—people who study the brain and brain activity—see gut feelings in a very different way.[5]

Emotions, from the neurologist's perspective, begin with sensations within our internal organs and tissues, from the hormones in our blood and the activity of our immune system. The basic feelings that accompany us throughout the day, whether pleasant, neutral, or painful, arise from ongoing inner processes that deliver, minute by minute, a flow of sensations. This flow of sensations is called *interoception*. Every thought and decision is colored by these sensations, so the distinction between "thinking with your gut" and "thinking with your head" disappears. The head is always shaped by the gut.[6]

Introspection is the process of examining our own thoughts, feelings, and ideas. When we engage in introspection, we are aware of what we are doing and of what we are thinking. Interoception, on the other hand, is largely automatic and often unconscious. It has been called the sixth sense we have about our body,[7] the internal state of our organs, the pumping of our heart, the digestive activity in our stomach, the filling and emptying of our lungs, the heat, wind, touch, and texture on our skin—indeed all our physiological processes. Interoceptive signals are transmitted to the brain, producing a spectrum of feelings from calm to jittery, from pleasure to pain.

Our brain then interprets these signals. Interoception is an active and highly individual process. Every person's interpretation of inner states is unique, shaped by past experience, present hopes, and values. Every emotion has input from this interoceptive network—as does every thought, plan, or idea.

Think how challenging it is for teens to confront new emotions within a host of new interoceptive signaling, from the revamping neural circuits to the strange new hormones in their blood. Children take their shifting feelings for granted and have less at stake when they construct their emotions. Grown-ups have more experience to draw on when they construct their emotions. Teens, however, examine and evaluate their emotions without a road map, yet they feel that their life depends on getting the right answer to the question, "What do I feel?" and "What do these feelings mean?"

Trusting our emotions is crucial. Emotions reveal what we

value and shape our goals and guide our attachments and even our beliefs. Our feelings are never 100 percent trustworthy, yet constant distrust or skepticism of emotions would cut us off from our core engagement with others, and ourselves. As teens reflect on and test and construct their desires and needs, they ask, "What makes me happy? Will I always feel angry? What kind of person do I love? What is their gender? What do I have to be for someone to love me in this new strange way?" Many typical teen interests—such as music and lyrics, TV shows, and poetry—become aids in their efforts to learn their new emotional language.

NEGATIVE BUT NECESSARY FEELINGS

When teens are asked to list their greatest concerns, top of their list is the threat of being overwhelmed by negative emotions, particularly anxiety and depression.[8] Parents want to protect their teen from negative feelings, and wish that they could provide a buffer between a teen and the inevitable upheavals of teenage life, but many struggle with how to do this effectively.

"I was a hormonal mess when I was a teenager," Tessa tells me. "I felt awful most of the time. My dad would walk into a room, and that was enough to make me angry. I'd look at a friend's new pair of jeans and be awash with dissatisfaction—you know, how could I ever look that good? I could be horribly lonely, and yet wouldn't feel like leaving my room. I looked at people who seemed happy and even-tempered and I really thought they lived in a different world. I hate to see Miriam going through the same thing, but I guess you can't escape biology."

Anger, fear, worry, loneliness, boredom, irritability, and

sadness can be felt by people of any age, but as we move from childhood into adolescence, these negative emotions increase markedly.[9] In one study, researchers asked children, teens, and adults how they were feeling at various times throughout the day. The differences were clear. Teens experience difficult emotions more frequently and more intensely than either children or adults.[10]

Sometimes parents say, "It's your hormones talking," to reassure a teen. The message they want to convey is "You're normal" and "Your difficult feelings won't last forever," but teens hear, "Your feelings aren't real" or "I can't take them seriously."

Teen hormones affect physical maturity, triggering the "secondary sexual characteristics" including pubic and underarm hair, girls' breast and hip development, and boys' chest development and voice changes, but, contrary to common belief, there is no direct relationship between hormone levels and emotional turmoil. Instead, the hormones that trigger puberty also trigger teen brain development, and it is this development that generates emotional intensity.[11] These emotions should not be dismissed as "teenage turbulence" that will soon "go away." Instead, they lay the groundwork for the teen's identity.

Teens' expanding intelligence and empathy and advanced reasoning generate emotional intensity. Sometimes this intensity has a negative charge, and this is a source of anxiety for both teens and parents. But negative emotions—sadness, hurt, worry, loneliness, anger—serve a purpose. They signal a breach between what we value and need, on the one hand, and what is really happening, on the other. Negative emotions prompt us to mend this breach. They are useful as long as we do not remain persistently overwhelmed by them. Teen brains, with their loud alarm systems and circuitous, inefficient neural pathways, often need someone to share, understand, and help moderate those feelings. The person who does that most effectively is the parent.

HOLDING THE TEEN IN MIND

When sixteen-year-old Miriam tells her mother Tessa how "down" she feels and how she wishes she "could just bury [her]self and forget [she] ever existed," Tessa initially shows sympathy. But as Miriam elaborates her feelings—"The whole world seems like it's going to topple over, and everything is scary and even simple things make my head buzz"—Tessa tells her, "You're really morbid. You have to pull yourself up. You're just wasting energy."

Tessa is sympathetic, but she is frightened, and, she explains, she does not want to "indulge" her daughter in her "morbid thoughts."

Fifteen-year-old Jonas tries to talk to his parent about his negative feelings, but complains that their responses "pull the carpet from under me. It's like, 'Oh, don't think that way.' And then my mom goes on about 'hormones' and just, like, 'being a teenager.' I heard them talking—you know, they've split, and they never talk, but there they were, sitting at the kitchen table, and my dad said, 'He's depressed. You should take him to the doctor,' and my mom said, 'It's just hormones.' But their voices were creepy. Not that they were yelling at each other, but sort of yelling about me. It makes me feel awful. *Ugly*. Like they're suffering because I'm ugly inside. It's like they're putting my mind in a specimen jar and it's on display. They're peering at it, but it's all alone."

A parent's fear of the teen's emotions magnifies a teen's own fear. It takes a special kind of guts for a parent to steady herself and remain present—responsive and respectful—when a teen seems to be falling apart. Parents want to make things better and do their best to respond positively; after all, it is painful to witness a teen's distress and difficult not to try to banish or fix it. But that is not what the teen needs. The teen needs to feel that someone is "holding them in mind"—which simply means that you can think about teens' experience from their perspective. To do this, you need to show that you "both know in your mind and feel in your body what [your teen] is feeling"[12] without becoming overwhelmed by their—or your—distress. As Jonas says, the worst thing is that his mind is alone.

Just as a child needs a grown-up she loves and trusts to show her that her terrors are understood, a teen needs a parent, still, to assure her that her mind is not alone, that someone she loves and trusts can help her frame feelings that threaten to overwhelm her, and that she is lovable whatever she feels. Teens need a parent to remain with them, to be there for them, even in their darker moods. (In Chapters Eight and Nine I will discuss dark emotions that go beyond what parents themselves can help the teen manage.) But while "holding a child in mind" comes naturally to many parents who automatically tune into the child's developmental level, the skill of holding a teen in mind needs to be learned—yet, until now, parents have had very little guidance.

NAMING EMOTIONS AND TAMING THE BODY

When we were children, grown-ups were able to manage many of our difficult feelings. They would hug us when we felt lonely, perhaps offer a treat when we felt sad, and assure us there was "nothing to worry about" when we were anxious. Teens' emotions are too complex to be soothed like a child's. Both teen and parent need to learn new techniques.

Emotions, as we have seen, are influenced by the interoceptive network, the signals that are carried to our brain from our inner body states and that our brain then imbues with meaning: "I am in love," or "I am falling apart," or "This is too painful," or "I'm drowning." A good starting place for managing difficult emotions is attending to the churning stomach, light-headedness or dizziness, the wobbly legs, the tight throat. Grown-ups don't have to be reminded, quite so often, to do this because their adult brains more efficiently switch off the alarm. They have learned that this embarrassment, this rejection, this uncertainty will not kill them, and while they may still be upset or hurt, they are not overwhelmed.

Teens' negative emotions are problematic because the alarm, once raised, persists. Once the breathing loses a normal rhythm, once the heart starts racing, once the stomach tenses, teens are caught in a cycle that is difficult (but not impossible) to break. First, the body's alarm rings out and then, when the brain doesn't switch it off either by reinterpreting the physical signals or messaging the brain that things are really okay, the body's alarm signals escalate. Any adrenaline released stays in the teen's body and keeps on signaling, "Something bad is happening" and "You are in danger." As the physical sensations linked to difficult emotions persist, so does the emotion.

Subsequent alarms now sound, because the emotion itself is frightening.[13] Teens spin in a fear-adrenaline-fear cycle, where fear (or anxiety or pain) produces adrenaline that leads to physical sensations associated with fear. A surprisingly effective first step is moderating the physical signals accompanying negative emotions.

"Take a deep breath," we are told when someone thinks we are upset. This advice does not always go down well. It can be heard as a criticism of our response, that we are "overexcited" or "losing it." We can feel that someone is trying to manage us instead of helping us. But "take a deep breath" is actually good advice when you are anxious and the brain—particularly the teenage brain—is running on alarm mode, preparing to address a threat by minimizing the intake of oxygen (so more can go to limb muscles in case you need to run away from danger).

Taking deep measured breaths delivers much-needed oxygen to the brain. But breathing, something we do all the time, is surprisingly easy to get wrong. When we are frightened or anxious, we often take deep breaths through our open mouth. These fast-paced open-mouth breaths are attempts to get more oxygen into our system, but they do the opposite. It is the nose, not the mouth, that is perfectly designed to get us the air that's needed. Deep inside the nose, folded membranes warm or cool the air to body temperature. When the air we breathe reaches the sinuses—the air spaces connected to the nose—it is bathed with nitric oxide that relaxes the blood vessels in our respiratory system, and more oxygen passes into the blood.[14] Regular breathing, the kind you would do if you were calm, helps achieve what's called "the relaxation response."[15] The body is no longer fixated on self-defense. The surge of neurochemicals telling your body to prepare for danger ceases, and soon the storm eases.

Once oxygenated blood is no longer directed towards the muscles for fight or flight, the brain gets the oxygen needed to reflect on our feelings. What is bothering us? What do we need? What name can we give this emotion? Is it a combination of emotions—sadness, self-doubt, irritability, anxiety, impatience, or fear?

There is a mysterious phenomenon, demonstrated over and over, that naming emotions—particularly negative emotions—has the power to tame them.[16] Words, the right words, activate the brain's control center. This requires more than giving feelings a highly general name, such as "mad" or "sad." This requires turning a light on the emotion to examine its particular quality and context. It involves sifting out the central anxiety ("I'm worried that I'll get in trouble/I won't have anyone to talk to/Someone I like will snub me") from the escalating anxiety teens experience when they are afraid of the emotion itself. It involves holding on to the negative feeling, focusing on it without fear, observing its impact on the body and then working with the body to ease the urgency and pain of the emotion.[17] This process—sometimes called "negative emotion differentiation," or NED—may not solve the problem, but when teens find the right words to describe emotions, they are in a better position to look for a solution[18]—and, until they find that, keep calm enough to feel comfort and connection.

Thinking about the right words for our feelings focuses our attention on them, and this focus awakens the brain's prefrontal cortex—the part of the brain that is able to reflect, plan ahead, and reason, the part that integrates good information. Riding out the initial storm, naming the painful emotion, and observing that it does not destroy you foster a healthy neural flow. The emotional intensity eases, and suddenly the teen is in a "better place."[19]

When we stand at the foot of a steep hill with close, supportive companions, the path seems less steep than when we are alone.[20] Automatically, we synchronize our breathing and heart rate with the people close by, particularly the people we trust. Nothing calms emotional pain as effectively as being "held," whether in our body or our mind. Challenges seem less daunting, and problems seem to shrink.

OVERVIEW AND EXERCISES

Teens are trying to figure out how to manage changes in their bodies, their relationships, and their minds. They feel the pressure of new demands and ever-widening uncertainties. Parents want them to work hard in school and to take on more responsibility at home. Teens still want to please their parents, but they also want to be their own person. They sense an emerging self that is unique and wonderful, but still undefined. Within a single day, they swing from euphoric self-confidence in which they feel strong, invulnerable, and immortal one minute, to despair, emptiness, and terrifying vulnerability the next minute.

Many parents feel helpless in the face of raw teen emotions. Many assume that teens' unregulated frustration and overwhelming irritability and self-consciousness are "merely hormonal" and should be ignored. Yet "being there" for your teen means being willing to acknowledge those difficult emotions and assure the teen that these emotions, however uncomfortable, do not damage the bond between you. Showing that you understand—or are willing to try to understand—helps, just as it did when your teen was a young child, when you stood by tantrums and tears until they went away.

"Emotional coaching" is a term that is now familiar in books about parenting children, but is badly neglected in books about parenting teens. The basics of emotional coaching for children involve prompting them to think about what others feel. "Why do you think your little brother is crying? Do you think he is sad because you snatched his toy?" Or a parent might say, "Are you feeling sad because Daddy is cross/Granny can't come/Your friend is sick?" Through conversations like these, a child's attention is drawn to the context in which emotions arise.

Emotional coaching also directs the child's attention to the feelings that prompt her behavior. "Are you feeling left out?" a parent might say, when a child sulks during a sibling's birthday party. "Are you disappointed your mother has to leave?" a parent might say, when a child refuses to play.

Emotional coaching is equally important with teens, though it requires different techniques. The words that parents use to help a child learn about emotions are not always helpful to teens who want to find their own emotional language. The empathy that a parent can offer a child is not always welcomed by teens, who see the parent as "babying" them. Emotional coaching in the teen years demands more patience, and is more of a collaborative effort.

We can start with a list of things to avoid in emotionally coaching a teen:

Don't dismiss the emotion.

This chapter explains the importance of accepting emotions, even difficult ones. So, while emotionally coaching a teen, parents should not work on the principle that their son or daughter should always be happy.

Don't try to "fix" the emotion.

Sometimes, as we empathize with a son or daughter, we want to "fix things." "Forget it," we might say to a teen who is distressed by a fight with a friend. "She's not worth it. Don't give it another thought." This minimizes her emotion. "This unhappiness can just be brushed aside," is the implicit message. But sweeping aside unhappiness is not the best way to manage negative feelings.

Unhappiness, hurt, and disappointment have a habit of sticking with us even when we avert our attention from them. Moreover, by minimizing the teen's feelings, we miss an opportunity to learn from our teen, and to hear about the teen's own experiences, to discover where difficulties lie. This means we also miss out on opportunities to comfort and advise.

Minimize the use of distractions to help the teen.

Distracting a toddler with a treat or a story or an activity or a joke works well because at this developmental phase emotions are usually short-lived. Sometimes parents try similar techniques to ease a teen's mood. You prepare a favorite meal, or promise to buy him something he wants, or suggest an outing. While an unhappy teen might benefit from comforting shifts of focus, relying on distractions leaves teens feeling unsettled and unacknowledged. At best, the distractions you offer signal your sympathy, and your teen may appreciate that, along with the meal, purchase, or outing, but it is your empathic love that is central to helping the teen regulate powerful feelings. Distractions do not prompt the self-understanding a teen needs to moderate anxiety about intense emotions.

Don't show disapproval of the emotion.

Sometimes parents say, "My teen is in a permanent funk," or "My teen constantly mopes." Or, as Tessa said to Miriam, "Stop being morbid." Their patience tested, parents demand, "Why can't you be happy about anything?" and "Do you always have to complain?" The message here is "There's something wrong with you for being unhappy/depressed/frustrated." In response, the teen feels either anger at their unsympathetic parent, or shame for these negative feelings. Neither of these will help the teen understand and manage emotion.

Don't worry that talking about difficult feelings will make them worse.

Sometimes parents worry that talking about negative emotions is bound to lower the teen's mood further. It is important to focus on the positive, and teens can benefit, as everyone does, from appreciating good things that are going on, but talking about negative feelings does not, contrary to what many believe, crystallize them. In fact, when you prompt your teen to reflect on difficult emotions by, for example, differentiating disappointment from despair, or the pain of rejection from shame, or sadness from anger, you are prompting skills that will help your teen identify and resolve emotional problems.

Here are suggestions for things to do, with the aim of assuring your teen that difficult emotions are normal, that you sometimes feel them too, and that there are different ways of managing them.

Show interest in the emotion, and a willingness to hear more about it.

Give the teen time to find the words needed. If, in answer to the questions, "How do you feel?" or "Is anything wrong?"

you get back, "Nothing's wrong!" or "I don't know!" or "Leave me alone!" then the teen may need more time, and clearer signals of your willingness to listen. So pay attention to your own body language. A relaxed, still body suggests a willingness to take time to listen. A focused, neutral gaze invites disclosure. Your steady breathing shows you have stamina for the conversation, and may even help calm your teen.

Engage with the teen, even when the teen suffers emotions you yourself do not want to think about.

At the end of Chapter Nine there is guidance for managing acute anxiety, including panic attacks, but with everyday emotional coaching the aim is to manage emotions by encouraging a teen to name and reflect on emotions. When teens can call emotions by their name, and explain the context in which they occur, then the physiological storm eases, and strong emotions no longer seem so threatening.

Once your teen is assured that you are reflecting on the emotion alongside him, it may be possible to suggest different ways of looking at and addressing the underlying problems.

Again, with your teen as guide, ask what might be done to ease her distress. Though I advise parents against trying to fix the emotion or offer distractions, encourage the teen herself to come up with possible ideas for self-care. What would make her feel less stressed, or less helpless, or less anxious? Again, you can assure your teen that these feelings are normal, and that learning how to continue pursuing interests and follow routines is an important skill.

A parent's persistent, positive engagement with a teen, even during times of turmoil, has been shown to promote the pruning of the cortex and calming of the highly reactive amygdala.[21] In short, the parent's steady engagement—being there for the teen—helps the teen develop a brain that is better equipped to moderate and manage intense emotions.

No parent will manage this "coaching" or collaboration every time. As with most parenting guidance, getting it right, more or less, about 30 percent of the time is enough to partner positively your teen's remodeling of the adolescent brain.

4

"Only my friends understand me."

Are Parents Really Replaced by Teens' Friends?

ONE OF THE most common myths about adolescence is that parents lose the power to influence their teens. According to this myth, the importance of friends replaces the importance of parents. Sociologists who trumpeted this in the 1960s[1] adhered to two false assumptions. The first is that attachment is a fixed quantity, like a pie, so if teens become more attached to their friends, then they must become less attached to their parents. But attachments are not like this. We do not love one child less when another is born to us. Attachments, like love, are elastic.

The second false assumption is that when the influence of friends increases, as it does in adolescence, then the influence of parents must diminish. The influences people have on us, however, have many shapes and dimensions. They are salient during one phase of our lives, then lurk in the background while continuing to shape us. Research over the course of the past four decades shows that parents' influence remains strong throughout the teen years. Yet the constantly repeated myth, "My teen doesn't care about me. He only cares about his friends," continues to distort parents' views of their teens.

In the next two chapters I look at the world of adolescent friendships, at broad differences between teen girls' and teen boys' friendships, and at the many roles parents play as these friendships change and develop. This chapter highlights the potential of teen friendships to wield positive influence, while the following chapter addresses parents' worry about pressures and risks posed by peers. We will see ways parents can promote positive friendships and manage the risks.

A VERY BRIEF HISTORY OF THE GROUP

Humans are fundamentally social beings. Our ancestors would not have survived as loners. The long span of human childhood—longer than in any other species—requires many years of care. Initially, children need help with the basics of survival—obtaining food, warmth, and safety from predators. But human sociability extends beyond this. It extends to the brain-building forces of love and attachment and mutual understanding.

Many of a growing child's needs are met by close family members, but a family is not an isolated unit. It is embedded in a society with rules for inclusion and exclusion, with norms for participation and contribution. Children rely on more experienced adults to pass on their knowledge, but as young people move into adolescence, they also need people like them, people who are at a similar stage of learning about the world, to pool and exchange knowledge. Alongside their peers, teens assess, revise, and update what the adults teach. And, like all people, teens learn best from people to whom they feel close.

Learning from other people involves trust and connection.[2] Before we accept the information someone gives us, we ask, "Can I believe what you are telling me?" and "Are you showing me something that matters, something I might find useful?" We also ask "Do you have my best interests in mind?" so that we can be assured that the informant is not trying to cheat or harm us. This is one reason friends who are liked and trusted wield such influence.

As teens learn from one another, they imitate one another. Mimicry is part of both learning and attachment. Infants mimic a parent's smile and speech, and by watching other children they learn—by imitation—rules of interaction and play. Their talk is peppered with "Me too," and "Same here."

In adolescence, when teens feel pressure to shape their personal identity, when they take control over their grooming and behavior, mimicry extends to what they do and how they look. Teens listen to the same music as their friends, watch the same TV shows, and follow the same influencers on social media. They share distinctive greetings, and talk and walk like one another. They also mark their similarities by dressing alike—indeed, all forms of grooming, from hairstyle and makeup to body piercings, reflect the norms of their group. Similarity becomes a code for belonging. Hence some parents say their teen has been "taken over" by their friends.

A sense of belonging not only to a family but also to a network of friends is fundamental to human happiness.[3] Throughout our lives, whatever our age, friends provide benefits to our mental and physical well-being. But teens feel the absence of friends more keenly than either children or adults. Any mark of social isolation, such as being excluded from an activity—even a transient one they don't particularly care about—lowers their mood and raises anxiety.[4]

Teens sometimes refer to friends as their "armor"[5]—a term that suggests just how threatening the everyday world is without them. A teen without friends has to survive in what seems like an unprotected and precarious social environment.[6]

THE TRIBAL SELF

Friendship changes its gravitational field in adolescence. Teens long for social acceptance, and most teens will change their appearance, their behavior, and their ideas to fit in. Their urgent need to connect and belong to a peer group unsettles many parents, who then conclude they are "losing their teen to friends." Below, we see three parents puzzled over the impact friends have on their teen's character and well-being.

"Philip has always been a nerdy child—in the best possible way," Stan explains. "He was mad about train sets as a very young boy. He built complicated tracks all over the house, and when I put him to bed, he'd talk about what he'd build tomorrow. He always had one or two friends. He wasn't a loner. But he wasn't all that social, either. And it didn't matter. Being deaf wasn't really a thing then, you know? It was just what he was and no one seemed to blink. Kids would say 'hi,' just like normal, when I took him into the schoolyard for lineup. Now I see him at school and he kind of skulks on the sidelines. And the skulking isn't only at school, I can tell you that. He comes home. He throws that school bag on the floor like there was some bad electricity running through it. And then he goes to his room. He slams that door like he hates the world because the world doesn't like him. Suddenly at fourteen he seems lost without friends."

Amanda also describes her fourteen-year-old son Garth as, once, a "little boy fixated on trains and cars. Then it was computer games, all in his own world with no need of real friends, just the odd little boy now and then as a mischief mate. Well, it started maybe a year ago, and suddenly he's looking at what other boys are doing. And their stuff! He never gave one tiny thought to what he wore. Now he has to wear what the others wear. And his Dad could always get his hair cut just the way his Dad thought it should be. Just try that now! No, it's got to be just like Keith's or Jim's or Amin's. The way he tries to blend with this group is funny, sort of, because it's just *not him*. But it also makes me—like—sick, because that *is* him, for now."

Sandra says her thirteen-year-old daughter Wendy "was always a social little thing and had friends and best friends and then worst friends and so on, and they were constantly changing. Sometimes there was drama. And you know sometimes there were tears. Now it's on a different scale. I swear, her friends jerk her around. They're doing one thing, so this means she has to do something, all the way down to the eyebrows and the braided wristband. You see them all together, those friends, and they look like some *tribe*."

Sandra's word "tribe" suggests something larger than a group of friends. Tribes include all generations, with shared customs and values and beliefs. Friendships are different. They form within and are limited to the teen's own generation. Nonetheless, I enjoy her use of the word. *Tribe* has a softer feel than the word *gang*, with its associations of aggression and delinquency, but it has a similar resonance of exclusivity and ritual. Sandra, like Amanda and many other parents, feels her teen is being taken over by foreign customs and practices.

Few teens are indifferent to either inclusion or exclusion from their peers. Wendy and Garth reshape themselves to ensure inclusion, while Philip replaces the "armor" of friends with a distinctive teen mix of anger and feigned indifference.

Why does the need to be included in a peer group gain new urgency in adolescence? Why do Garth's long-term interests fall by the wayside as he adopts those of his friends? Why does Wendy prioritize being with her friends, even when it means giving up doing something she loves? Why is Philip's belonging within the family no longer enough? Why do adolescents without close friendship face higher risks of depression?[7]

To understand the importance of friends in adolescence, we have to reflect again on the looking-glass self and teens' social brain.

THE LOOKING-GLASS SELF

The name "looking-glass self" might suggest that teens identify who they are with their reflection in the mirror. A looking-glass self, however, is obsessed not so much with what the teen herself sees in the mirror, but what others see. This is a fragile, ever-changing self, packed with self-doubt as a teen wonders,

"How do I look to other people?" and "How are people seeing me as they look at me now?"

As we saw in Chapter Two, the changes taking place in the teen brain mean that teens have to work harder than either a young child or an adult to process social information.[8] This additional effort increases teens' uncertainty about how others see them. Accompanying a teen as she walks into a room or around her school is an internal critical, edgy audience that second-guesses what other people are thinking. This internal observer delivers verdicts that shift in an instant from "You look great" to "You look like a freak."

In childhood we look to parents to be our "mirror." They express pride and pleasure or anger and anxiety about what we do, and we generally accept what they reflect back to us. Sometimes a child is "gorgeous" or "cute"; sometimes he is "filthy" or "disgusting," as he picks his nose or eats with his fingers. A child accepts that this is how he is viewed. Parents present a mirror in which his behavior is good or bad, and provide reference points for his judgments of other people. As a child observes other people, he checks his parents' responses before he decides whether a person can be trusted. In this way, parents convey information about other people, too.

But teens constantly seek information about how people outside the family see them. As thirteen-year-old Liba grapples with her rapidly developing body, her mother tries to reassure her: "You're gorgeous. You're turning into a stunning young woman." But what matters to the teen is what she looks like to people in her social world. Nina, her friend, is the arbiter of whether jeans or a top suit her. "We go shopping and it's really great because we're both in the dressing room together, and, like, I'm looking in the mirror and she's looking at me, and when she says what works and what doesn't really work, I can see what she means, and it helps me when I wear it for real. If I just look in the mirror myself, I don't know what I see."

Friends reflect an image that might be okay—or not. Sometimes what a friend reflects back mocks, taunts, and demeans a teen, but often a friend supports and consolidates or "fixes" an acceptable image. Liba uses what Nina sees to boost her confidence as she walks down the school corridor, into a classroom or a party. Nina can measure what her peers see in a way her mother cannot.

These friends, these new mirrors, are not just "there" as family are. The teen is now an agent in her choice of mirror. Herein lies the special excitement and power of friendship. A friend is selected as someone worthy to mirror a teen. Perhaps a friend is chosen as someone who they would like to be like, or a friend may be someone who knows what the teen should look like. A friend puts a teen in touching distance of a viable, acceptable persona.

Garth, fourteen, tells me that he "can't really believe [he's] lucky enough" to be included with his new set of friends. "I knew them back in grade school. They'd be all together and there was this pause in the whole yard when they came by. I'd be doing hoops, but when these guys were by, I just started bouncing the ball, biding my time, watching them. I didn't even want them to notice me. I just wanted to watch them. Now I'm one of them, and I get, 'Come on, Gar,' and, it's like whoosh—I'm inside that magic center." Garth takes note of the shoes his friends wear and the bags they carry and the ways they style their hair, and he wants the same shoes, bag, and hairstyle because, with an as-yet fragile looking-glass self, he hopes that looking like his friends will ease or at least camouflage self-doubt.

Self-doubt is common in teens because they have not yet grown or invented[9] a sense of self, with a steady register of character traits, with a range of passions and interests, with a working feel for their abilities or limitations. The great psychologist Erik Erikson called adolescence a time of identity crisis. In coining this now familiar term, Erikson described teens' intensive exploration of the different ways they might see themselves. They practice being one kind of person and then another. If an adult changes persona day after day, it would be considered a pathology, but it is a normal part of a teen's life.

Teens discover who they are by experimenting with or trying out different identities.[10] This is what Wendy does as she presents herself as just like her friends, keen to do what they do, changing herself to fit in with her friends. She thinks, "I don't know who I am, but my friends seem comfortable with who they are, so I'll try out their persona and see how it feels."

Some teens, however, are uncomfortable with this chameleon effect. With a firm sense of their own temperament and interests they seek a good match in a friend. Philip is irritated by his father's "nagging to invite my so-called friends to the house." He would rather be alone than spend time with people who are "just not like me at all. There are guys I can hang out with, when I have to. But I feel like a fake."

Teens are so intolerant of anyone they consider "fake" or a "phony"[11] because they are themselves uncertain what within them is genuine and what is "fake." They despise in others the trait they fear is theirs. But if they see themselves reflected in their friends, then their own self seems more clearly defined and real. Strangely, as they mimic their friends, they feel less fake.

Choosing a friend as a mirror, however, is only the very

first step in the friendship work of adolescence. After a teen chooses her mirror, she and her friend shape how each sees the other. Using their new skills in self-reflection, they talk. Friendship talk is centered on, "This is how I feel," and "This is what I love," and "This is what I fear," and "This is who I want to be." And in friendship talk, they bring a new self to life.

SELF-EXPLORATION WITH FRIENDS

Parents sometimes bemoan the time teens "waste just talking" to friends, or hanging out, or exchanging views via email, text, or social media. But in this mix, real work is being done, the work of self-discovery and self-expression.

"I knew you'd understand!" is a cry my colleague Ruthellen Josselson and I frequently heard when we talked to teens about their friendships. In childhood friendships, children learn the basics of positive sociability—turn taking in games and in conversations, joining a group activity, and abiding by the social rules. In adolescent friendships these prosocial routines continue, but a deeper and more personal mutuality emerges. Friends begin to talk about their feelings and fears, often feelings and fears they thought were theirs alone. Vicky, whom Ruthellen and I interviewed when she was fourteen years old, said, "I thought, before I got to know Clare—before I got to know her like I know her now—I thought I was the only one in the school, maybe in the whole world, who thought about things and wondered about things like I do. There are things you can't talk about to other people. I sometimes feel so weird, the way I look at everyone and see them. But with Clare, I can talk about this without feeling I'm such a weirdo."[12]

Ruthellen and I observed the hours of practice teens put into friendship talk. We, like many others at that time, thought such mutual self-exploration was specific to teen girls' friendships. But our studies about girls' friendships shone light on widely shared teen experiences. When, for example, researchers looked at boys, particularly boys in early and middle adolescence, they saw the same efforts to articulate who they are and what they feel, the same eagerness to hear who the other is, and to use these exchanges to clarify their own thoughts and feelings. Teenage boys, like teenage girls, coach their friends into speech. "How do you feel?" and "What do you think?" and "What is it like inside your head?" and "What do you hope for?" and "What do you fear?" Teenage boys, like teenage girls, are relieved and delighted when a friend says, "I understand" and "This is what it's like to be me." For teens who feel they do not fit in their assigned gender, or either gender, having a friend who, as fourteen-year-old Matt says, "sees through this stupid disguise of a body and sees who I really am," is a precious gift. "It helps me feel real, and helps me get to know myself."

Friendship work marks a new stage in the mentalizing exercises that began much earlier in life between infant and parent. Friendship offers teens space to name their shifting, confused feelings, and to recognize shared difficulties. The endless talking that parents complain about helps teens focus on their thoughts and feelings and motives. Teens also learn about their power to offer comfort and understanding to others. As we saw in the previous chapter, naming emotions has the power to tame them,[13] providing teens with another route to self-regulation—the ability to experience intense and changeable feelings without being overwhelmed.

Self-revelations within friendship help organize the teen brain. In his excellent book *Brainstorm*, Daniel Siegel writes, "People who use their minds to reflect on the inner nature of their mental lives grow circuits in the brain that link widely separated areas to one another. This linkage, called 'neural integration,' creates the coordination and balance of the nervous system."[14] Like warm and engaged relationships with parents,[15] good friendships guide brain growth.[16]

OPTING OUT OF IDENTITY WORK

Not all teen friendships, however, allow genuine exploration.

For both teens and adults, explaining ourselves to a friend and responding in kind to our friend's disclosures are hard work. We concentrate on facial expressions and modulation and emphasis in voice. We take in the rhythm of breath, the sudden freeze in muscles, the swerve or fix of eyes, and adjust our responses according to whether we note interest or boredom, sympathy or criticism. Sometimes we don't get it right. We want to offer sympathy, but we find we have given offense. We reveal our feelings to a friend, but instead of empathizing with us, he condemns us. Teens want to "be real" with their friends, but often have difficulty negotiating their need for belonging with their need for authenticity.

"Siobhan and me—well, we understand each other perfectly," Wendy tells me. "Me and the other girls—Dori and Elodie, too—we all think the same, and like the same things. Sometimes, especially with Siobhan, we don't talk for a while, like we're in a situation, and then we look at each other and I'll know exactly what she's thinking, and she'll know, like, what's in my mind, and we'll just laugh, because we don't even need words to know we're in sync."

Wendy is describing stage one of teenage friendship—the excited discovery of someone outside your family who, you think, is "just like you." In this stage, teens often idealize friendship. It has a magic, almost romantic enchantment. Each feels safe in the approval of the other. The satisfying "click" or "match" when they feel "my friend understands me" leads some teens to believe a friend is "exactly like me." This "solves" the identity crisis, because they believe they know who they are now: they are just like their friend.

But what happens when teens change and grow, when their interests shift, when enthusiasms fade? What happens when a friend changes? If the friendship is based on being exactly alike, it is highly constrained. When friendships change, teens face a dilemma: either they change to be, again, just like their friend, or they are back to square one, wondering who they are.

When Ruthellen and I explored the world of girls' friendships, we found that fourteen years was the pivot age, when friends who felt like identical twins (or how they imagine identical twins feel) often experience a brutal betrayal as one goes her own way. Ruthellen relayed the story of Tamara, who, in the ninth grade, saw her best friend, the one who was "just like her" turn up on the first day of school dressed all in black—a sign that she identified with the group of Goths. "I felt that she betrayed me to be cool . . . for some guy with green eyes who could play the guitar." Tamara and her friend talk for hours on the phone every evening, promising each other to reestablish the oneness they once had. But "then the next day it would turn sour as soon as we met in the school hall."

Later in this book we will see how resistance to being "just the same" is played out with parents, but teens also mark out their individual identity with their friends. They discover that they feel different with different people and in different contexts. This is why Tamara and her friend genuinely feel they can be "one" when they talk in private, but feel very different at school, where they feel like "different people."

When differences between friends emerge, teens face a dilemma: "Do I continue to voice my real thoughts, and risk creating a rift with my friend, or do I hide who I really am to keep my friend?" As teens tread a narrow path between genuine attachment and desperation for inclusion, their friendships can be unstable and unpredictable.

THE IMPORTANCE OF GOSSIP

In friendship, teens practice building stories about their lives and the lives of others. Telling a story about what's happened is a way of processing and organizing our experiences. Simply setting events in context and noting their sequence helps us put our thoughts in some kind of order. This apparently simple process helps us store memories and manage the emotions associated with them, so that distressing events do not continue to plague us. Given teens' raw and turbulent responses to ordinary social interactions, storytelling can be a great healer.

People have been storytellers as far back as we can trace humans, but scientists have been slow to appreciate the importance of these narratives. It was not until about thirty years ago that psychologists realized how our sense of self is built up by the stories we tell about our lives. From the raw data of experience we shape heroes and villains, successes and failures. Teens' sense of self is both expressed and formed by these stories.

We found that friendship talk was a way of practicing and testing the stories that define who we are. Sixteen-year-old Kelly told us, "We spend hours talking. Just talking. Sometimes it's about just one thing. Like, what happened last night, or yesterday at school when she was away. Then she asks a hundred questions: 'What happened then? What did she say? How did she say it? Tell me exactly how she said it. Do her voice! What did you say then? How did you feel?' That's why she's my best friend. She wants to know all about my day and who I am."[17]

Many stories teens relate and receive are referred to as gossip. Today the word *gossip* has a bad name, but originally it just meant conversations with "god-sibs" or people in a close-knit group. It is often thought to be "a female thing," but all genders and ages alike engage in gossip.[18] It is through gossip that we learn how people live behind the public face, behind what teens often think of as a façade.

Given teens' obsession with a "real" or genuine self versus a fake or phony self, it is clear why gossip takes hold in the teen years. Grappling with their own identity experiments, teens are endlessly curious about other people's lives. Gossip explores the unofficial version of people's lives, the experiences and drama behind the carefully presented self.

As Wendy talks to her friends, who seem "one just like the other" to her mother, she learns that Gayle, who used to be Wendy's friend before she joined this new group, "hooked up" with a boy who she thought, and thought others thought, was "fire." On the breakup of this brief liaison, Gayle posted pictures and tweets mocking the boy, calling him a "plain pussy." Wendy wants to know more. She follows the social media exchange, both appalled and intrigued by the words and images used. "We were in a way just being silly about it, but it really meant something to me. I was finding out about someone who used to be my friend, kind of like keeping up with her. There was this 'Whoa! She's having a life without me,' and I was also, like, 'How did this happen? Does she miss me? Where is she really at now?' "

Gossip slakes teens' curiosity, but what they learn can be very upsetting. When I ask Garth about recent stories he's heard about other people, he tells me that a friend of his described how another friend had sex with a girl he knows and likes. After sex, the boy abruptly left, took a shower, and felt "stoked, real pleased with himself, but the girl was like 'nothing.' He didn't call or text her again. He didn't do anything. It was just like, 'I've had a good time.' It makes me feel sick. I want to be nice to the girl. I want her to feel better. But I don't want to let on that I know."

What Wendy and Garth learn through gossip deepens their responses to people they know, raises further questions, and triggers reflection about the meanings of these events. Gossip stimulates storytelling beyond our own experiences, connecting us to others.

Gossip is also used to signal the strength of the bond between friends. Kelly knows that her best friend wants to hear all about her, but she also knows her friend wants "the lowdown" on everything that happened at a party she went to but her friend didn't. The content seems empty to her mother, who "can't understand why this stuff is so interesting" and chides Kelly for "spending hours chewing over a whole load of nothing," but for Kelly and her friend, information about who talked to whom, who snubbed whom, who left early, who stayed late, and who got drunk all form significant pieces in the social puzzle they constantly assemble and rearrange.

Gossip also measures trust in a relationship. When Wendy is included in the gossip about one of the group—that Tina was "bothered" by a friend of the girl's brother, and was "nearly raped," Wendy experiences "that really yucky feeling when you see what can happen," but she is also reassured that she is among the trusted inner circle of the group. "They know I won't spread this around. They know I can be trusted."

Sometimes, however, even a friend cannot be trusted with gossip. The unease someone feels about information puts pressure on them to talk to others. "I wanted to find out what was going on with Tina. I wanted to know whether she's okay. But when I asked her about stuff she got real nasty. She wanted to know like, 'Who told you that?' and I had to tell her, and she just walked away. Then [another girl] asked me, 'You know Tina. Why is she being so weird?' So I kind of wanted to defend Tina, because she has a good reason to be—you know? And I wanted [the other girl] to know this guy was someone to avoid. I wanted someone else to hate him in the queasy way I hate him. I don't think she'll tell anyone. But I worry, because I think the guys will know it was me who let it out, if it gets around that other people know."

Whereas Wendy's mother thinks her daughter is "stewing over things that don't matter," friendship talk involves mind-stretching exercises. Wendy grapples with issues of trust, truth, and duty. Her conundrum is "I am trusted not to say anything, but I have a duty to protect others from the harm Tina suffered." She engages in complex perspective taking: "My friends know I know about the assault on Tina, and they see me, the new girl, as the one most likely to betray the group's rules." She considers how background knowledge helps make sense of Tina's "weird" behavior, and she seeks help with emotion management (she "had to" tell her mother to ease her own distress). In adolescence, when the social life of friends has paramount importance, this is not "nothing" nor does it involve "things that don't matter."

But no teen or parent would claim that gossip is only a force for good. Gossip's special language—"*What!* Did she *really* do that?"—with the short intake of breath and shake of the head, contains brutal social judgment. Messages signal what's acceptable and what's not. This alerts teens to the reputational risk not only of what they actually do, but of what others think they've done. At any moment they themselves might be the person other people "say bad things about." With their fragile looking-glass self, the question, "Who will say what about me?" is a constant concern. Getting wind of negative gossip about *you* is torture.

Teens develop their understanding of others and their sensitivities to how others see them just when their emotions ignite most easily. They are more interested in gossip, learn more from it, but are also far more anxious than children or grown-ups about being the subject of gossip.

The convergence of heightened social awareness and social anxiety has been called the "neuro-biological storm" of adolescence.[19] It can cause such havoc that some teens try to avoid being a social victim by victimizing others. Behind the Queen Bee, mean girl, and schoolyard bully is often no more than a confused teen trying to manage this storm. She becomes the dictator who determines what others are, how they should be treated, and what names they should be called, all in the hope that she can deflect attention from her own vulnerabilities.

However painful it is to hear behind-the-back stories about themselves or a close friend, the shock of unjust stories delivers important lessons. Teens learn that stories are often simplified and distorted and even falsified. They then begin to reflect, as Wendy does: "I always, like, start thinking about what it's like for the other person. There are always two sides of a story."

Understanding what friendship talk offers can adjust parents' impatience with what Judy calls "the non-stop non-event chatter I get when Kirsty comes home from school. It's full of 'she said this' and 'someone did that' and then suddenly she's asking me if I agree with her about such and such, and I think, 'What? Where's this all going?' I lost the plot ten sentences back, you know?" But this "non-stop non-event chatter" is teens' way of mapping their social landscape. The more parents understand about the importance of friends, the better they will be at allowing their teen to get the best from their friends.

FRIENDS IN A DIGITAL WORLD

Until the pandemic crisis, with lockdowns and school closures, most parents and teachers worried about the negative effects of screen time, particularly on social media. Parents' fears were stoked by claims that virtual communication reduced empathy, limited teens' attention span, and put their well-being in jeopardy.[20] When the Royal College of Psychiatrists issued a report on the effect of screen use on teens, they asked, "What are the harms?"[21] The questions, "What are the benefits and how can these be protected?" were lost in the moral panic over a new technology.

If digital communication is harmful, then the alarm is understandable. Ninety-five percent of teens in the US have, or have access to, a smartphone, and 97 percent of teens aged thirteen to seventeen have a social media profile.[22] The majority of teens spend more than four hours a day on various social media sites[23] and nearly half say they are online most of the day.[24] Parents were warned that, as a result, teens were becoming superficial, language-deficient, and narcissistic.[25]

These concerns shifted abruptly during the pandemic crisis that began in 2020, when the more salient concern was about the very special dangers teens faced from social isolation. Loneliness is unhealthy for anyone, at any time, but in adolescence the risks are much higher with potentially far-reaching consequences.[26] Friendships, as we have seen, are often a source of anxiety and insecurity, but isolation does not ease anxiety. Without daily contact with friends, teens' mood and outlook plummet.[27]

Weeks into the pandemic, scientists and parents began to fear depression and anxiety more than screen time. "Thank goodness this didn't happen fifteen years ago," parents and teachers and scientists said. The benefits of new technologies were suddenly obvious. In lockdown, teens could engage with friends, gather information, gossip and gripe and joke, while protected from contagion. They had some access to the social stimulation they require on an hourly basis, and they could avoid the lows of social isolation. They could share and manage new fears about their health and that of their family. They had the comfort of companions who also saw their plans about school and college and work fade into the distance. Once-maligned digital devices offered a lifeline to teens who constantly form and revise their identity with their friends.

What the lockdown brought home to parents and teachers and scientists is that smartphones, tablets, and laptops have a variety of impacts, depending on how they are used. The passive scrolling through accounts of people they do not really know—celebrities, influencers, lifestyle gurus—can isolate teens further as they view but do not actually enter the lives of others. They end up being "stoned" (as fourteen-year-old Tina put it) on the gloss of others' lives, and "sink deeper into a funk about [their] own." Digital communication with friends, however, provides something like ordinary companionship, and can, for a limited time, fill the gap imposed by physical distance. When the world itself seems scarier than ever, when teens lack the daily structure of school and outside activities, the neural exercise of social interaction with friends could calm anxiety and relieve boredom.

Some parents nonetheless remain anxious about the time their teen spends on social media. "Isn't it bad for their brain?" they ask, drawing on high-profile claims that screen time rewires young people's brains.[28]

The metaphor of "wiring" is often used to describe the brain's communication system. Just as a home is wired via clusters connected with separate circuits, so too does the brain work via clusters of cells that then send signals across various routes. A special feature of the brain's "wiring system," however, is that different circuits develop according to what we do, and routes are constantly created and modified. Digital devices do "rewire the brain," but so does reading or running or telling jokes or doing physics experiments.

"Screen time" covers many, many things, and virtual communication can be used in many ways. It can be used to give a sense of belonging when a teen is different from classmates. Philip follows a variety of hashtags for deaf teens, where he discovers that "the thing that makes me a freak at school is just the baseline normal. Some stuff is about being deaf, like how you deal with so-called sympathy and those stupid questions about whether you were born deaf. But most of it is just talk, about things everyone cares about." Kirsty, who has diabetes, follows an active diabetes community on social media where she can post questions to diabetes nurses directly "without going through my Mom, and having her get all worried and need to suss out the answer herself."

Teens also use social media to try out their different personae. Wendy shows me posts where she is sexy or bluestocking or cute or sophisticated. She tells me about a friend who is good at the "real tough don't mess with me look." Their posts on Instagram or TikTok are a leisure activity, where they play at being in control of the looking-glass self.

Of course, friends respond in negative ways too, and I discuss new vulnerabilities teens face from social media in the next chapter. But social media is also just another way of interacting with one another, sharing and commenting on information about friends, parents, school, films, music, and TV soaps. Teens post information about their feelings, their arguments with parents or siblings or friends, their frustration with schoolwork, and their sense of a messed- up world. They share, and co-regulate, emotions. Their responses to eye-to-eye contact, facial expressions, and laughter are, according to brain image studies, the same via a screen as in person.[29] Nothing can replace the vast information friends get from one another as they sit or walk together, eat together, watch each other listen to music, or interact with others or fall silent, but the digital world offers enough contact to keep a friendship ticking over during periods of separation.

OVERVIEW AND EXERCISES

Social interaction with friends is of paramount importance to teens. Much of the time, teens use friendships to learn about other people and the context in which others make decisions, act, and experience emotions. As teens explore others' minds, they also reflect on the nexus of ideas, beliefs, and goals that define them.

Studies of teens across decades show that when parents get to know their friends, teens are at less risk of friendship's potential negative effects.[30] Encouraging teens to bring their friends home presents parents with the opportunity to understand and monitor the friendship.

Many parents find, however, that even the most basic introductions to their teens' friends are problematic. "He brings his friends home, but they hunker down in his bedroom. I never get to say 'boo!' " parents often tell me.

There are simple ways to diffuse the awkwardness that drives teens' shyness. The first step is to show that the friend is welcome. The best techniques are minimal techniques, such as greeting the friend directly, with some version of "Nice to see you." Second, don't linger or indicate that your greeting is an opening for a conversation (which the friend and your teen are likely to see as an interrogation).

You can seek out opportunities to extend your knowledge of your teen's friends. When you go on a family outing, suggest your teen bring a friend. This might make the teen happier about joining you, and it enables parents to see the friendship in action.

When you think the friend has been at your home "long enough," and you know your teen has homework to do or you want his or her input with meal prep, instead of knocking on the door (a brutal intrusion) or calling to the teen (it will sound like you are shouting), text your teen to give warning: "You need to be in the kitchen/doing your homework in 15 minutes." Advance warning goes a long way in reducing the teen's sense of being "bossed around."

When the teen and friend emerge from their private space, you can ask the friend, "When are you expected back home?" This is a gentle way of exploring whether your teen's friend is monitored by his or her parents.

Welcoming your teen's friends, of course, does not mean giving them and your teen free rein in your home. Teens crave more independence, and they want you to trust them, but they also need rules about where they can go and about when they need to be home. The rules should be clear, realistic, and enforceable.

Social life is of great importance to teens, but it can also be a source of physical and mental dangers. There will be low points when a teen feels awkward and isolated, when even a reliable friend seems unable to understand him, or when a once-trusted friend betrays him. Some low points seem like the end of the world.

Parents suffer when they see their teen in such pain, and they often want to "fix" it or "make it go away." "You shouldn't care about such a bad friend," or "Just ignore him," they advise. A more effective strategy is to listen and observe a teen's distress without minimizing it. From their place on the sidelines of friendship dramas, parents can offer sympathy (devoid of anxiety) and suggest small compensatory comforts that remind the teen of family belonging (such as watching a film or game together, sharing a meal, putting up shelves). As parents quietly show they are "there" for the teen and gently refocus the teen's attention, the teen can stay with her unhappiness while seeing that it is not ending her world.

Embarrassment and self-consciousness wield a special power in teenagers. As we have seen, with their particularly fragile looking-glass self—the part of all of us that is shaped by awareness (and fear and hope) of how others see us—teens are preoccupied with what other people think of them. Hypersensitive to social cues, they often misinterpret them. One common misinterpretation (as I discuss in greater detail in Chapter Seven) involves "reading" a neutral facial expression as one of anger or disapproval. As a result, teens suffer great social anxiety unnecessarily, seeing anger or disapproval where there is no such thing.

When a teen allows a parent to see his or her social anxiety, the parent should grab this as an opportunity to connect with the teen. Rather than brush the teen's anxiety aside, as many parents wish they could do, with instructions such as "You're imagining things," or "You shouldn't care what other people think," parents can open conversations about how difficult it is to know what other people are thinking and feeling. "What makes you feel you've been rejected or criticized?" and "Why do you think they said that?" Encourage your teen to think what might be going through a friend's mind. Then you might ask, "And how many other people think [these negative things] about you?" In a low mood, the teen might say, "Everyone." This presents the opportunity to ask, "Can your friends really all think the same thing?" and "Can you think of something nice a friend said about you recently?" Such questions remind the teen that there is a vast social space outside the particular problem he is focusing on now.

Teens' friendships deserve respect. Offering respect, however, does not mean shelving your own views about your teen's friends—and there is more discussion of this in the next chapter. Helping a son or daughter choose trustworthy friends is one of the most important parental tasks. In adolescence, however, parental help requires a give-and-take approach:

parental opinions will be tolerated only if they are shaped as a gentle hypothesis: "I think Lucy is the dominant one here. Is that right?" Or "Does Joe change his plans for you, like you do for him?" Presenting a teen with something to think about, and showing interest in the teen's response, are far more effective than telling her what you think.

5

"I just did it. Stop asking me why."

Hot Zones and Pressure Points

WE HAVE SEEN how friendships encourage and guide teens' mental and emotional growth, yet parents put "concern about the influence of peers" among the top two or three worries. Are their worries unnecessary?

Alas, the answer is no. Throughout adolescence there is an increased risk of friends destabilizing a normally trustworthy teen. The likelihood that teens will break the law, or drink alcohol or take drugs, is closely correlated with the behavior of their friends.[1] It is not surprising, then, that for many parents, a teen's friendships top the list of their concerns.

No one gets to be parent of a teen without facing battles about who a child should befriend and what activities with friends are allowed. "No, you can't go there with your friends; it's not safe" and "I don't care what other parents let their child do" are standard fare in a parent's life with a child, and, during the teen years, as teens resist parental control, such routines often become brutal.

Lynn, mother of fourteen-year-old Aaron, shudders at the sound of her own voice as it strains with anger. "I hear my mother's voice when I forbid him from meeting up with [those other boys]. It's the same voice I hated as a teen, but I don't know what else to do. The guys he thinks are his friends are trouble, big time. And I'm at my wits' end."

In this chapter, we see why many parents feel at their "wits' end," and why protecting and monitoring teens' time with friends is so difficult and so necessary.

THE PERILOUS HABITAT OF TEENAGE FRIENDS

Parents often fear the bad influence of friends. Each parent is haunted by his or her personal scenario, the thing that seems most likely to endanger a teen's well-being and potential, whether it is the lethal introduction to drugs or a perilous dare in a speeding car. So parents advise their teen, "Don't let your friends lead you astray" and "Don't give in to your friends." This advice is sound, but it ignores the crux of problems in exercising good judgment among friends.

Teens sometimes do coax or coerce or bully one another, but the pressure is more likely to come from what happens to a teen's own brain in the company of friends. We all, whatever our age, enjoy social rewards such as praise or admiration or even simple attention, but, as we saw in Chapter Two, teens' craving for rewards is easily triggered and not so easily controlled. Combined with their hypersensitivity to how others see them, looking cool can be a powerful motive for doing just about anything. Avoiding looking "uncool" is an even more powerful motive.

While teens' intellect is perfectly capable of assessing the risk of a dangerous activity—whether it is drug taking or driving too fast or smoking—the company of friends produces a "hot zone" in which the thrill of the risk and the delight in impressing friends dominate their actions.[2] The urge to please friends, to gain their admiration or attention, to impress them, does not arise because your teen's friends are leading him astray. The urge comes from within your teen's brain.

Teen drivers, for example, are as sensible and reliable as the average adult when they are alone in a car. But when teens are with friends, they are much more likely to drive after they've been drinking, to speed, and to leave their seat belts unfastened. The risks teens take increase with each additional friend in the car. With one friend, a teen's risk of having a crash is 40 percent higher than that of a grown-up. With two friends along in the car, the risk is 80 percent greater. With three or more friends accompanying a teen driver, the risk of crashing is 300 percent higher than that of an adult.[3] Teens are four times more likely to die in a car when they are with friends.

The psychologist Laurence Steinberg has spent decades looking into teenagers behaving badly—particularly at their risky behavior. Steinberg and his colleagues measured the brain activity of both teens and adults during a driving game.[4] This was essentially a video game in which players had to make quick decisions as to whether to stop at a red light or risk speeding through an intersection. He observed the teens playing the game twice, once on their own and once in the presence of friends.

There was no difference in how teens and grown-ups played the game when they were alone, but teens played the game very differently when their friends were looking on. The adults "drove" the same, whether or not their friends were around, but the teens took far more risks, such as going through red lights, when their friends were watching. Later, Steinberg discovered that the friends did not even have to be in the room to wield their influence. It is enough for the teen to be told, "Imagine your friends are here," and—presto!—teens' risk taking escalated. Steinberg writes, "Most people think that adolescents are more reckless with friends because of peer pressure—that teens actively encourage each other to take chances. . . . As it turns out, peer pressure isn't necessarily the culprit . . . simply knowing that their friends are nearby makes them take more chances."[5]

Several regions of the brain contribute to what is called "the social brain." There is the complex and extensive mentalizing part of the brain that figures out what other people are thinking.[6] There is the more primitive emotional part of the brain with its active reward center and its quick-fire responsiveness to other people, assessing whether they are friend or foe. Then there is the region of the brain that is sensitive to social acceptance or rejection. All switch on when a teen is asked to think about friends, or about being liked, accepted, or rejected. Acutely sensitive to the rewards of risky behavior—the attention, the thrill, the kudos—the teen brain's (already compromised) control center is easily suppressed, creating a hot zone that destabilizes even a normally sensible and responsible teen.

Alcohol presents another risk to teens' good judgment.

Drinking affects everyone's judgment, whether adult or teen, but teens are particularly vulnerable to its ill effects. "I know he's going to drink at those parties," Dee says about her seventeen-year-old son Simon, "so I tell him, 'It's okay as long as you take responsibility. Know what you're doing. Keep track—you know—keep a kind of score. And he says 'Yeah, sure, Mom. I'm not stupid.' But later he'll come back sick as a dog, totally out of things, and miserable as hell the next morning."

Simon is not stupid, but as a teen he is slower to notice the effects of alcohol, even though his teen brain is more sensitive to alcohol than that of an adult. When Simon drinks half the amount of alcohol that a grown-up drinks, he gets twice as drunk as an adult would from the same amount.[7] So when he insists, "I didn't drink that much," he may well be telling the truth, but that doesn't mean he did not drink enough to be drunk. Not only do teens find it hard to track what they drink when they are with friends, they are also measuring "enough" and "too much" on a scale that is not appropriate for them.

Nor do adults measure teen behavior on a realistic scale. Len says he is "absolutely flummoxed" when his sixteen-year-old daughter Sophie is charged with shoplifting when she is out with her friends. Bea is "mortified and furious, like someone kicked my guts out" when the police arrive with her fifteen-year-old son Ravi in tow to report that he and his friends were vandalizing cars. "My first thought was, 'This can't be right. That's just not my son.' But then I looked at him and I saw it *was* right. What happened to that boy? Who is he?"

Bea's son is both the boy she has known and loved, a boy with sound values, capable of care and respect, and a teen whose brain's reward center is highly reactive and easily overwhelmed. The excitement of social rewards and the inefficiency of the brain's pause button create a fault line in teen friendships, where smart and sensible teens do utterly stupid things. Yet we live in societies in which older teens are, by law, expected to meet the same standards as adults.

Many psychologists have called for changes to justice systems, noting that so-called delinquency, or typical young people's crimes such as vandalism, theft, and assault, peak in adolescence and then rapidly decline in adulthood.[8] Eighty percent of teens who are charged with delinquent behavior prove themselves to be perfect citizens by the age of twenty-four. Any parent whose teen has been hauled through criminal justice for a single, impulsive act can attest to the harm of a legal system that fails to acknowledge the hot zone of the adolescent brain.[9]

GENDER PRESSURES FROM PEERS

Parents tell me they want their teens to be true to themselves, to find their own voice, and to follow the goals that work for them regardless of their gender. Today's parents often express irritation with gender norms, or social rules about what's right for a girl and what's right for a boy and the need to fit into gender roles. Parents want to preserve for their teen a breadth of choice. All too often they find that the tolerance they encourage is undercut by their teen's social environment.

Gender takes on a new importance in adolescence. Teens' sexual development is now visible and inescapable. While teachers and parents complain about gender stereotypes in films and TV shows and social media and advertisements, they often overlook the power teens exert over other teens to set down rules, enforcing them through teasing or gossip or outright condemnation.

During early and middle childhood, friendship groups tend to be segregated by gender. If boys at that stage try to join a group of girls, they often mean to make mischief. If a girl tries to join a group of boys, she is likely to be rejected.[10] By adolescence, two different genders have unique codes or rules for what counts as a good friendship. Teens who do not feel at home in either gender, or in their currently designated gender, are particularly uncomfortable with these codes, but all teens are aware what they risk by nonadherence—exclusion from their group.

For girls, exchanging compliments, offering reassurance about appearance and character, being a friendly mirror to one another are high on the list of rules for being a good friend. Teen girls compliment a friend's skin and face and dress, and offer reassurance about appearance ("You look great in that. No, you don't look fat" or "I don't see one darn spot from here, and I'm only five inches away from your face"). Teen girls also compliment a friend's character. They use their deepening human understanding to highlight qualities in a friend that the friend herself may not have noticed. When Dori admires Kelly for her courage or her humor, Kelly sees new qualities in herself, too.

A lot of friendship work goes towards managing one another's self-doubts, heightened by teens' growing moral sensitivity. This may involve revising the story a friend tells about herself, or refuting stories other people tell about a friend. Kelly, sixteen, needs to talk to her friend Sandy when she feels she has "messed up." Kelly explains, "Sandy always listens. And then she'll say, "No you didn't mess up. You did the right thing. I don't see how your mom can say you're inconsiderate." Or "You weren't mean [to another girl]. You were honest. And she should appreciate that. It's her problem, not yours."

Together friends reframe the story from one in which Kelly is to blame into one in which she deserves praise. This technique will be used over and over in our lives, either in our internal dialogue or with a close friend as we ruminate over questions such as "Was I fair?" and "Did I do the right thing?" and "Is he right to criticize me?" At any age we are sometimes uneasy about whether we have done "the right thing," but the unease a grown-up or a child feels cannot compare to the acute anxiety experienced by teens. Friendships can help diffuse these anxieties, but in doing so they draw on codes of conduct, many of which are strict and constraining.

Kelly discovers there are limitations in what she can tell her best friend. "I sometimes really, really hate my mom. I mean I have these five-minute daydreams where I kill her. It's awful, yes, I know, I know, but you *said*, you know, you said you would just listen and not condemn. Right? Well I have one friend who also listens and doesn't put me on a blacklist when I say this stuff. Or so I thought. But when I told her how I get into this frenzy of hatred—well, I was expecting some kind of, 'Oh everyone thinks like that,' but her face kind of froze and the way she looked at me completely changed. I felt like I'd just walked off a cliff. I tried to backtrack, you know, to say, 'It's not really like that. I mean, that's really extreme.' And we sort of got back to an okay place, but it's a sign that there are some things I really can't tell her. Things that show she's wrong about me being a good person." Because naming feelings is so important in managing them, a friendship in which feelings have to be silenced can induce shame—the belief that one's real self is unacceptable.

Gossip, too, contains a host of reminders about rules of conduct, particularly gender norms and sexuality. "She's a slut/slag/whore" does not merely attack the gossip's target. It reminds everyone who hears it that certain behavior will incur disdain from friends. Similarly, "She's so full of herself" and "All she does is brag, brag, brag" and "She thinks she's some Real Housewife with those fake designer shoes" instruct a group that boasting is a culpable offense.

In the female code of friendship, friends don't criticize one another, or compete with one another. These female codes can constrain and distort not only the relationship but also how a teen sees herself. "I am bad to have such negative thoughts about my friend" and "I must be a bad person, really." Or "I can't go for editor of the school paper because that would be stepping on my friend's toes. I know she wants that." Or wanting to be "like" a friend, she avoids taking subjects that a friend thinks are "too nerdy." The stakes for compliance are high, particularly for teen girls who are exquisitely sensitive to the fine detail of social interactions. Teachers and parents report how upset girls can be by even small conflicts, how they stew on them for days, pouring time and energy into sorting out what happened, and who said what, and who was in the right.[11]

Teen girls list personal courage and ability to speak one's mind and not be afraid of any pushback among the traits they most admire in others, demonstrating their resistance against the stereotype of "the good girl." But when it comes to their friendships, they dread conflict[12] and want to comply with the female ideal of "the good friend who never argues."[13] They then confront a dilemma: to choose between social rejection (a common trigger for teen depression) and silencing their own thoughts—also a trigger of depression.[14]

PEER PRESSURE ON TEEN BOYS' FRIENDSHIPS

It is often said that girls' friendships involve more intimacy—more personal and intricate storytelling—than boys' friendships. This isn't true. Boys also form close friendships. They spend hours talking to one another while "hanging out" or shooting hoops. As with girls, much of their talk is gossip or exchange of information about what others are doing, about who is friends with whom, about people in their school who are not friends, and about sports figures or other celebrities. As with girls, the delight of belonging has a dark side that emerges when certain gender codes are broken.

Listening to the voices of boys, William Pollack realized that "boys have described to me how every day of their lives they receive covert messages that they do not measure up, and yet they feel they must cover up their sadness and confusion about plummeting self-esteem."[15] Pollack found that boys, even as young kids, are warned against being "soft" or "needy" or even "loving."

In early adolescence, however, boys' friendships defy this guy code. Fourteen-year-old boys form warm, passionate bonds in which they freely reveal their self-doubt and vulnerability. It's not that they directly challenge guy code rules, but they simply ignore them in their friendships. The language they use to describe their friendships is as rich with love and intimacy as that of girls. Like girls, they sing the praises of their friends, who are "there for them" and "loyal" and have empathy. These teen boys are also open about needing a friend. As one teen boy told psychologist Niobe Way, he would "go wacko" without his friend to talk to.[16] Hence they defy the macho code of autonomy and self-reliance.

Later in adolescence, however, around the age of sixteen, the grip of gender norms tightens. Teenage boys no longer speak so easily and openly about their attachments. In her original and sensitive exploration of boy friendships, Niobe Way observed how older teens would freeze, look abashed, and backtrack rather than disclose their tender feelings towards a friend. "I'm not a homo, or anything," they insisted, and the conversation would switch gear, becoming halted or jokey. Questions were met with that shrug familiar to parents of boy teens—an irritable, often voiceless shrug signaling, "Whatever" and "I don't really want to talk" and "I don't know, anyway."

This discomfort infects private conversations between friends, too. When one teen boy begins to tell his friend about how important he is to him, his friend warns him not to "get hormonal." Soon, the more tender feelings are denied and derided. The boy who in early adolescence praised a friend for "being understanding" now praises him for being tough and independent and fearless.[17] As these traits become the ideal, teen boys become hypersensitive to "not measuring up."

One route around such gender policing, some boys discover, is forming a friendship with a girl. The gender segregation that is strictly enforced in childhood friendships eases in mid-adolescence. Being teased about being romantic or lovey-dovey or even "soft" with a girl does not pose the same threat to the guy code as does being "soft" or "hormonal" with another boy. Mixed-sex friendships offer new paths to emotional development. Here, however, it is parents rather than friends who are alarmed. Some parents struggle to see mixed-sex friendships as anything other than a disguise for sexual attraction, and, as a result, overpolice the closeness, or express cynicism, and unwittingly starve an important blood supply to the teenage brain that thrives on intimate conversations.

NEW TECHNOLOGIES MAGNIFY OLD DANGERS

In the previous chapter I highlighted the benefits of digital communication through virtual contact or text or social media. However, there are instances when parents' concern about the harms of digital communication—particularly social media—is justified.

Top of parents' concerns is the risk of cyberbullying that extends from casual dismissals ("Who is the lame girl fooling?") to threats ("We should all shoot him"). The special force of negative, nasty comments—often anonymous—gives momentum to cyberbullies. As Naomi, age fifteen, explains, cyberbullying comes from "people you don't know but think they can trash you. And, you never know, maybe it's from someone you do know. But you never really know what's it about you that they're attacking." I ask her if that makes it better—after all, if they don't know you, or are attacking you for no reason, isn't it easier to dismiss? She says, "No, it's worse. Because you can't see how you can change. And it's not a specific thing. It's somehow you, the deep core of you, that they're saying is shameful." As fifteen-year-old Diana says, "It's like someone spitting straight at you."

In a sample of just under two thousand parents, eighty-nine percent said their teens had received messages that mock, denigrate, or threaten them.[18] More than half (55 percent) of all teens see bullying as a major problem;[19] even when they themselves don't experience it, they see its effect on their friends and know it might at some point affect them, too.

Parents often plead with their teen, "Don't look at it. Ignore it." But, as thirteen-year-old Ewan tells his mother, this advice is useless. "Ignoring what's going on is even worse. Even when they tell you to 'go hang yourself' because you're such a pathetic dick—well, like, at least you know the worst, instead of turning up at school when everyone else knows you're a target, and you don't know anything." For teens, ignoring social media is a fast route to feeling excluded.

Another common parental concern is how screen time takes precedence over teens' real-time world, so they lose focus on conversations and activities around them. Garth's mother Amanda said, "He went through this phase, at thirteen and fourteen, when he'd be staring at that screen for six hours a day. I had to grab the tablet away from him to get him to stop, and that would make him explode. He'd say, 'I hate you!' And he meant it, for sure."

Digital activities are designed to grab attention and keep hold of it. They are designed to provide excitement and pleasure, to offer a combination of adrenaline and dopamine—hormones of excitement and reward—that encourages repetition. Because they deliver a hormonal cocktail with a buzz and a thrill, video games and social media can take precedence over the real world and its complex, often slow-burn rewards.

Garth, at fifteen, has left his obsession with games behind, but a year ago he and his mother Amanda experienced terrible battles over screen time. "It got really physical—you know," she explained, "with me pulling the tablet from him and him shouting, 'Don't snatch it!' It was scary. Breaking that habit took a monumental effort of will on my part, and seventy-two hours of hell, when he locked himself in his room and kicked the wall, shouting, calling me all sorts of names."

Teens can develop a range of useful skills from video games, but the carefully designed allure of these games, sometimes leading to behavior that shares some features of addiction, comes from predictable challenges and reliable pleasures—unlike those gritty issues of real life.[20] Why engage with the messy world where you cannot replay everything, where you cannot track your improving skill, where the rules can never be fully known, when instead you can be fully absorbed in a game?

A third concern about screen use is how social media extends teens' vulnerability to social norms that restrict their goals and damage their self-esteem. Teens, as we have seen, are building, dismantling, and rebuilding their identities. As they ask, "Who am I?" and "Am I okay?" they look to their friends. They copy the friend who walks "in a cool way" that exudes confidence. They try out a friend's gestures because, they believe, everyone else is impressed. They copy another friend's makeup and hairstyle. Teens are quick to believe that someone who appears "cool" and confident feels confident and cool inside. But face-to-face, over time, they have opportunities also to see rough-edged realities this friend confronts, and the initial idealization shifts—sometimes to disappointment, sometimes to a more nuanced admiration. Social media provides little opportunity for any reality check.

The life source of social media is superficiality and glamor. The glitz, the show, the poses, the filters that remove imperfection and context set a standard against which anyone falls short. Teens try to match up by posting their own carefully presented "selfies"—photos taken by the teens themselves, usually on a smartphone, which they then share via social media. The looking-glass self then turns to other social media users to ask, "Do I look tough/sexy/desirable/handsome/strong?" Teens seek the answer from friends they know, as well as from "followers" who may be no more to them than anonymous profiles. The "likes" or comments on their posts become a measure of their own acceptability and worth.

It isn't that teens aren't aware that social media images are manipulated. The problem is that they respond to these images as though they were real even when they know they're not. In one study, a teen girl spoke about the "masks" others put on, and which she also wore when she posted images of herself.[21] Teens know that the photos are edited, but, as Liba tells me, "They just glow." "OMG!" she exclaims as she scrolls through her feed. "Wouldn't it be awesome to look like this?"

The novelist Marian Keyes touched the nerve of teens' responses as "relentlessly comparing my insides with everyone else's outsides, and finding myself always coming up short."[22] Carrie, sixteen, articulates but still cannot resist the false allure. "You assume so many things about people on social media without really knowing the truth, and it makes you think crazy things, based on the wrong information."[23] But what she knows and what she feels do not match. Scrolling through images that promote the fantasy of a perfect looking-glass self, she grows increasingly dissatisfied with her own physical and personal self.

Teens know these images are unreal, yet use them as a standard against which to judge their own lives and appearance. Photos on Instagram that attract lots of "likes" from their friends, set their brain's reward center alight,[24] so they imagine the pleasure they would have if one of their posts attracted such admiration. The envy-generating features of social media disrupt teens' self-satisfaction.

It is surprising that few researchers or policymakers address concerns about social media by asking "How can teens' use of social media improve?" The most common approach to managing the harms of social media involves limiting screen time. But, as many parents tell me, efforts to limit teens' time on social media give way to arguments and counterarguments that are exhausting but have little effect. In any case, keeping teens away from social media does not seem to make them happier or less anxious.[25] Ask a teen, and you will be told, "Without social media I wouldn't have a social life." Teens would not know what their friends are doing or whom they are meeting up with, and would not get alerts to tell them where and when they should meet up.

If limiting screen time does not work, can anything be done?

In 2019 I joined forces with the education charity The Female Lead to explore whether we could intervene in some way to reduce the negative impact of social media on teens' self-esteem.[26] We began with data showing that teens—and teen girls in particular—use a limited, shallow vocabulary on their social media sites when they describe themselves and their interests. They focus on beauty and makeup and lifestyle tips and boy bands. Boy teens register a somewhat wider range of interests when they use social media, but they also focus on how cool, confident, or sexy (and sexist) they look.

In asking "What can we do to shift teens' narrow and shallow focus when they use social media?" we (The Female Lead and I) had to devise an exercise that teens would actually do. This meant we couldn't ask them to limit their time on social media. Instead, we simply asked them to follow at least five profiles from a list we sent each of them. It included people we thought were positive role models, people doing interesting things, people who were aiming at excellence and who wanted to make a contribution to others' lives.

The list was tailored to each teen's interests and aspirations. In an initial interview with each teen we got to know what she cared about and how she saw herself in the future. We asked her to tell us whom she admired, and why. With this information, we drew up the list of people she might follow in her usual social media accounts. After eight months we met these teens again, and again asked how they were using social media. We were amazed and delighted by the transformation.

The twenty-eight teen girls who participated in this exercise still used social media to check in with their friends and get headline news and gossip about celebrities, but they were also using it to explore deeper interests. Leila, seventeen, said, "Following these people has given me a completely different outlook, because it's not, well, obviously it's social media, but it's not the materialistic side of it. It's about people doing really good things. . . . I didn't know it could be used for that." Fifteen-year-old Theresa, who had been following a concert pianist we sent her, gained insight into the pressure, grind, and delight of daily music practice, about which she had previously "no idea." Explaining what inspired her about these posts, she said, "Some of these people were gorgeous, but that wasn't the point, because some of them weren't. What inspired me was the woman who posted clips of herself practicing day after day, and how she was preparing for a competition. You saw her getting from A to B, and working at it. I guess that was it, the fact she didn't start out on top of things. That's what inspired me."

These teens told us that they learned most from the people who posted nitty-gritty details of what they were doing and why it was important to them. They were intrigued by posts showing the routine grind involved in achievement, including the slipups and disappointments in pursuing their goals. Given a choice of substance over style, teens chose substance.

But it wasn't only the profiles we sent them that transformed their use of social media. The algorithms built into social media platforms—those calculations that manage which posts appear according to an assessment of what will grab the "user's" attention—extended rather than limited these teen girls' horizons. When sixteen-year-old Amelia added an aspiring astronaut to her social media feed, she was directed to the NASA site, and she became a fan of the NASA Explore section. "It's like a keychain of events," we were told.

Social media is a relatively new phenomenon, and researchers are just beginning to get to grips with its impacts on teens' well-being. As with any new technology, it can be used badly, depressing teens' mood and restricting their interests. Much like a junk food diet, it offers short-term pleasure, but leaves the user feeling rotten. Extricating teens from social media seems futile, and at present the companies that benefit from this dependence appear to have little motivation to improve its impact. But parents and teachers can go some way towards transforming a junk food diet into a healthy one by introducing profiles that show the daily processes and challenges and disappointments that underpin real aspiration and achievement. In this way, the algorithms that often reinforce teens' more simplistic and superficial interests can be reset to support their better angels.

After participating in our exercise, many of the teens, like Leila and Subeta, decided to "clean up their social media feed" and unfollow people they came to realize were "getting them down" or keeping them "in a bad place."[27] They realized that they envied but did not admire many of the people they had been following and used the term "cringe-binging" to describe their their "obsession" or "wallowing in a kind of envy for really superficial things." But as they followed people they valued, the teens no longer felt envy. Instead, they felt inspired.[28]

THE NEED FOR CO-REGULATION

The hot zones and pressure points of the teen years pose the greatest challenge to parents. Teens approach life as an adventure and see their role as explorer. The child's fear of strangers gives way to intrigue and attraction to new people. Familiar comforts of home and routine seem stifling. The excitement of discovery takes the driving seat, while safety and sound judgment are left behind, ousted by the presence of friends.

It will be a long time before the teen can reliably manage her impulses, make reasonable risk assessments in heated moments, sensibly solve problems and reliably sustain intelligent goal-directed behavior. Until this cluster of skills—known as "self-regulation"—is consolidated at about the age of twenty-four the reactive, reward-hungry teenage brain needs to be partnered. Parents can use their continuing influence, and the teen's continuing love and trust, to *co-regulate* their intense and reactive emotional system.

Co-regulation is the near-magical comfort that occurs when someone we love shows curiosity and warmth toward our inner world.[29] However chaotic the emotion, however distressing the thoughts, we are calmed by another's understanding and engagement. As parents show their desire to share their teen's perspective, they fine-tune and strengthen the hectic, overdriven teen brain. As parents coach their teens to name their feelings and thoughts, they help their teens with a higher-level brain activity that eases more primitive impulses of the fear and reward centers.[30] As parents offer a relationship in which it is safe to speak out, to air thoughts that go against the group's grain, to experience stress and distress, they support teens' self-regulation, helping them manage their emotions and thoughts well enough to make decisions that separate them from their friends.

We have already seen the calming effect of a parent who "holds the teen in mind" and helps a teen name and tame emotions that otherwise seem unbearable. Co-regulation is a byproduct of "holding the teen in mind." A more common term is "being there for a teen"—acknowledging their feelings, reflecting a manageable version of their heartache and confusion, thereby allowing them to reflect on problems and eventually solve them. This is a challenge, because the teen's feelings affect a parent's feelings. States of high emotional arousal, such as anxiety, despair, and passion, are contagious, but by remaining steady, patient, and open to what your teen says, you will be able to moderate your teen's powerful feelings. Your steady breathing, patience, and receptiveness lower the teen's arousal.

Teens' need for a co-regulator is less obvious and more complex than it was in childhood. Though a hug may no longer provide the "Everything's now okay" feeling it did in childhood, some form of physical comfort—such as a hug or a cuddle—is still mightily effective. Even taking a hand or pressing a shoulder has an impact—partly as a gesture of sympathy, but also to remind teens of their physicality. In times of emotional upheaval teens can forget the substance and comfort of their embodied self. Hence a teen feels "all over the place" or "as though the ground is pulled from under my feet." A touch brings them back to the assurance of their physical self.

But some teens, when distressed, are in such a "hot zone" that they cannot tolerate being touched. In this case, a parent can nonetheless "be there" by staying in the same room, extending a hand without actually touching the teen, and remaining calm, even when the teen rejects an embrace.

One of the hardest tasks of parenting a teen is learning a new set of responses. What comforted the child may not comfort the teen. The words that soothed the child may irritate the teen. Moreover, teens themselves change, so parents may have to learn new techniques over and over again. The specific expressions of co-regulation can take many forms, but always involve warmth, focus on the teen's feelings and assurance that you yourself will not be crushed by them. Empathy, attention, and calm provide a scaffold that steadies the teen's volatile emotions.

OVERVIEW AND EXERCISES

Teens, as we have seen, form friendship tribes. They learn from one another and imitate one another. Sometimes the need to belong to a tribe overpowers the need to find a tribe that shares the teen's own values and interests. So important is the ability to trust *with discrimination* that, in the view of many psychologists, knowing whom to trust is the most important thing parents can teach their children.[31]

The first step in guiding teens to place trust wisely is to promote their personal courage—the courage to speak their own mind in the presence of friends. This means that we, too, have to tolerate a teen's outspokenness in the family. We have to listen and show respect even when a teen expresses views about people or politics or the family that disturb us. Instead of meting out punishment, we need to register and explore the teen's ideas.

A few possible ways to show interest and give the teen's views some authority include: "I didn't know you thought/felt that" and "I'm not sure I understand. Can you tell me more?" and "You've clearly given this some thought. I need to think about this too."

When parents demonstrate tolerance—even delight—in the teen's individuality, then the teen finds it easier to stand up to peer pressure. The message is "Being yourself and being different won't threaten your connection to others." But sometimes a parent feels uneasy at the teen's emerging identity. "You were always such a sweet little girl. Why do you have to hide your femininity?" Linda asks of her fifteen-year-old daughter Diane.

It is probably inevitable that parents have expectations of what kind of woman or man a child will become. Teens often test these expectations, and if parents refuse to modify theirs, the relationship suffers. Showing a willingness to learn what your teen wants—even simple things, such as what they choose to wear, and how they choose to style their hair, and what being male or female or neither means to them—goes a long way towards maintaining the bond and helping the teen resist peers' pressure to comply with the tribe's styles and attitudes and personae.

Being the parent of a teen requires humility. A parent (as teens are quick to remind us) is not always right. The teen's needs and thoughts sometimes change too quickly for parents to track. Parents' role now is to listen while teens mark out their different opinions and preferences. When teens are able to do this without receiving contempt ("How dare you say that!") or denial ("You can't really think that!"), they are more likely to stand their ground with their friends, too.

And what can parents do about risk taking with friends?

Risk taking is an inevitable part of adolescence,[32] but parents can manage risks by monitoring a teen's limitations. If allowed too much risk taking, teens become habituated to that level of risk and the next level up does not seem so risky. The potential danger escalates the more used they become to taking risks.[33] This means that every risk avoided represents a significant win, allowing the teen to assess risk more reliably.

Friends' influence, as we have seen, can be positive. Sometimes friends help keep each other safe and give one another courage to avoid risks.[34] Encourage your teens to reflect on whether their friends have their best interests in mind with questions such as "Does your friend listen to you?" and "Are you able to say what you think to your friend?" and "Are you able to decline a friend's request or suggestion?" These questions should not be fired one after the other, but emerge within a range of questions to pose as opportunities arise. Having real conversations with a teen requires a watch-and-wait approach, moving forward when the teen seems open to talk, and respectfully backing away when the teen is too anxious to talk, or needs time to organize thoughts in private.

Teens are intrigued to learn about the science of emotional regulation.[35] Understanding the special challenges of teens' self-regulation makes sense of their energy and of their urge for adventure. The science of the teen brain also shows why teens, with their tendency to slide into the hot zone, need some constraints on their freedoms. A parent's insistence on some control, in this context, seems more reasonable and becomes less personal.

Control is most effective when shaped via rewards: "When you show how responsible/sensible/careful you can be, you will be able to do more." Necessary punishment is most effective when it is geared to the consequences of recklessness, and also focused on rewards that come when the teen demonstrates improvement: "You damaged the car and this is the way you will repay the cost. When you do, and demonstrate more responsibility and care, you will be able to drive friends again."

When it seems that you and your teen are at an impasse, when the teen insists that you are being unreasonably restrictive, there is always a way forward, a way of acknowledging the teen's anger while standing your ground. You can try outlining your thinking processes to the teen, and invite her input. "I know you are responsible/capable/trustworthy much of the time. But I am worried that in this specific situation (staying out very late/going to a club/mountain biking/partying), things might be a bit much for you. There will be a time when having this independence will not be problematic, but now I think it is. Can you suggest a way you can show me what you can manage?" Offering the teen input in solving the problem tends to reduce the heat in the conflict.

Digital health is a concern for many parents, particularly when they worry that their teen is addicted to screen-related activity. The teen is furious at being deprived of a device because, he believes, this absorbing focus is the only way his anxiety or depression can be managed.

There are different ways through such digital addictions. The first, more extreme approach, is to force a reset with a cold-turkey pathway. This will be difficult, as the teen is likely to remain in meltdown for two or three days. This needs to be followed by a longer period of separation from digital devices for several weeks, while the teen does other things, preferably physically active, such as gardening, construction, exercise, or sport.

Another, far more moderate approach involves tracking the number of hours spent with the device, and then cutting down by ten or fifteen minutes for a few weeks, and then cutting down by a further fifteen or twenty minutes for another few weeks. During this time, physical exercise is essential to manage the anxiety of digital separation, before the teen gets used to more subtle cues that engage attention.

Banning or strictly limiting screen time, with its opportunities for sharing social interests and maintaining social networks, however, is usually unnecessary. In the majority of cases improving social media health is much easier than many parents suppose. Introducing just a few positive profiles to the accounts they already use has been found to transform how teens use social media. The passive, envy-generating scrolling through superficial images then gives way to more goal-directed interests. But to introduce your teen to new more positive profiles, you need to hear about their updated interests. Some of the questions we asked the teens who participated in our study were: "Do you admire the people you follow?" and "What would you pass on to your friends?" and "Can you give an example of an exciting post?"

Teens can be remarkably receptive to parental input as long as the parent is collaborator rather than director. When parents encourage their teens to focus on their emotions and thoughts, they help them organize their behavior and work towards their goals. But influence goes two ways: teens see their task as reorganizing and refining a parent's mind by introducing the new person they are becoming—though they do not always proceed elegantly or clearly.

6

"No one's ever felt this before!"

Teen Love and Teen Sex

ONE EMOTION that emerges during the teen years, new, strange, and powerful, is romantic love. It feels marvelous but can wreak havoc.

At fifteen years, Ira is noticing the changing physique of the girls in his class— girls he has known since childhood, but who now create an impact beyond anything he has ever experienced. For a while this distraction was "just around, like in the air, and not real important." Now he focuses on one girl, Carlita, who was once a childhood playmate but whom he hasn't spoken to in a couple of years, and who now takes up "like maybe 100 and 10 percent of [his] thoughts." Ira explained, "Sometimes it's like these images of her just come at me, and it's like they target me on purpose. I mean, it must be obvious—to her, to the other guys, even maybe to the teachers. I sort of expect someone to help me. Like, 'Why are you coming on so strong? Why are you doing that to him?'

But she's—I mean, she's just *there*. It's not, you know, it's not just her—her breasts, like—it's her hands, and her feet. You know, there's something about feet? There's the personality you usually don't see. And her shoulders, the way they move, and the breath that comes out when she laughs. It's as though I can smell her even though I'm not sure I really can."

When I ask Ira to name his feelings, he looks at me, dumbstruck. He looks at the corners of the room, as though searching there for an answer. "It's too big to give it a name. It's everything. It's, like, got a temperature, but I'm not sure if it's hot or cold, and it's like a kick in my stomach, and I can't stand it but I kind of like it, too."

I ask him to imagine being "close to her." He blushes furiously, then answers, "I can't imagine that, really. I mean, if she says 'hello' to me, it's like a blood volcano. I'm crazy for the whole day."

Many teens, like Ira, experience love as a physical upheaval. "What is that strange feeling in my stomach?" they wonder. "Why do I want to run and soar?" "Why do I freeze when she speaks to me?" "How can I feel this without exploding?"

It may surprise both teens and parents that though the upheaval of teenage romance is widely celebrated in song and film, it is not a strong area of research. This a sign of how little importance grown-ups put on these feelings: "It's puppy love" or "Just a crush." When I talk to Ira's mother, Karly, and ask whether her teenage son discusses any of his new preoccupations with her, she laughs and says, "You must mean this Carlita girl. Ah, yes, first love. I give it three weeks."

Karly dismisses the importance of Ira's feelings. After all, grown-ups think they know the arc of youthful infatuation, when someone suddenly becomes the center of a teen's life and represents every ideal. Just as suddenly, they believe, the teen's enthusiasm will fade.

This widespread attitude may be why it is so difficult to do research on teen love. Why would teens speak about these feelings to any grown-up who thinks they are "cute" or "funny" or "silly" and minimizes their passion? Why should teens open themselves to those who talk dismissively about "raging hormones," when teens know their feelings to be real?

Yet romance takes up a huge proportion of teens' emotional lives. Girls attribute 34 percent of their strong emotions to romantic relationships, whether fantasy or real. Boys attribute 25 percent of their strong emotions to these.[1] This is more than any other single topic—more than friends and more than school. While there is no comparable data about teens who do not feel at home in their assigned gender, they tell me that "thinking about who will love me and how it will be" is a constant preoccupation, "always there, even when it's not right in front of me."

Romance, for teens, is both mystery and self-discovery. There are practical questions, such as how to approach someone you are attracted to, what to say, and how to reveal your feelings. Then there are questions about a teen's identity as a lover. Are they worthy? Are they constant and kind? Are they strong enough to withstand disappointment or rejection?

Ira, as we have seen, is ambivalent about interacting with Carlita. A smile can mean very little to her, but to him it is "huge" and gives an emotional charge to the whole day. In the grip of love, teens' social brains go on overdrive. They hypermentalize—or overthink—every interaction, however minor. What, they wonder, does this smile, or word, or glance signify? How can they discover what someone else feels?

Teens need an entirely new social language to navigate

romance. The familiar discourse of friendship does not serve them now. The familiar cues that regulate friendly interactions now seem inadequate. They can pick up signals as to whether a friend welcomes their approach. They know how to start a conversation and propose a game. But they do not know how to ask, "Do you like me in a special way?" or "Do I mean more to you than anyone?" And if they try to ask these questions, and get something wrong, they risk pain and humiliation.

One month after our initial conversation, I meet Ira for a second interview. "I tried talking to her and there was this face freeze," Ira tells me. "Like she was looking at me, but she couldn't keep looking at me, her eyes kept kind of swerving. I felt really nauseous. Like she was looking to see if someone could help her. I just, like, left, right in the middle of this stupid conversation, and I couldn't see her, but she probably doubled over laughing. You know, 'What is this guy?' And it seems like everything I felt was suddenly dead. I mean, how can something that's real change suddenly, like it's there, and then it's not? I'm sort of ashamed of all those things I thought I felt. Like my feelings kind of let me down."

Ira's words flag one of the most important questions a person can ask: "What do my emotions mean and can I trust them?" While parents speak about "puppy love" and the quick turnaround of teen infatuation, teens believe the feelings of *now* are the feelings of forever. Except, of course, teens also learn that their feelings do change, suddenly and drastically.

DAYDREAMS AND HARSH REALITIES

Parents often complain that their teens idle away their time in daydreams. They see daydreaming as an indulgent waste of time. "Stop daydreaming and do your homework," Karly tells her son. "Did I lose you again? Are you daydreaming?" Tessa demands of her daughter, Miriam, when she ignores her mother's question. But for most teens daydreaming is a kind of child's play, and for children, play is a kind of work.

A daydream is usually defined as a series of pleasant visionary, usually wishful creations of the imagination that distract one from the present. Parents see teens' daydreams as mere escapism, devoid of the grit and constraints of reality. Some parents believe that daydreams are "all about sex." When I explore daydreams with teens, however, they reveal something more substantial.

As teens daydream, they are both scriptwriter and director. They choose the setting, characters, and plot line. At first glance, these plots seem full of clichés, such as the desert island scenario that offers time and space for closeness to develop without social competition or social vulnerability, or the rescue scenario, when teens save their crush from danger or death. The daydream, usually with the teen as hero, centers around someone the teen actually knows and imagines loving, or around someone known only from films or TV or social media.

Initially the daydream is safe from the constraints and embarrassment and uncertainties of real interpersonal interaction. In this very private setting teens are protected from rejection. But challenges soon creep in and dominate the plot. There are breakups and mishaps and shameful exposures. "What starts out as soothing and real sweet turns into a real tangle of awful stuff," seventeen-year-old Allison tells me. "It gives you a kind of jolt when this lovely world you've built kind of crumbles away. You can have nightmares in daydreams, too, you know."

In daydreams teens play and puzzle over the beginning and

ending of romance. Just as children explore the grown-up world through make-believe, teens imagine strange and wonderful possibilities in daydreams. This "idle" occupation is common to everyone, but far more frequent in teens than adults. It fosters neurosynaptic health by anticipating possible scenarios and outcomes. It is, in other words, good for the brain, encouraging it to cycle through different modes of thinking, from analysis to empathy, from wish and pleasure to threat and fear. The imagined conversations and interactions access information that is otherwise dormant, allowing teens to make new connections between scattered pieces of information, and this exercise will help them solve relational problems in the future.[2]

But no imaginary enterprise can protect a teen from the heartbreak of a love that goes wrong. Parents often make light of the pain caused by a romantic breakup. When seventeen-year-old Finley breaks up with his girlfriend of two years, his mother, Sophie, "feels sorry for the poor guy" and wants to help him, but she is also confident that "he'll heal. It will be over before he knows it."

While Sophie believes "He's down in the dumps now, but he'll be okay," Finley's perspective is very different. He tells me, "You know they talk about 'giving your heart away.' Well, that's how I feel about Annie. She has my heart, and if she doesn't want it that doesn't mean she can just give it back to me. I don't have it anymore. I don't know what I have. I walk around, go to school, eat and stuff, but I'm moving around with no ground underneath. Mom says, 'Oh, you'll cope,' but she doesn't see that I'm not coping. Sometimes I can't breathe, and I have to stop just so I can take the next step. I sit at my desk and there's this buzz in my head— you know it buzzes with emptiness, because I don't have her anymore."

Five years from now Finley will be more adept at compartmentalizing such a loss. The end of a relationship will still be painful, but it is less likely to drain all his mental energy. Now the primary emotions of love and loss fire in his brain, while the prefrontal cortex lacks the ability to "hug" or soothe the amygdala (a source of those primitive emotions). His teen brain imbues his breath and heart rate with dark meanings. He feels, "I have no one, no direction. I am lost." These thoughts reinforce the physiological effects, producing greater disruption to breathing and blood flow.

When Finley was close to Annie, when he knew he would see her and touch her, he had someone to help synchronize his breathing, his heart rate, and other physical signals. This helped moderate his interoceptive network. Internal sensations were then not so quick to signal pain, and day-to-day challenges of schoolwork and social interaction did not loom so large. In losing a girlfriend, he has lost someone who helped regulate his inner world.

BREAKUPS: HIS AND HERS AND THEIRS

It is often said that girl teens are more dependent on close relationships than boy teens. Girls are thought to feel greater attachment to a romantic partner than boys feel, and to be at greater risk of depression. But, once again, common assumptions about what girls feel versus what boys feel turn out to be false.

The surprising fact is that when it comes to romantic relationships, teenage girls are less vulnerable in the wake of a breakup than teen boys. Those on the frontline of teen mental health have known this for many years, but the knowledge has not reached parents. A high school counselor explained, "The boys fall apart when they break up with a girlfriend. They can't study. They [sometimes] start to drink. If they come to me with problems about their work or their parents, I can help them. But when they come saying they've just broken up with a girlfriend, I see a red flag."

As young children, girls deal with passionate friendships that often rupture. By the time they reach early adolescence they have undergone tough lessons in trust and betrayal. Every girl I have spoken to has, by the age of fourteen, had a trusted friend betray her by revealing the private thoughts that were shared "in secret" or bad-mouthing her behind her back or inexplicably casting her out for a different best friend. Girls suffer greatly from these breaches, but also learn that they can survive them.

Teen girls, in the wake of friendship betrayals, learn to seek comfort elsewhere, particularly from other friends. They have experience in "making up," and learn that damaged relationships can be repaired. If one relationship does prove to be beyond repair, they know that new bonds can be formed. But boys, because they tend to shut down friendship intimacy in later adolescence—when the guy code exerts its demands to be "strong" and "independent" (and carry emotional burdens in silence)—are more dependent on a romantic partner. They come to the intimacy of first love less practiced in rupture and repair. A breakup is a trauma that they are very slow to process. Nor are they as likely as girls to have friends who sit close, hug them, and listen to the constant ruminations that help manage their grief.

This explains why, over and over again, I have found, in defiance of expectation and stereotype, that teenage boys are more vulnerable after a romantic breakup than girls. While teenage girls describe breakups as "really hard," or "a shock," teenage boys use words such as "falling apart" and "shipwrecked" and "tailspin," which imply severe disruption and disorientation.

For teens who are unsure of their sexual orientation or are shifting away from their assigned gender, a breakup has an added dimension. The loss can disrupt their emerging gender or sexual identity, raising doubts as to who they are and who will love them. "The worst thing wasn't so much losing her," Jerry explained, "but losing the ground beneath my feet." At sixteen, set on transitioning to male, Jerry's heartache awakens anxiety about "ever finding someone [with whom] I can be really 'me.' " At such times, teens benefit from a parent who can co-regulate their feelings, assuring them that they do not have to suffer this teen upheaval alone. (Techniques for this process are described at the end of Chapters Three, Five, and Nine.)

SEX: ANOTHER POTENT EMOTIONAL FORCE

Research on teenage love has been sidelined because teen love seems, to grown-ups, far less important than teen sex. For parents, a child's sexual maturity is like a grenade thrown in the midst of comfortable family life. Sexual feelings mark the end of childhood, and leave their teen vulnerable to their own and others' desires.

Most parents do their best to offer support and provide useful information about sex, but anxiety skews their efforts. They worry about the health risks of sex. They worry about the power of sex to distract their teen from school and from future plans. They worry about the moral and personal impact of pregnancy. As a result, they focus on restraint: "Just say 'no' " and "Don't be pressured into anything" and, above all, "Be careful!" The pleasure of sex and the unique intimacy of sexual connection are all too often omitted from "the conversation"—the special talks parents plan to have with teens about sex.

Parents who have read Chapter Two on the adolescent brain might argue, "It must be good practice to highlight control and restraint when it comes to sex." After all, we saw how the brain receptors for the pleasure hormone dopamine proliferate in the teen brain, while message circuits from the prefrontal cortex (often referred to as the "brain's chief executive office" or control center) are slow and inefficient. The teenage brain is quickly aroused and, once aroused, isn't all that good with self-control, risk assessment, and forward planning. Hence, teens are prone to impulsive, unthought-through behavior, especially when the rewards are highly pleasurable and exciting. For teens, sex is often not a decision; it "just happens." Telling a teen, "Just say 'no' " or "Control yourself" is not useful advice, because it may be advice that teens are unable to follow.

While parents' influence on their teen's brain is complex and piecemeal, they can improve a teen's capacity to make a decision about whether to have sex. They can do this not by keeping an eye on the teen every minute, or by setting down strict rules of abstinence, but by talking to them about the pleasure—both physical and emotional—that sex should provide.

Most parents say they want to be better at talking about sex than their parents were. Most parents hope their teen will come to them with questions about sex. Yet most of the teens I talk to say, "When [my parents] talk about sex, it's as though they don't understand anything."

Parents generally want to have frank and open conversations with their teens about sex. "The last thing I want is for her to feel there are things she can't tell me," Tessa says. But her sixteen-year-old daughter Miriam says, "I get so annoyed when she tries this heart-to-heart thing about sex. First of all, I know that stuff already. But second, you know, she isn't really cool about it. Basically she can't stand how I'm not the kid whose body she can control. It's like I live in this dangerous world where everyone's trying to 'take advantage of me'—yeah! Those are her exact 'enlightened' words—as though I don't know anything. It's like miles away from the world I really live in."

Teens, as we see over and over again, are astute observers. They are quick to spot a parent's uncertainty, ambivalence, or anxiety—and just as quick to exploit it. Miriam notes, for example, when she needs to apply just a little more pressure to gain permission to go to her friend's house. She knows she can ease her mother's doubt by promising to work through the problems on a math sheet. But keying into her mother's anxiety about her sexuality and the dangers of sex heightens her own uncertainty and ambivalence. She tries to shut down the conversation with an insistence familiar to parents of teens, "I know that already!"

"She knows as much as I do," Tessa tells me. "They grow up so fast, and they have access to all this—this stuff about sex and everything. But it's one thing to have the information, you know? And another thing to understand it."

"Knowing all that stuff" and "understanding what's happening" are indeed very different. The most disturbing discovery I made in talking to teens about sex is how many of their stories about sexual initiation involve either intimidation and confusion or interpersonal carelessness. Teens know the facts but not the script of sexual engagement. It is as though they—

particularly girls—don't recognize the steps that lead to sexual intercourse or don't know how to assert themselves, and boys don't recognize the importance of respect and consent.

Supposedly savvy teens tell stories about hesitation and confusion when an encounter abruptly becomes sexual. "I didn't know it could happen so quickly," teen girls tell me. "I thought I would have more time," or "I was still thinking what to say, and suddenly he was inside me." They are unable to formulate, in the moment, a response that will protect them from what soon seems like an "inevitable" outcome. Their hesitation arises in part from reluctance "to call a halt to something he's so into," as Naomi says, or "to disappoint him when it's really no big thing," as Jemma says.

Over 6 percent of teen girls say their first intercourse was unwanted and forced.[3] They describe coercion that is sometimes emotional, sometimes verbal, and sometimes even physical. How are we failing the teens (mostly girls) who don't seem able to manage what's happening and the teens (mostly boys) who either lose sight of or don't care about their partner's feelings? Are we neglecting to teach our girls how to be the primary agent in their sexual activity? Why have we failed to dissuade our boys from acting as though they have a special entitlement to sex?

Teens today are more at ease with a range of sexualities, in themselves and in others, but girls remain vulnerable to "slut shaming" and the humiliation of (as Jemma says) "everyone knowing you had sex with some pig." Girl teens are supposed to be sexy but not sexual. They are supposed to please men, but if they "give in" to male pressure to have sex, they are shamed. In the catch-22 of female norms, girls are quick to blame themselves for what they see as their own "mess-ups." As one sixteen-year-old, shuddering in self-disgust, explained, "I thought it was okay, like, I was saying, 'Hey, you got to slow down there.' But it didn't come out that way. Then stupid sex just kind of happened. I got myself laid."

Boy teens, most parents insist, have been taught to value others' feelings and to be alert to any absence of consent. Yet the persistent male norm of being "strong" and "dominant" and the persistent, distorted female norm of compliance together obscure understanding of consent. As seventeen-year-old Josh argues, "I know I feel that [sex] urge more than she does. But this is important to me. We need [to have sex] for me to see us as a real couple. I know she gets this, really."

Many parents and educators blame the toxic messages of pornography that both glorify and normalize male sexual domination and female passivity for the pressure many teen girls experience—pressure to which they may succumb without desire on their part. Though parents dislike the images and associations of pornography, and though it is disturbing to learn that our teens have access to porn, we should distinguish its messages from its actual effects. There is no robust evidence that pornography's messages are more damaging than other out-in-the-open stereotypes of male power and female submission. The more a teen, whether girl or boy, endorses insidious male or female norms, where the boy's desire has more significance than a girl's, and where a girl's duty is to "get"—understand and comply with—the boy's needs, the more likely that teen, whether male or female, is to find male coercion acceptable.[4]

Teens badly need tools to manage sexual experiences, yet, as their experiences show, we are failing them. Are parents not talking to their teens and teaching them what they need to know, or do teens simply not hear what their parents tell them?

Teens tell me that they value loving, respectful physical

intimacy, but are confused as to what is "normal, in a kind of good way." They admit that their ideas and thoughts about sex are confusing, but say that it is "hard to get information that makes any sense."

Because teens know they do not *understand* the information they *know,* and because they don't like confronting their own confusion, they are often irritated by sex talk with parents. In the early teen years, they retain the child's response of "Yuck!" to the idea that their parents have sex. "You don't *really* do that!" a child thinks on first learning how they were conceived. "How can people talk normally to each other afterwards?" they wonder. A few years later, when they think of sex not in terms of what grown-ups do but what they themselves will or want to do, there is still the puzzle, "Do my parents really do that? Yuck!" and "It's totally different for me."

Many teens want to appear at ease with sex and their own sexuality. When parents say, "Teens today are blasé about the whole thing," teens don't challenge this image. Miriam is "okay with Mom thinking I know what's what just to get her off my back and give her some relief. It's obvious she's terrified of the whole subject—her little girl and sex." Sensing her mother's unease, Miriam does not want additional anxiety. She has plenty of her own.

"I like [my boyfriend] but there are these times when he really repulses me," she explains, "and I don't want him to touch me. And I don't know whether it's just then, like 'No thanks, not tonight' sort of feeling, or whether it's because I don't love him. And if we ever—you know, do everything—it will be so much worse. Because even now, when we just do some things, it can make me want to scratch my skin raw."

Her friend Jemma, eighteen, two years older than Miriam, who does have sexual intercourse with her boyfriend, faces a different set of questions. "Being 'intimate' is supposed to be some kind of euphemism, but it's not to me. It's this closeness. You slip into a new level of communication. And there's this bond. I see him and I feel it. So it doesn't make sense to me when it's not that to [her boyfriend]. It's a real letdown, what it means to me is just nothing to him."

Parent/teen conversations about sex remain important—and become a little easier—in late adolescence. When I ask twenty-one- and twenty-two-year-olds (who, as I show in Chapter Eleven, are still adolescents, brainwise) what they appreciate most about their parents, it is "being okay with knowing the worst about me," and "helping me put mess-ups behind me." When I probe for examples, these include "having sex when I didn't mean to" and "getting stuck in an infatuation with a really awful guy" and "being really supportive and not freaking out when I told them I was gay."

The discussions teens crave are those that go beyond physical and biological facts, and beyond reminders of restraint, such as "just say 'no' " and "be careful." Sex is not "just sex" but involves deep emotions and relationships. "You sort of expect that your parents have figured all this out, or they're past it," Jemma told me. "So it was really good to hear my Mom talk about her feelings and how she isn't certain, and that she's been let down by guys, or by her own feelings. It sort of makes me feel less—diminished—because of what I'm going through. Like I can mess up, or feel humiliated and still have self-respect."

Some parents and policy makers believe that talking about sexual pleasure and sexual feelings will encourage teens to have sex too often and too early. A remarkable finding is that teens who talk to their parents about sexual pleasure and desire are more likely to delay having sex. These teens are older when they first have intercourse and they are more likely to use contraception than are teens whose parents stick to "the facts" and "the dangers."[5] Moreover, teens whose parents talk about the importance of pleasure in sex—the teen's own personal pleasure—are far less likely to say that sex "just happened."[6] They are less likely to submit to pressure from a partner, and less likely to exert pressure on a partner, because they're aware that it isn't only someone else's desire that matters. They are better equipped in articulating to a partner, or hearing a partner say, "I don't want this." When they have sex, it is because they both want it.

When parents set aside their anxiety about teen hormones and raging sexual desires and focus instead on the teen's own sexuality, showing respect for her desire and pleasure, the teen gets the message, "You are an agent in this activity."

That prefrontal cortex may not yet be in its mature state; the networks between the brain's pleasure centers and planning center may be a little shaky, but conversations with parents can help teens be smart, even in the heat of passion.

HOW TO TALK ABOUT SEX, REFUSAL, AND CONSENT

We have seen in this chapter disturbing evidence that many teens (mostly girls) feel coerced into having sex and that teens' apparent sexual savviness covers profound ignorance and confusion. For boys, the most disturbing issue is lack of sensitivity to a partner's reluctance, a low threshold for what counts as consent,[7] and the supposition that their urgent desire takes precedence. For girls, the most disturbing issues are their self-blame when they are coerced into having sex and the embedded belief that their compliance is appropriate.

Exploring and challenging these gender norms with your teen is not easy. Researchers have noticed that teens routinely struggle against double sexual standards but have difficulty identifying and explaining how these emerge in their own romantic relationships. They embrace the principle of gender equality and complain of injustice when girls who have sex are pilloried and boys who have sex are glorified. Yet in teen girls' and teen boys' stories about their own unhappy sexual experiences—experiences that arise at least in part from a double standard ("I felt bad, so I kind of went along with it," or "She doesn't really want to admit she wants it")—that shrewd, articulate criticism is conspicuously absent.[8]

So how can parents have effective conversations about sex?[9]

First, make sure you go beyond biology. Straight talking about the physical and biological facts of sex is important, but good conversations include the emotional risks and the deep personal meanings of sex. Take the opportunity to include talk about relationships, respect, desire, and pleasure. The first two topics—relationships and respect—require emphasis in conversation with teen sons, while desire and pleasure need to be emphasized in conversations with teen daughters. Where relationship and respect are emphasized in personal education classes (as they are in Holland), the rate of unprotected sex in teens is low, the age of first intercourse is higher, and fewer teens report that their first sexual experience resulted from coercion.[10]

Second, assure your teen that confusion is normal. Anyone can be confused by emotions and desire. Try to avoid asking the teen how she or he feels about sex, but rather acknowledge that it takes time to gauge one's own needs and desires. Seek out opportunities, in films, ads, and Instagram, to raise awareness of mixed messages. Look out for messages that signal to girl teens: "You're supposed to instill desire in others, but say 'no' to sex, have no sexual desires, be sexy but not sexual." And look out for those that signal to boy teens: "You're supposed to dominate/perform/be the hunter" or "Reluctant girls need persuasion."

Any such message, in any context, not only a sexual one, should be challenged because these norms undermine both the ability of girls to see themselves as agents entitled to make decisions based on their own desires and the ability of boys to acknowledge the significance of a girl's reluctance to have sex. Parents can encourage more critical appraisal of gender norms in many ways, for example, by picking up on anything negative a teen says about a girl because she is sexual, whether with words such as "slut" or "slag" or remarks such as "She's easy," and "She'll do whatever." It also can be done by picking up anything a teen says, or is said within a teen's hearing, that presents males as sexual aggressors, such as "You can't fight testosterone," or "What do you expect? If it's on offer, he'll take it."

Third, show that you are interested in what your teen has to say about sex and gender. As often as possible, treat the teen as a collaborator rather than a pupil. Don't be afraid of pauses in the conversation. The teen may need time to sift through words, to test what it's safe to say, to think how much he or she wants to reveal and what must be kept private. Above all, avoid telling teens what they should think or feel, and avoid jumping to conclusions about what your teen does think or feel.

Keep in mind that talking—deep talking—is often opportunistic. When parents jump-start a conversation, teens tend to shut down. They feel that a parent is "lecturing" or "scolding." Intimate conversations usually take place informally, while doing other things together, whether preparing dinner, folding laundry, shopping, or on a journey to school. It can continue over weeks and months. The parent's best option is to wait patiently for a window of conversation to open. Remember, patience and a willingness to listen show respect. And, as many parents know, when real conversations with a teen go well, they are a joy.

7

"You always say the wrong thing."

The Real Aim of Teen Criticism

"Every time I open my mouth, she pounces. Every word I say is wrong. The simplest thing is wrong. 'It's not a '[TV] soap, it's a Netflix series' or 'It's not a party, we're just hanging out. You don't understand anything.' She looks at me, eyes like daggers. She's such a sweet kid, you know, underneath . . . but it really wears me down."

Vella, mother of fifteen-year-old Clara, voices a complaint familiar in parents of teens: "Everything I say is wrong."

Kieren says that his fifteen-year-old son Sam "scowls when I try to have a conversation with him. You can see the anger in his face, and he squirms until I just give up. I try. I ask him what he wants to talk about and he says, 'Nothing. I don't need to talk.' I don't think he means to hurt me. He just can't help it."

Caleb says that his thirteen-year-old daughter Mercy "doesn't need any reason to find fault with what I do. I can bite into an apple, or drink a Coke, or settle myself in a chair, and I'll be doing something that mightily offends her, though I can't fathom the reason why. I've stopped asking, 'What the heck's the matter?' because all I'll get is 'You're so annoying.' She can burst into tears over this, and I don't know which way that sorrow is going, whether she's sorry for me because I have such a touchy daughter or for herself because she has this dad who goes out of his way to annoy her."

Not using just the right word, trying to engage a teen in conversation, and simply biting into an apple are not reasonable grounds for heated criticism. These three parents are confused, hurt, and also concerned for their teen. What many parents do not know is that teens feel awful even as they appear so self-righteous. "I know Dad's trying to, you know, support me, like, *show an interest*," Sam says. "But this dad-to-son cheeriness doesn't suit him. It's not exactly fake. But it's kind of put on. I clam up when he tries it on. And then I feel bad."

Mercy, too, knows she is "really unfair. I guess he can't help the way he swallows. And I don't know why, but sometimes it just makes me want to cry. He's in the room and I can't concentrate on anything, and then there are these little sounds. It puts me in this awful rage."

PARENTS IN THE TEEN'S MIND

Parents' understandable confusion arises from the belief that the teen's criticism or annoyance is directed at what the parent is saying or doing now, in the present moment. But teens' intense responses to their parents are embedded in a long emotional history, a history that began when—in the child's mind—the parent was always right, when a parent's presence filled the entire room, making it safe and secure. In adolescence, as teens constantly test out their newly emerging, highly individual self, they feel ambivalent about that comfort. The parent is still the most powerful person in the room, but teens want to challenge that power. As they lodge one complaint after another against their parent, their real problem lies within themselves. Their irritation is directed towards the parent who dwells in their own mind.

So teens' apparent wish to excise or "oust" a parent isn't quite what they want. Their message is "You're wrong," and "Go away," and "I'm uncomfortable with you," but they also feel, still, a child's love and dependence. They squirm under its weight, frustrated with themselves for their need of a parent's presence and a parent's love. Teens then vent against their parent, as though *their* ambivalence is the parent's fault.

Teen ambivalence explains a range of behavior that puzzles parents. Vella says of her teen daughter Clara, "One day I'm the worst mom in the world and she wishes she didn't have anything to do with me, and the next morning she's the sweetest kid, showing me her artwork for school and coaxing [her little brother] to get ready when she knows it's time to leave. She's full of her news in the car [on the way to school] and happy as a lark. Sometimes I think having a fifteen-year-old is the most wonderful thing, and then sometimes it's like you're in a vise and any which way you turn you are in the wrong. It's the most confusing thing."

Vella is describing the changeable behavior many parents recognize. At times teens are as lovable and openly needy and affectionate as a contented child. Kieren pauses in his account of how difficult his son Sam can be. "You know, I get to the stage when I think, 'There's nothing I can do that works with this boy.' But that'll give you the wrong idea. Because some of the time, a whole lot of the time, he's the greatest companion. I can do so much more with him now. And he impresses me. We were setting up bookcases in his sister's room, and we're the smoothest team. There's a rhythm when we work together, and we have the same goal. Well, that's pure joy, you know, that you can only get from an older kid."

It is this "pure joy" and getting the rhythm of a smooth team that teens are trying to achieve even as they criticize a parent. But, as so often with teens, their messages are distorted. When Clara complains that her mother Vella doesn't "understand anything," she seems to be saying, "There's no point in talking to you," but in listening to Clara explain her criticism, something very different emerges. She tells me, "I try to explain stuff to my mom. I really do. Like maybe I've decided to switch a few subjects next year. And she'll keep doing what she's doing, like putting dishes away or braiding [my little sister's] hair, and there's that set of her mouth, and I can see she doesn't like it, and I wait for her to say something, and then all I get is 'Mmmhmm.' I hate that. What am I supposed to do with 'Mmmhmm'? Like, is she not really listening? Or is it, like, 'No way'? I can feel all sorts of stuff going on inside her head, but she's not giving me anything back."

Teens know their parents well. They sense every expression, sound, or shift in muscle tension, and guess its underlying meaning. Vella is trying to process her daughter's new plans for next year's school subjects. The proposal—or, as Clara presents it, the "decision"—to switch from geography to history and from calculus to computer science brings up a host of questions: "What's going on? What are her motives? Is it because of what classes her friends are taking? Is it because of how the different classes are scheduled? Is she struggling in her current classes? What impact could this switch have on her college applications? Has she discussed this with an academic adviser?"

Clara has opened up a huge issue, but wants a simple "Sure, fine," from her mother. That is not going to happen. Clara has a teen's impatience to have things sorted out immediately, in accord with her impulsive proposal. Anything else feels unnecessary and frustrating.

HOW TEENS "READ" A PARENT

There are two additional ingredients in this mix of teens' criticism and ambivalence. The first is the distinctive teen reactivity in which anger is quick to rise and slow to resolve. Once something annoys teens, they remain in that negative state for longer than either a child or an adult. This is a byproduct of their more volatile emotions, the easily excited limbic system in the brain, and the less efficient prefrontal cortex or control center.

The second ingredient arises from their long history of reading a parent's face and voice. Before they can walk or talk or even crawl, babies understand that minute shifts in facial muscles have important interpersonal significance. A parent's face reflects both who they are—good or bad—and the wider world as either safe or threatening. But at around the age of twelve, just as adolescence begins, their interpretation of emotional expressions becomes *less* reliable.[1]

The dip in face-reading skills is linked to the tangled mass of gray matter described in Chapter Two. We saw how the teen's executive brain (the prefrontal cortex) is less efficient at forward planning and controlling impulses. The teen's social brain (the network of brain regions involved in understanding others) also processes some things less efficiently and less reliably. One common error, scientists have found, makes them particularly touchy.

When a grown-up sees a human face, the reasoning part of the brain (the prefrontal cortex) gets to work on the complex task of interpreting its expression. When a teen sees the same face, it is the more primitive, emotional part of the brain (that includes the amygdala) that is activated. The amygdala, when activated, puts us on high alert. Our heart beats faster. Our muscles are poised for fight or flight. Since our body is behaving as though we are in danger, we feel threatened. And when we *feel* threatened, we believe we are really under attack.

The result is that teens are likely to interpret as hostile or frightened or angry the very same facial expressions that a child or grown-up would see as neutral. And when they look at a face that does express fear or anger, teens' brains (in two regions of the frontal cortex) become exceptionally active.[2] As we have seen, once teens feel strong emotion, they are slow to calm down.

Knowing the brain science behind the teen's heated response to neutral looks or remarks may go some way to reassure parents. "So that is why my teen jumps on everything I say. She's angry because she thinks I'm angry" and "I see why my teen gets so angry so quickly. He's being defensive because he thinks I'm hostile." Sarah concludes with relief, "So it isn't my fault. It's the way she sees me, and this hair-trigger irritability will go, some day."

As most parents know, however, in the thick of teen/parent bickering, "some day" can seem like forever. After the initial relief in the discovery that "my teen's criticism of me and my responses are not my fault, but a result of how that pesky teenage brain processes information," there remains the nitty-gritty reality of interacting with the teen day to day. In these daily interactions, both teens and parents can be reassured—and helped—with a deeper understanding of the purpose of teen criticism. After all, the brain story doesn't tell the whole story.

THE CHANGING FACE OF LOVE

Over and over again, teens complain about what a parent fails to "see" or "appreciate" or "understand." Through their criticism, teens are working hard to secure a parent's support and recognition for the person they are trying to become. Their impatience is partly with themselves: "Why can't I explain myself so that my parent understands?" Nevertheless, they blame the parent for being "dim" or "slow" or "uninterested."

The gist of many teen complaints is "You are talking to me as though you think I'm still the child you think you know, but I am much more." But teens themselves do not know who that person is. Ambivalent about their continuing need for a parent's recognition, teens' responses are both vehement and confused.

Let's take another look at Clara's impatience with her mother, Vella. Clara talks to her mother and waits for her to "say something . . . and then all I get is 'Mmmhmm.' I hate that. What am I supposed to do with 'Mmmhmm'? Is she listening, or not?" Clara wants a particular response. She wants her mother to show respect for her decision, and to trust it. Yet she knows that her mother won't see all the reasons (that Clara can't quite articulate) that clinch her argument. Clara admits to me, "Even before I opened this subject I knew she would put me in a really bad mood."

Clara, like many teens, wants to shed her childhood dependence. At the same time, she wants her parent's recognition and admiration. She is frustrated that her parent is slow to learn who she is—though it does not help that she herself doesn't know. This need for recognition emerges as teens articulate what frustrates them about a parent: "My mom thinks I'm still a kid. She doesn't see that the cousin I once liked is now a big bore" or "My dad wants to run my life according to his blueprint." In a teen's view, parents need reminding, time after time, that they should update their knowledge of "who a teenager is." It is not that teens doubt that a parent loves them, but to them, when they are unsure of who they are and also dependent on how others see them, love is not enough. "How can you really love someone when you don't know who they are?" they demand. Teens want a parent's help in defining a self, just as they did in infancy and childhood.

The first book I wrote on adolescence, nearly thirty years ago, had the title *Altered Loves*. The title came from a sonnet written by Shakespeare in which the speaker reflects, "Love is not love which alters when it alteration finds." In short, real love does not end when the person we love changes. The sonnet draws on the notion of unconditional love ("You can be and do anything and I will still love you"), but in looking at the teen/parent bond, I saw that alteration was necessary. The love itself had to change to be effective. "I still love you," is never quite enough. The love has to be the right fit. And as the teen changes, so must the love.

This is one of the biggest challenges in parenting teens. Psychologists often speak of developmental tasks. In childhood these involve developing motor skills, both little and large. The finer (little) motor skills involve the muscle control needed to pick something up, pass it from one hand to the other, and draw a line or circle. The larger motor skills involve balance and limb movement. Then there are the verbal skills of understanding and acquiring language, and the social skills of interacting with others, with the give-and-take of conversation. Parents, too, have developmental tasks—the task of keeping up with their children's stages, providing language and interaction and encouragement that make sense to their child at each phase of development. Parents are awash with information on how to perform the tasks of responding to children. Until recently, parents have had very little information to support them in the developmental tasks required to raise teens.

LISTENING TO IDENTITY REMINDERS

The rapid changes teens undergo are easily recognized, while the changes parents undergo in response to their teens are ignored.

Parents delight in each discovery about the infant and young child but often feel anxious as they witness rapid changes in their teen. They worry what a teen might do to jeopardize their future. They fear they are losing influence as guide and protector. Teens pick up on that hesitation and concern, and they miss the all-embracing curiosity parents showed them as a young child.

The reassurance that parents give—"I love you, no matter what"—is heartfelt, but does not provide what teens need. "Oh, I know she loves me," Clara says, somewhat dismissively. "But do you know why she loves me? It's because, one, she has no choice, I'm her kid. Two, though, she loves me because I'm still her little bitty baby. She loves me because of who I was, not because of what I am." Clara, like many teens, is not satisfied with being loved simply as a parent's child. Teens believe they deserve a new kind of love—and to get it, they try to focus a parent's attention on their new, more mature self. Sam tells his father, "I hate it when you say, 'Oh, he's such a history buff.' " And Philip complains to his father, "It's not my thing anymore. You keep saying, 'He thinks this, and he wants that,' and you really don't know. You don't listen."

I call remarks like these "identity reminders." Teen/parent exchanges are packed with them: "This is who I am/am trying to become/think I may be" and "I am neither the child you think you know nor the alien you fear." Teens' complaints about a parent, and their quick-fire criticisms, are generally efforts to influence and refine parents' responses. Without understanding their teens' positive aims, parents often interpret efforts to retune and update the relationship as, instead, rejection and hostility.

When parents ignore, dismiss, or simply fail to be impressed by their teen's critical input, conflicts escalate, leaving each anxious and isolated. Clara knows she has trouble explaining herself: "My ideas about what I want to say are huge, but they sometimes come out in broken little bits. It's like one of those speech bubbles fills my brain, but only tiny circles come out. I either dry up or start shouting." Clara puts part of the blame on her mother: "If she'd only sit down and pay attention it would be easier to get this out. I feel like I'm talking to dead air. She doesn't really listen."

Without her mother's full attention, without reassurance that her words resonate with her mother, Clara feels that her own thoughts break into "little bits." She believes her choice is between remaining silent and screaming. While to a parent such responses seem disproportionate, the teen feels moral outrage at a parent's failure to engage fully. After all, in a close relationship "not listening" is a betrayal.

"I FEEL LIKE THEY'RE RIGHT, AND I HATE IT"

Listening to parents and teens as they talk, joke, and quarrel, it becomes clear that teens are skilled at rooting out parental weaknesses and prodding them until the parent "loses it," thereby transforming the grown-up into something very much like a reactive teen. When Sam's father tries to engage him in conversation, and then complains, "You're hard to talk to," Sam says, "You think I'm hard to talk to? Mom says she has to drag you into a room and lock the door before she gets you to say what's bothering you, or to listen to her problem." Father and son glower at one another. After a beat, Kieren says, "Like I say, you're hard to talk to." As he walks away, Sam mocks him, " 'Like I say . . . ' Case in point, Dad. Perfect example."

Teens know their parents' faults and failings. When they feel under uncomfortable scrutiny or criticism, teens use this knowledge to "get back" at a parent. They expose traits that parents themselves may not admit to, and a defensive parent is likely to be an unreasonable one. Parenting teens, Kieren says, "requires a good pair of shoes." I ask him to explain. "It's a long and bumpy road. You have to be prepared to travel far. And some of it's uncomfortable. Your ego is constantly getting pinched."

Many parents tell me that parenting teens erodes their self-confidence not only as parents but also as people. "I've learned," Vella tells me, "that anything at all about me can suddenly be 'wrong.' " What surprises many parents is that part of that distinctive heft of the teenager's criticism stems from teens' unease at retaining their blind trust in a parent. Teen criticism, although it seems so vehement, is hedged with doubt. The parent's views and beliefs remain signposts embedded in the teen's mind. The teen's criticism, apparently directed toward the parent, is actually directed toward the still-powerful parent residing in the teen's mind. Sam tells me, "There's nothing I could say to my dad that is big enough to match what I want to say. It's like my words aren't going to get to him, not really. What's really maddening is . . . what really makes me mad, is how sure he is and how I sort of believe he's right, and I kind of hate that."

The criticism a teen lodges against a parent harkens back to all the times the teen, as a child, accepted the parent's version of the world. In contrast, a teen's own personal voice seems halting and uncertain. By criticizing a parent, teens hope to hear the not-quite-formed voice within themselves. To correct this imbalance between (what they see as) a parent's certainty and their own self-doubt, teens decide, "I must be on my guard and always challenge what they do and say." But when parents show they are willing to hear the teen's—as yet unformed—voice, they ease that distinctive teen frustration. When they feel their emerging self is respected, teens no longer have to fight so hard to make it heard.

IT ISN'T ONLY THE TEEN WHO'S TOUCHY

As we have seen, teens are quick to react to negative emotions. A heated argument is likely to become more heated and less rational. It is difficult for anyone, teen or adult, to remain calm in the company of people whose emotions run high, and the teenage brain's reactivity often infects the parent's responses. Emotional arousal is contagious.

Parents are more sensitive to their teen's criticism and hostility than they were to a child's. The same words uttered at the same decibel level will mean something different when they come from a teen than when they came from a child. "I hate you!" and "I want to leave and never see you again," uttered by a four-year-old are momentary outbursts, not statements of real feeling. When a parent of that four-year-old is at his wits' end, and he too loses it, he might reply in kind ("I hate you right back!"),[3] but the fire and fury ebb quickly on both sides and love washes away all bad feeling.

When fourteen-year-old Leis tells her mother, "I want you out of my life!" and "I hate you!" she feels, in many ways, like a four-year-old.[4] She is frustrated that she cannot get her own way—her mother insists she cannot meet a friend until she cleans her room and does her homework, and that frustration, at that moment, fills her entire world. Like a four-year-old, Leis is unable to see beyond the present pulsing anger.

But Leis's mother does not respond to her teen's outburst as she would to that of a young child. Instead, Annette sees before her a daughter who, over the past year, has become highly articulate, who can discuss other people's perspectives and values as well as if not better than any of Annette's friends. Annette hears the terrible words, "I want you out of my life" and "I hate you!" as coming from a person who knows her own mind. Stunned and deeply hurt, she retorts quickly and coldly, "The feeling is mutual."

It is from Leis that I hear the report of Annette's words. "I couldn't believe my mom was saying that to me. I mean—sure,

I get mad, too" Leis told me. "But Mom knows that. I've been real mad before? Like, I know I can say even worse things. But what she said really shook me. It stopped me dead. And I was about to apologize but—you know—it takes a while to get to that. And then she just walked away. She didn't speak to me for twenty-four hours. It was scary."

No one likes to hear "I hate you," and this is particularly painful to hear from a close relation. So why is Leis caught off balance when her mother retaliates so coldly to *her* words? The fact is that Leis still sees her mother as she did when she was a child: super strong, assured, the one who's always in charge. The teen who is good at discussing other people's perspectives does not yet see her mother as an ordinary mortal. Leis continues to see her mother magnified, many times her normal size, through a child's perspective.

Some parents disguise their vulnerability to their teen's criticism. "I don't care what you think," Vella says when her teenage daughter Clara "jumps on every word that comes out of my mouth." She reasons, "I have to be the grown-up here. I can't let her see how she gets to me. Here's this super darling daughter who once thought I knew everything now telling me I'm up the creek without a paddle. Like I don't know *anything*. It isn't easy."

It seems like common sense to feign indifference to an unreasonable and sometimes hostile teen. But parenting teens comes with unexpected dynamics, and common sense is not always a reliable guide. When Vella disguises her vulnerability and pretends to be unmoved by her daughter's criticism, she endorses Clara's view of her mother as super strong. Clara then becomes the super attacker. As Vella notes ruefully, "She just will not step back. She says things to me that she wouldn't say to anyone whose feelings she cares about."

Clara believes her mother when she says, "I don't care what you think." The feedback she gets from these exchanges is that however angry she is, however cruel, she is not hurting her mother. The message Annette gives to Leis is very different. Annette's surprising comeback to Leis—"The feeling is mutual"—puts parent and teen on more or less equal footing. Her words shock her daughter, who then realizes that she does after all have power to hurt her mother in a way she has not had before. "I didn't mean to hurt her so much," Leis tells me. "I was just mad, and I wasn't thinking."

This is not a recommendation to "lose it" when your teen loses control. "Losing it" is not something, generally, parents should model. Instead, we want to show our teens how to regulate even difficult feelings. But breaches between parent and teen present us with opportunities.

First, there is the opportunity to apologize to our teen. In doing so we admit that everyone has trouble, sometimes, in managing emotions. Second, we have the opportunity to explain why we lost our temper, what we felt at the time—perhaps we felt betrayed, or terribly hurt, because we value our teen's love. Third, having set out our perspective, we can then invite the teen to do the same. We can model the capacity to reflect on our responses, to put behavior in the context of feelings and intentions—and in so doing we collaborate with, or co-regulate, the teen's neural storms.

For the teen/parent dynamic enacted by Vella and her daughter, where Clara feels that her mother shows disrespect by "not listening," Vella could articulate her anxiety and present it as a point of discussion. "Changing subjects is a big decision. Can you help me understand why you want to do this?" This would invite Vella to update her mother about her interests, and Clara would be assured of her mother's willingness to hear her out, even if they cannot agree. If Annette were to say to Leis, "It really hurts to hear you say [that you hate me]. I hope you don't mean it, but knowing you feel it, even for a moment, is hard because I love you so much," then Leis could take on board the power she herself has in the relationship and avoid that painful (albeit temporary) breach between them. In speaking about strong feelings, not to attack the other but to reach out and connect, parents model ways to repair intimate bonds when they seem at the point of rupture.

In every strong bond there are occasions of conflict and fury. Learning how to repair these ruptures is crucial to maintaining the bond. Moreover, conflict can deepen the relationship and bring greater closeness when, in the aftermath, each clarifies the feelings that underpin the quarrel. When a parent explains her response to the teen and seeks a teen's help in understanding the teen's perspective, then teen/parent arguments are likely to achieve the teen's aim—getting a parent to take a new look and show appreciation for who the teen is becoming.

MORAL CHALLENGES

Teens enjoy countering the family views they once took for granted. They are critical of once-accepted rules and examine their underlying principles, regardless of whether these rules are set by parents or school or government. They delve into abstract concepts, such as fairness and justice, and are quick to challenge familiar notions of what's right or wrong, what matters and what doesn't, what's shallow or what's profound. As Shakespeare observed, teens show "irreverence to their elders,"[5] and this can exhaust and exasperate parents.

With their expanding horizons, teens engage with broad complexities and abstract issues. They question what it means to live well and be fair to others. Teens are now capable of feeling empathy for distant people who face very different hardships from those they themselves experience, and this capacity both enriches and unnerves them. "What can I do," they ask, "to make this a better world?"

Proud of their newly acquired reasoning and thinking skills, teens see moral issues with pristine clarity. They don't yet know how difficult it is to get good things done, how what is obvious now may not have been obvious before, and how many compromises may be needed in the course of fashioning a decent life. They enjoy taking the high moral ground to point out that their parents have been reckless, that they have failed to think ahead, that they have not taken responsibility for pollution, waste, and damage to the climate. Once teens identify a solution, they believe achieving a good outcome is straightforward. This can give them the fierce moral energy of a Joan of Arc or Greta Thunberg, but it does not make for easy discussions within the family.

Another criticism parents often hear from a teen is "You're a hypocrite." Like Holden Caulfield in *Catcher in the Rye*, many teens see the grown-ups around them as "phony." Parents sometimes lie when they say that it is wrong to lie. They complain about a teen's diet or alcohol intake when they bemoan their own tendency to be tempted by fatty food and beer. They complain about the teen's screen time, but are often glued to their own phones.

Teens are unforgiving partly because they have not been tried and tested by competing duties and needs and values. Remember how the teenage brain approaches significant risks and imminent rewards? Teens are so excited by possible rewards that the downside of pursuing these disappears from view. When they look at a big-picture concept, such as how to solve a crisis for refugees or climate change or personal integrity, they imagine the reward of putting things right. The eagerness to "do something" arises from the teen's hyper-rationality,[6] whereby only the positive outcome of a challenge or a risk is seen, and any negative impacts of implementing a "good idea" are irrelevant.

Such drive and idealism have many benefits, and parents can help teens put them to better use. Engaging in moral arguments is an opportunity to challenge teens' (often) simplistic approach. But to engage a teen, parents need to avoid simplistic arguments themselves. They need to resist the temptation to take a position diametrically opposed to that of the teen. They need to manage the heat of argument and be nuanced and collaborative, showing willingness to listen to and be moved by their teen's views. While parents find such discussions exhausting, teens get a thrilling sense of agency when they are able to shift a parent's views.

HOW TO WEATHER TEENS' CRITICISM

Given teens' frustration with a parent who "doesn't get" or "understand" or "see" or "appreciate" them, it is surprising to discover what teens say when they are asked, "Who understands you most?"

When I put this question to teens, they mention friends, often a special friend they can "always talk to" and who "won't ever talk behind my back" and who "is always there for me." Friends come high up on the list, but they come in at only second place. Highest on the list of people teens trust to be there for them and help them work out personal problems are parents. Most teens say that a mother or father is likely to understand them, and that, when they are struggling, it is a parent in whom they are most likely to confide, and that the person they would trust most with something private and "awful" is a parent.[7]

When parents are asked what they hope for in their relationship with their teen, they are very likely to say: "I want her to trust me" and "I want him to be able to confide in me" and "I want her to feel she can tell me anything" and "I want him to know I am always there for him." Showing a willingness to engage with a teen, even when engagement exhausts you, is mightily reassuring to the teen.

Another concept to keep in mind as you weather the storms of teen criticism and conflict, is antifragility.[8] This term describes systems that strengthen as they repeatedly endure normal shocks. Bones, for example, need pressure and jolts from walking and running to develop and retain density. Our immune system requires exposure to a variety of germs and allergens to function well. Some vaccines make use of this feature by introducing a small amount of a pathogen (such as a virus) into a system to trigger an immune response. The result is a system that can withstand a higher viral load without getting ill.

Antifragility provides a useful frame for understanding the positive aspect of teen/parent opposition. In a dynamic known as "mismatch and repair" teens show dissatisfaction with a parent's response: the parent assumes the teen is still the familiar little child, and fails to acknowledge how the teen's thoughts and needs and abilities have changed. The teen challenges a parent's assumptions. The heat of the argument directs a parent to re-engage with the teen's current feelings and needs. These quarrels, when understood and managed, refresh and revitalize the teen/parent relationship. Repeated experiences of repair strengthen the bond, so that it is no longer threatened by inevitable mismatches.

Without this dynamic, a teen may give up on getting genuine recognition from a parent, and instead opt for surface harmony while presenting a "fake face" to parents. If a parent cannot tolerate the relational tussles with teens and closes down a teen's efforts to mark out the differences between them, then the teen confronts a dilemma: "Do I suppress my individual needs and hide my knowledge of my difference in order to maintain harmony with my parents?" Or "Do I continue to resist my parent's need for me to comply with her current sense of who I am and remain constantly at odds with her?" A relationship that goes through mismatch and repair many times becomes stronger. A relationship that avoids disagreement and dispute, on the other hand, remains fragile.

Conflict with those we love is not pleasant. It jars our emotional equilibrium, but when the mismatch is corrected through argument and explanation, the resulting "repair" reassures both parent and teen that their bond is responsive and secure.

MAKING USE OF TEENS' CRITICISM

Many parents insist, "I would never let my teen get away with talking to me like that" and "I don't stand for such disrespect." They also ask, "Are you saying we should put up with back talk and a bad attitude?" My answer is "The best way to change unacceptable behavior is to understand what it is trying to achieve, and the underlying need it expresses."

Seeing criticism from a teen's perspective offers parents

deeper understanding of behavior previously deemed disrespectful or offensive. No longer do the words "You're wrong/ You don't understand anything" signify a rejection, but a plea to take a close, curious look at the teen. No longer is criticism evidence that "my teen is a bad/ungrateful/disrespectful person." Instead, the teen is valiantly dealing with the enormous challenges of being a teen.

Teens too, could benefit from understanding the driving forces behind their constant criticism. As they reflect on what they want a parent to "see" or "understand" or "appreciate," they will learn how more effective "identity reminders" can guide parents to seeing who they are, who they are becoming, and who they want to be.

My approach rests not on assessing what teens should or should not "get away with" but on an assessment, based on decades of working with teens and parents, of what works and what does not. When parents view the common flow of teen criticism as rejection or disrespect, they become hurt and anxious. They are then quick to hit back by criticizing the teen. They signal rejection by refusing to hear what the teen is saying. They sometimes lose their temper and then share in the chaotic emotions of their adolescent, instead of helping the teen regulate those emotions.

Common advice given to parents of teens is "Don't expect to be successful when you put a reasonable argument to a teen; don't be surprised when your teen frustrates you; the problem is that they are caught in an immature/irrational/pig-headed phase."[9] My approach is more challenging, but also, in my experience, more helpful to both parent and teen. My message is "Try to see what your teen is seeing; try to understand what your teen is feeling. Your teen's thoughts and feelings and perspective carry genuine meaning."

The hard work of being a teen and parenting a teen serves a purpose. In the heat of an argument, teens are trying to reintroduce themselves to a parent. When parents pick up on those "identity reminders" that pepper teen/parent arguments—"I know what I'm doing"/"I don't like that anymore"/"I'm capable of making the decision myself"/"I am so frustrated that you don't trust me"—they can interpret the teen's underlying meaning and see the positive goal of the argument. It is hard to listen to criticism, but listening to a teen's criticism is part of recognizing the teen herself.

The teen's broader criticisms—of religious, political, ethical beliefs they once shared with parents—exhibit courageous attempts to think for themself. They are exercising the skills humans need to advance, and which each individual teen needs to find the path to adulthood. But however confident teens appear when they proclaim that their own views are more valid than those of a parent, part of the teen feels dependent on a parent's opinion. And while teens wish they might be strong enough not to care what a parent thinks, they do care desperately. So when parents listen to the messages beyond the criticism and irritability, they encourage their teens to keep doing the fundamental task of adolescence—remodeling their brain and their identity.

BUFFERING CRITICISM

Since criticism, especially from someone we love, is hard to take, it may be helpful to have some reminders of the teen's real aims and some tools to diffuse it.

Teen criticism is usually an effort to recalibrate and update the relationship. Parents' understanding of this goes a long way toward reducing defensiveness and bringing arguments to a halt. Parents can then use the teen's criticism as an opportunity to explore what it is the teen wants from a parent. Instead of retaliating with, "There's no point talking to you" or "You think everything I say is wrong," you could try, "I'm clearly upsetting you. Can you help me understand why?"

A parent may then hear something like, "Just because," or, "Because you're so annoying." Your challenge is to show, by looking at the teen and waiting for the teen to compose a response, that you are willing to hear whatever the teen says. If the teen says something like, "Because you never listen!" you could show you are listening by seeking clarification. One example worth modeling is: "You feel I don't listen. That's pretty serious, if your parent isn't listening to you. It seems I need some help in this area. Can we start now? I'd love you to give me a chance. Can you tell me something I need to hear now? Can you help me be a better listener?"

The teen may need some time to ponder this. Sometimes teens don't know what they want. However, a teen might say, "You look at your phone when I'm talking," or "You get up and start clearing the table when I'm in the middle of saying something," or "You always interrupt me!"

Parenting teens is a humbling endeavor, and it is hard to hear such things. But you can coach your teen to articulate the basis of criticism by acknowledging their efforts. "What you say is really helpful" should be followed up with questions that relate to what your teen has told you. When the teen complains about what you say or do, or what you seem to feel, you can use this as an opportunity to repair the mismatch. Something like, "It's hurtful, but that's okay. I wasn't aware I did these things. But I can see that does seem I am not listening. I'll try to do better."

When parents use their teen's moral enthusiasms as an opportunity to elevate conflict to a real conversation, there are ground rules to keep the argument on track. A discussion about religion, politics, or climate change, for example, should not include personal criticism or mockery. Sweeping challenges such as "You don't know what you're talking about" or "I've never heard anything so stupid" or "You don't know what it was like in my day" have no place in such discussions. Remember, the parents' views already have added weight, and the teen's vehemence is shaped by doubt rather than certainty. When a parent shows willingness to learn from a teen, the extreme heat of argument is turned down.

8

"I don't think I'll get through this."

Vulnerability and Resilience

TEENS RIDE an emotional rollercoaster as they learn what it is like to desire other people, to be disappointed in them and sometimes in themselves, and to care passionately about social and moral issues. Most teens gradually learn to maneuver, manage, and even enjoy inevitable emotional peaks. But in some cases the ride is too rough. Things go wrong and, for a time, the ordinary tasks of teenage life—studying, socializing, eating, and sleeping—present overwhelming challenges.

As I talk to teens, I see how alert they are, how curious and deep, how capable, and yet how very, very young. They seem so smart, so proud, so "together," but I know things may feel very different from their perspective. "How will they fare?" I wonder. "How many will grasp what they want from life, and whose life will be a series of constricting compromises? Who will flourish and who will falter?"

Adolescence is a time of immense opportunity. The heightened plasticity—or remodeling potential—of the teen brain allows a rapid acquisition of skills and knowledge. As each brain circuit is strengthened, chemical changes impact nearby brain circuits, so that learning other, very different things also becomes easier.[1] Positive growth during the teen years helps shape an agile, adaptive, and resilient adult brain.[2] The energy and urgency with which teens explore, reflect, and challenge serve us all well; we need original, out-of-the-box, creative thinkers to address the big issues of our day.

But along with enormous potential comes vulnerability. Some of the risks teens face have been discussed earlier in the book. In this chapter, we look at risks of a different order—the risk of mental illness. Among people who suffer mental illness, 75 percent will have had symptoms that first emerged in adolescence.[3] In this chapter we focus on the most common signal of a teen in mental distress—self-harm. Affecting between 10 and 30 percent of teens,[4] self-harm is linked to depression, social anxiety, and even suicide. Like most challenges to teen well-being, however, self-harm can be overcome, as long as we also understand the mysteries of teen resilience.

THE PARADOX OF SELF-HARM

Most people will do anything to avoid physical pain. The sight of a wound, however minor, sends signals to nerves that widen our blood vessels, and our blood pressure plummets. Teens, keen to focus on their invulnerability, seem particularly prone to this vasovagal reaction. Yet a very high number of teens deliberately inflict damage to their body by hitting, cutting, or burning themselves. The actual damage to body tissue is often minor, but the concern extends far beyond the injuries themselves because self-harm is the single most significant predictor of suicide.[5]

Self-harm is diagnosed when "in the last year, the individual has on five or more days, engaged in intentional self-inflicted damage to the surface of his or her body." It can take many years for parents to become aware of this disturbing practice. Toby, now sixteen, began self-harming when he was fourteen. It started with small cuts on the inside of his thighs, areas ordinarily hidden from view. Scars and fresh wounds now extend along his arms, forming criss-cross patterns, almost like a game of tic-tac-toe. The pain and the sight of blood, which in most people would intensify anxiety or sadness, induce very different feelings in Toby. The pain, Toby explains, "makes me calm. I get this—oh, wow, it's relief, but it's more than that. It's peace, really I feel peace. Just seeing my blood. . . . It's kind of reassuring—showing that I'm real, after all."

In teens who habitually self-harm, pain becomes a method for regulating the whirlwind of emotions, particularly self-consciousness and social anxiety.[6] As teens like Toby take a knife to their thigh or press a burning match to their inner arm, they leave behind the constant worry that they are being criticized, rejected, excluded, or ridiculed. Pain halts his endless rumination about whether he is disappointing and burdening his parents or losing friends. "The shame of being me," Toby says, "just drains away." But where does this shame come from? How can a much-loved, smart, and healthy teen like Toby be ashamed of being himself?

In Chapter One we learned about the teen's alien self. This arises in part from the rapid physical changes of puberty and adolescence, when the once taken-for-granted body feels strange and its flaws all too noticeable. At the same time, teens take a leap forward in their ability to mentalize—to see other people's behavior in the context of their thoughts, feelings, intentions, and motives. Psychologists working at the forefront of this common, disturbing, and puzzling teen behavior believe that underlying self-harm is mentalizing gone haywire.[7] Self-doubt and self-consciousness lead to overthinking every situation in a process known as hypermentalizing. Here teens' probing mind becomes their enemy, generating wild and usually negative assumptions about the minds of others.

When his friend cuts short a conversation in the school corridor, Toby concludes, "He doesn't want to talk to me. He thinks I'm worthless." Toby does not consider, "Something else might have been going on. This might have nothing to do with me." Once he becomes upset, the negative interpretations escalate. Instead of shrugging it off ("These things happen" or "I'll have a chance to have a better conversation later"), he sees this single incident as a global experience: "I mess up every relationship. I'm no use to anyone."

Eventually this negative guesswork forms a core belief about who the teen really is—someone who is worthless and repulses others. As Trudie Rossouw, a child and adolescent psychiatrist, explains, "The inner experience of the alien self is akin to the experience of an inner tormentor. It is the constant experience of inner criticism, self hatred, lack of internal validation and expectation of failure."[8]

Burdened by negative expectations, teens' interpersonal world appears hostile and unmanageable. Teens who self-harm are unlikely to talk about their feelings because they do not believe others would be sympathetic or helpful. Ordinary techniques for reducing anxiety and problem solving—such as talking to friends or parents—elude them. Instead, teens like

Toby withdraw, and isolation reinforces their sense of exclusion. Toby grows increasingly irritable and hostile. Anticipating rejection or contempt, he rejects others. "I'm fine," Toby hisses to a friend who phones to ask how he is. "And what do you care anyway?" The alien self instigates responses in others that confirm the core belief, "No one understands me/wants to help me/thinks I'm worthwhile."

HOW DANGEROUS IS SELF-HARM?

Parents are appalled to see the daughter or son in whom they invest so much love and care willfully damage the body that they are primed to protect. Nothing is more frightening than to see a teen deliberately counter every instinct of self-preservation.

A great worry is that self-harm seems only a heartbeat away from suicide, the most common cause of teen death after (usually reckless) accidents. Tragically, teen suicide and self-harm have both increased over the past decade, but most teens who self-harm are not thinking about suicide. They are searching for some relief from self-punishing, self-reinforcing thoughts. They seek the distraction and the strange tingling calm that, for them, come in the aftermath of pain.

A common and counterproductive belief is that teens who self-harm are seeking attention. But nothing could be further from the truth. They try to hide their wounds, and feel shame when these are exposed. They interpret any questions about the cuts or blisters as an attack. "It's nothing/Leave me alone/It's not your business!" are common replies to people who show concern.

"What triggers self-harm?" parents often ask. "How can we protect our teen from it?" The puzzling thing is that any social interaction can generate self-loathing and anxiety in a teen who interprets even mundane experiences as proof of the alien self within. A close friendship might sour, and the teen sees confirmation of his overall lack of worth. Conflict with parents convinces a teen that he is a disappointment, a problem, a burden on everyone. The teen then concludes that no one is there for him, no one to help manage the turmoil within.

Sometimes self-harm starts as a one-off act of self-punishment or anger. But as the knife cuts into flesh or the hot match presses against skin, there is a rush of relief, and the teen concludes, "Yes, this is wonderful. This is the answer." The neurological responses that in most people would raise an internal alarm, produce calm[9] and temporary reprieve from self-torment.[10] We do not yet understand why some teens experience this very peculiar neurological response to both pain and the sight of blood, but—as discussed at the end of this chapter—parents can coach any teen to manage emotional pain more effectively.

SOCIAL MEDIA: CAUSE OR COINCIDENCE

Self-harm and suicide in teens decreased steadily during the last decade of the twentieth century, but around 2008, the same year as the first-generation smartphone was introduced, cases began a relentless rise.[11] Now that 95 percent of fifteen-year-olds look at social media daily, often for several hours, the possible link between this increase and social media is a common question.

When Ian Russell found his fourteen-year-old daughter Molly dead in her bedroom, he was filled with rage as well as grief. Insisting that Molly had not shown any signs of mental health problems, he blamed social media.[12] Molly had been looking at sites that valorized self-harm and suicide. It was such content, the grieving father concluded, that had pushed his daughter to take her life.

We have seen how social media offered some protection to teens' well-being during the pandemic lockdowns. Without social media, teens would have been hit even harder by loneliness, boredom, and frustration. But as we have also seen, social media opens routes to criticism, derision, rejection, and bullying, all of which are huge stressors to teens who are enormously sensitive to how others see them. The problem is compounded by social media's notorious "nasty effect," whereby brutal put-downs and sneers attract more attention than supportive messages.[13] The brevity and speed of social media messaging promotes superficial values, emphasizing appearance over character and gloss over substance—though we have also seen how small modifications, such as adding positive profiles to their followers, can improve teens' social media health.

The initial promise of social media was that it would facilitate supportive connections, and sometimes it does. Philip (introduced in Chapter Three) is deaf, and while able to manage academically in a mainstream school, enjoys "chatting" to other deaf teens across the country. "How do you chat up a girl who isn't deaf?" is one question he can ask others. "What ways do your parents embarrass you?" is another. Tips on lip reading and arguments in favor of persuading your family and friends to learn sign language are others.

But some shared interests have a terrible darkness. Some

anorexic teens find sites that offer techniques for cheating parents' and doctors' efforts to make them eat. Some sites offer bulimics advice on techniques for purging after eating. There are also sites where depressed teens can reinforce their view that life is not worth living, that they will never find fulfillment, and that the only relief is in death. These sites also present steps for a "successful suicide," and beckon a distressed teen towards the worst possible response to her or his problem.

Many parents believe social media is the cause of such distress and disaster. Some researchers, too, claim to have found a causal link between the increase in teens' self-harm and suicide over the past decade and the increased use of social media.[14] But the most extensive and fastidious analysis of all available information does not find evidence that social media causes teen suicides, or even increases anxiety and unhappiness in teens. The best research shows that though the rise of social media coincides with the rise in cases of teen self-harm and suicide, any causal links are complicated.[15] Teens who are depressed and anxious often turn to social media in search of companions in misery.

This measured argument, however, goes against parents' gut feelings that social media is responsible for their teen's unhappiness. They insist that before looking at these sites their teen did not display any sign of mental distress. But teens are surprisingly good at hiding their unhappiness. While they sometimes seem intent on spreading their misery through the entire household, teens often want to avoid making a parent worry. Parental anxiety would, they believe, only add to their woes. Sixteen-year-old Sunetra explains that she does not want to talk to her parents about "the darkness inside me. They'd be bummed out, and it would make everything worse."

Parents insist that the dark material available on Reddit

threads or certain hashtags "causes depression" or "incites teens to self-harm." But teens themselves seek out such spaces because they are already depressed or thinking about self-harm. The danger is that these online communities amplify and normalize their negative feelings, and the algorithms adopted by these platforms to "serve" the interests of the "user" lure distressed teens towards distressing material. The teen forgets about the friend she is going to meet, or the report he is nearly finished writing. Their in-the-moment misery eclipses everything else.

While social media can lower teens' mood, so can a sour look from a friend, a quarrel with a parent, or a film that for some reason confirms a teen's sense of being overwhelmed. Moreover, teens who think about self-harm and have suicidal thoughts tend to have a narrow circle of friends. They seek out friends as companions in misery, and they reinforce one another's hopelessness. Dangerous bubbles do not occur only on social media.[16]

What sometimes happens, tragically, is that teens, whether in an online comment section or in private conversations with a friend or in isolation, lose sight of everything but the misery of the moment. As Toby explained, "It's no good telling me things will be better next month or next year. What I worry about, when I'm in that state, is how I'm going to survive the next five minutes." With his teen brain's tendency to be captivated by the emotion of the moment, he forgets the many things that provide pleasure, interest, and satisfaction.

This is what makes it so difficult for parents or friends or teachers to "see it coming." Even professionals who have worked for decades with troubled teens struggle to assess whether a teen's unhappiness poses a significant risk.[17] But most teens do survive, in spite of, sometimes, the inability to see beyond the next five minutes. And when we understand the sources of teen resilience we can guide our teen to safety.

GENETIC VULNERABILITY AND GENETIC RESILIENCE

New understanding of adolescent vulnerability and resilience has caused a significant shift in the approach to mental health in teens. Instead of asking, "Why has this teen fallen prey to mental illness?" psychologists now ask, "Why, given that teens' normal environment is so challenging, do so many teens thrive?"[18] Instead of looking at causes for each and every mental illness, psychologists today focus on one mysterious quality—resilience, the ability to ride out adversity. Why do some teens manage the pressures of friendship, the uncertainties of their future, the demanding expectations (sometimes unreasonably high, sometimes insulting low) of parents and teachers? Why do so many teens experience adverse experiences in childhood—family disruption and instability, bias, stress, social upheaval, or even violence—yet go on to flourish? What is the secret of teen resilience, and how can we foster it?

In previous decades psychologists have looked to one of two explanations of mental health and mental illness in adolescence. The first drew, roughly, on the question, "How good is the home environment?" A number of adverse experiences in the home environment—violence, abuse, neglect, parental death, mental instability, substance addiction—were seen as predictors of teen difficulties. Secondly, intrigued by the discovery that specific genes were linked to alcoholism, or depression, or schizophrenia, psychologists looked at genetic makeup. There also appeared to be genetic markers for resilience, and the notion of a "dandelion" child versus an "orchid" child became popular. Dandelion genes—named for the hardy flower—allowed children and teens to bounce back from adversity; orchid genes—named for a flower that only thrives in a carefully controlled environment—exposed children and teens to greater risks of mental distress.[19]

This genetic model of resilience suggests absolute endowment or absolute deprivation, as though to say, "Some teens are resilient, and other teens are not." Fortunately, the science of human development has moved away from this model. First, it was discovered that orchid children often retain good mental health. It is only when they are mistreated in childhood, usually through abuse or neglect, that they have an increased risk of developing depression.[20] The key orchid element, scientists realized, was not strength or weakness, but greater sensitivity to the environment. Therefore, orchid teens may be at greater risk than dandelion teens when their environment is compromised, while they benefit more than dandelion teens when they are surrounded by positive influences. In one environment the orchid gene posed problems, but in a different environment it provided benefits.

New discoveries in how genes change in response to environment showed the interplay between nature and nurture to be so intricate as to make the two factors indistinguishable. Though we keep throughout our lives the same DNA we had at birth, many genes switch on and switch off according to our experiences. Poverty, or war, or grief can switch on a gene for illness or depression or violence. A strong friendship, or an inspirational teacher, or a concert or chess game we attend by chance might switch on one gene that contributes to talent or switch off another gene that contributes to aggression.

Furthermore, single genes or even a single group of genes do not determine one trait or another. Instead, they interconnect in ways that are very difficult to predict. So variable are those "resilience genes" that most young people sit in a middle camp—now given the label "tulip." Neither as delicate as orchids nor as robust as dandelions, their indeterminate resilience shows the variability among young people with similar genes. If teens with dandelion genes grow up in adverse circumstances, they too are more likely to be negatively affected by additional stress, and if teens with orchid genes live in a supportive and stimulating environment, they are as robust as those born with dandelion genes.[21] Which traits emerge from specific genes depends both on how these connect to other genes and on whether a gene is switched on or off.

The secrets of teen resilience are most clearly revealed by teens who show resilience even when both their environment and their genes make them vulnerable. When we see how even these teens can thrive, we have clear guidelines for fostering our own teens' resilience, regardless of their genetic makeup, and even when they endure adverse experiences.

RESILIENCE AGAINST GENETIC ODDS

About half of the populations that have been studied for genetic resilience have at least one orchid gene, and 17 percent have two such genes, making them purebred orchids. These are precisely the teens who would be expected to have an elevated risk of life-long difficulties, particularly when they lack a supportive family and experience stress and setbacks.

So why are some teens who are genetically vulnerable to mental illness *and* who lack a supportive family *and* experience adversity nonetheless resilient? How do teens from very difficult backgrounds and who are genetically vulnerable to mental illness bounce back to health? What strengths might orchid teens acquire to reshape their troubled minds into healthy ones? How can the people who care for them discover life-preserving skills that, in their chaotic or threatening environment, are obscured? How can their thwarted vitality be nursed back to life?

Studying mental illness in adolescents is complicated by the fact that normal adolescents can seem disturbed. Irritable, sensitive to rejection yet needy, with a negative self-image and prone to inexplicable outbursts, the normal teen exhibits many of the core diagnostic features of several mental illnesses. Low mood, tearfulness, irritability, and disturbed sleep patterns are also normal in teens but can be symptoms of mental illness. To distinguish normal adolescent crises from those symptoms that are unlikely to resolve without special intervention poses a challenge to researchers.

This challenge was brilliantly met by a group of psychologists who traced the transition of sixty-seven teens who had suffered such severe mental illness that they had been confined to the locked wards of a residential psychiatric hospital.[22] The family environment of all these teens had been difficult and chaotic. The majority had been subjected to various kinds of abuse and neglect. No genetic testing was needed to know that these were vulnerable teens—the proof was in the severity of their conditions.

The recovery rate among these disturbed teens was not high. Twelve years after their hospitalization, most—over 86 percent—were still troubled and deeply unhappy. But nine young people—over 13 percent of the group—recovered to become capable, trusting, and successful adults.

What was different about these nine resilient teens? What was their secret strength? The life stresses they had experienced, in the form of neglect or abuse, were similar in all cases. The mental illness they suffered in their early teens was as severe as that of those who remained troubled. Why were some of these teens able to negotiate a path through adversity and go on to thrive?

Developmental scientists were inclined, initially, to look more deeply into genes or how adversity in teens might alter the brain. But as they pored over the interviews held throughout the teens' hospitalization and subsequent care, they found what they were looking for. The key differences lay in the way the two groups of teens—the group of nine that recovered and the larger group that did not—told the stories of their lives.

When the troubled teens whose difficulties persisted talked about their lives and reflected on why they did something or why other people behaved as they did, they lost focus. Their descriptions were disjointed, and their stories meandered. They shrugged when pressed for more details. Things "just happened." People "just did things." When asked about their own feelings, they fidgeted, grew distracted, or fell into a sulky silence.

The nine teens who sprang back to health and were leading positive lives as adults spoke about themselves and others very differently. They reflected on their changing lives and their relationships. They emphasized the importance of others' feelings and needs. They were responsive to other people's views and intentions. They saw their own behavior, too, in the context of their needs and hopes. Their dense and complex narratives were in sharp contrast to the simple, flat, or disorganized stories of the others.

The resilient teens did not always begin with nuanced

and coherent narratives, but they showed a willingness to understand their feelings as well as the feelings, thoughts, and motives of others. Here is Rachel age sixteen, inching away from a vague account of her family as "more or less like a family—but not really—just like a family set up—sort of." Rachel persists in her efforts to clarify her point and soon grasps the importance of understanding people via their thoughts. "They're upset, but you know, I don't really know how they feel if they don't say anything; it's just that they get mad."[23] Rachel does not yet understand why they get mad, but she understands the importance of the question, "What do they feel, and why do they feel as they do?"

At the age of fourteen Pete stole a gun and brought it to school. Initially he shrugged and tapped his foot when asked why he did it. Gradually, the therapist's questions prompted him to pinpoint his motive: "If you only feel safe when people are scared of you, they might not want to hang around. But if they aren't scared of you then maybe you don't want to hang around [them]."[24] Once he understands why he wants a gun—to scare other people so he can feel safe—he reflects how, even without a gun, he might avoid people who make him feel unsafe. He realizes that he is an agent who might choose different people to hang out with.

The teens who learned to tell a story about why they did something, who paid attention to context, and who then could reflect on their and others' motives, thrived. In stark contrast, the teens who did not recover were at a loss to explain why they did something. They grew irritated when their motives were questioned. They had a narrow repertoire of responses, most of them counterproductive. They saw danger when it was not there and reacted to innocuous and friendly remarks with inappropriate defensiveness or aggression. They seemed unable to learn that their environment could be different from the difficult one they experienced in childhood.

Among the teens I interviewed, too, when fixed, narrow and negative responses gave way to reflective understanding, resilience followed. Seventeen-year-old Mel, whose self-harm injuries required stitches and antibiotics, initially resisted new information and was hostile to any request to explain her behavior. When we first met, she first denied that the wounds were self-inflicted, then denied that they "meant anything," and closed with, "I just did it. Okay? What else do you want?" She shrugged off questions about her feelings. Was she angry? "Why would I be?" Was she anxious? "Not really." Was she sad? "What's the point of that?"

The next time we met she was back at school, preparing for exams, and grateful to her family. "I was really angry [at that time] and thought everyone was just useless. I hated seeing anyone, and everything they said made me feel worse. I think my Mom couldn't talk to me . . . you know, it was hard. The only time I felt in a safe zone was when I was cutting. Mom cries when we talk about it. She says she was scared stiff. I try not to scare her now."

There is nothing comfortable or predictable in the strategies of resilient teens. Their early efforts fail; they make lots of mistakes and suffer many self-generated setbacks, but with strong personal narratives, or stories that give sense and meaning to their lives, they are better equipped to navigate the inevitable challenges of the teen years. When teens are able to name their darkest feelings, when they understand adversity or maltreatment, they can put painful experiences into a broad context—a context in which good things are also possible. They acquire the ability to ride out stressful or hurtful situations and examine their choices so that they can do better in the future.

Resilience is more than absence of illness. It is the capacity to remain confident and whole in the face of disappointment or hurt or stress. Resilient teens see behavior—both their own and others'—through the lens of emotions, thoughts, and intentions.[25] They understand how their own behavior affects other people, and they are able to adjust their actions accordingly, giving them agency in their interpersonal world. They are equipped to repair the glitches that occur in all relationships. They are open to feedback from others, and are flexible enough to modify beliefs about others' feelings and motives. They develop emotional granularity—the ability to name and see nuances in a range of emotions. (See Chapter Three for an explanation of how reflection and emotional granularity affect the brain and the body.) They see themselves as agents who make choices, construct plans, and decide how to behave.

All these skills are packed into mentalizing. This fundamental mode of understanding helps teens form the close relationships that support them. When teens understand others' actions in terms of their feelings and intentions and desires, and when teens understand that how they behave affects other people's feelings and intentions, they make and keep friends more easily. When teens can name and reflect on negative feelings such as anxiety, disappointment, and sadness, they are more likely to reflect on their emotions than to express them by hitting someone.[26] This basic self-control increases positive exchanges with others who might then offer understanding and appreciation.

The capacity to mentalize, as we have seen, is learned. Initially it is learned in infancy, but in the fast-paced mental changes of the teen years, the necessary expansion and refinement of this capacity can flounder. Sometimes it is relearned in a therapeutic relationship, with a therapist who holds in mind the perspective of the teen and offers a "coherent (understandable) approach that provides hope."[27] But teens also continue to develop their capacity to mentalize within close relationships, as long as the people they love hold them in mind by listening, engaging, and supporting those rapidly developing brain circuits.

OVERVIEW AND EXERCISES

Parents want to understand their teen. They feel empathy for teen struggles. But when they try to talk to a teen, they are often accused of "prying." Or, when they ask a teen what's going on and how he or she feels (because they want to understand and help), the answer is often "I don't know."

Though teens do not want a parent to know everything about them (they value privacy) or to make assumptions about them, they want to feel understood. One aim of this book is to remind parents that, in spite of teens' awkward signals, they do want support. Another aim is to help parents spot the "get to know me better messages"—the identity reminders, the impatience with a parent's misunderstandings, and the pressure teens put on parents to acknowledge and correct their misunderstanding.

When communication stalls, when you feel alienated from your teen, there are extra steps you can take to show your willingness to "be there" for the teen, to hold the teen's difficult mind in your mind.

A simple step is to ensure you greet your teen as you and the teen come and go. A level gaze and an interested look send the basic message that you want to see who the teen is. The questions "How was your day?" and "Are you okay?" sometimes seem perfunctory to the teen, and they answer with a mere grunt. But remember the importance of body language: limbs relaxed but still, a steady, neutral gaze, and regular breathing to signal, "I have time to hear you, and I will be patient while you talk, and I am calm enough to take in whatever you tell me." Sometimes a parent's task is not to start a deep conversation right away, but to watch for an invitation or opening.

When you do talk to the teen, ensure that the conversation does not focus solely on your agenda. The parental agenda includes reminders of what you think they should do, what their attitude should be, and what you think their priorities should be. When communication is difficult, the parent's agenda may need to be put on hold. Without the teen's trust that you are in principle receptive to her ideas, she is unlikely to comply with your agenda.[28]

Avoid negative-sounding comments (including questions) about the teen's mood, temperament, character, or nature, such as "Why are you so edgy all the time?" or "Why can't you cheer up/go see your friends/get more exercise?" Even when such questions are genuine, a teen sees them as criticism—and while teens expect parents to accept a hefty dose of criticism, they are deeply hurt or irritated by "being judged" by parents.

Instead, try to engage with your teen's interests and activities and thoughts. If, when you ask, "What can we do together?" or "How are you feeling?" or "Why did you do that?" the answer you get is "I don't know!" you need to ask more not fewer questions.

The aim is to draw a story out of them. If you are inquiring about their feelings, you can suggest a menu of possible emotions: Are you sad/angry/pleased/relieved/frustrated? From there you can ask about the context or event in which a feeling arose. You can start with something that isn't controversial, such as a positive school report or a first driving lesson or an outing with friends or a sporting event. The point is not, initially, to get information but to (re)establish a conversation where the teen feels able to voice thoughts, opinions, and feelings.

It is also important to track your own behavior and your feelings. Are you showing that you are listening? Do you pose follow-up questions and refer back to information they have given you? Do you sometimes get anxious or angry when you hear what they want to do or how they feel?

Don't deny what you feel, but focus on your feelings rather than blaming the teen for "making you" feel this way. You can then tell a story about why you are worried ("I had a friend at college who was unhappy because she never wanted to do anything. I tried to help her, but I don't think I did. She is fine today and we are friends, but I remember how helpless I felt then. That may be influencing how I feel now.") You can explain why you got angry ("When you don't want to talk to me, I sometimes feel like you're rejecting me, or my love. I know that's just my interpretation, and it may not be right, but that's why I shouted. I felt hurt.") In this way, you model how to reflect on feelings and behavior.

If a teen self-harms or thinks about suicide, parents need a crisis plan. This plan includes a list of professionals to call and locations of emergency centers, and it includes a list of things to do to ensure the teen's safety in the short term, such as sleeping in his or her room.

While self-harming teens need professional guidance and monitoring, the powerful parent/teen relationship plays a huge role in recovery and resilience. As we have seen, self-harm arises from distorted mentalizing,[29] whereby the teen looks upon an interpersonal landscape of humiliation and rejection. Parents can help teens make sense of their own and others' thoughts and intentions.

During episodes when you feel your teen's well-being is seriously at risk, you will need to listen to a teen's dark thoughts—a very difficult ask for a parent. Some parents worry that if a teen talks about very negative thoughts, then their risk of serious self-harm increases, but that is not the case. Talking about these thoughts (sometimes called suicidal ideation) and acknowledging the teen's feelings reduce the intensity and urgency of the impulse to self-harm. Being there for them and listening to them, whatever they say, is likely to steady and soothe them.

After you listen patiently to the teen's negative thoughts, ask her to talk about something she likes doing. Is she planning to meet a friend later that week? Is there some new makeup she wants to try? Try to find some way to remind the teen of those different pockets of being, where they are engaged and have fun.

Gradually the vulnerabilities of the teen years give way to resilience. The demands for understanding and appreciation, for attentive listening and empathy, do not end, but are easier to meet. As the teen brain takes its adult shape, managing their own impulses and communicating their needs will come much more easily. Until then, the hard work of parenting must continue.

9

"I can't talk to you, but listen to my body."

Mind and Body Puzzles

TEENS ARE LEARNING to name new emotions and to interpret sensations within their changing bodies. At the same time, they are trying to decipher both who are they are and how they look to other people. Their minds and their bodies are intricately linked, but sometimes the messages from one to the other increase their confusion about what it is they feel, who they are, and who they should be. It is in the context of such mind and body puzzles that common teen problems arise. These include dangerously unhealthy attitudes to eating, panic attacks, and symptoms such as pain or lethargy that seem to have no medical explanation. These conditions are deeply disturbing to parents, who feel guilt ("What did I do to cause my teen's problem?"), helplessness ("I don't know what to do"), and a profound sadness as they mistakenly conclude that the teen is "damaged" or "broken" or "will always be at risk." Yet teens who have parents on their side are very likely to recover fully.

EATING DISORDERS: THE PROBLEM ISN'T MY MIND, IT'S MY BODY

Just when teens are most self-conscious and most likely to be dissatisfied with how they look, acceptance and admiration of their peers are of paramount importance. Full of self-doubt, they wonder, "How can people I like and admire find *me* appealing?" Their looking-glass self obscures what they actually look like. When they stare into a mirror, they do not ask, "What do I see?" but "What do other people see?" They cannot assess the evidence of their own eyes, and search for flaws others might detect.

Teens do not seem to know what a normal teenage body looks like. Their measure of what they "should look like" includes elements of late childhood (prepuberty) and an idealized body encased in skin smooth as plastic. To assess just how realistic—or unrealistic—teens are about normal physical development, I asked a group of fourteen-year-olds to guess the age of teens from a series of photographs. At age fourteen, both girls and boys think photos showing twelve-year-olds represent fifteen-year-olds, and that photos showing fifteen-year-olds represent eighteen-year-olds.

Next, I showed groups of eighteen teen girls four versions of a photo of themselves.[1] The first photo was untouched; a second was modified so that they appeared 5 percent lighter in weight; a third was modified to show them 5 percent heavier than their actual weight; and the final photo was modified so that they appeared 10 percent heavier than their actual weight. More than half the girls, when asked "Which photo of you is the most accurate?" selected a photo in which they appeared heavier than they actually were. Only eight out of the groups of eighteen girls identified the unmodified photo as the most accurate image, and only five preferred their unmodified image to the others. Forty-two percent of the girls wanted to be thinner and believed they were heavier than they actually were.

The questions uppermost in many parents' minds are: "How can I assure my teen she is gorgeous?" and "How can I protect my teen from persistent worry about how he or she looks?" Parents have lobbied, with limited success, for advertisers to use normal-sized models[2] and for airbrushed photos to be labeled, hoping that a label—"This photo is airbrushed"—will issue the warning, "Don't think that what you see is real."[3]

Many parents take this mission into their home. Some parents ban unrealistically modeled dolls (such as the classic Barbie doll) from the toy chest. When they hear a teen complaining about her body, they try to counter self-doubt with compliments. At the same time, they do not want to endorse the message that appearance is important. "I tell her she's gorgeous," Liba's mother says. "But I also keep it low key. I don't want being gorgeous to be her great success." And Gavin's mother says, "I insist both my teens (son and daughter) do a lot of sport to remind them what their bodies can do."

Few parents feel their efforts are sufficient. "The force is just too much," Liba's mother tells me. "I remember that horrible wish to carve myself a new body, but at least I could shut the door and be what I was to my family, who were fine with how I looked. My poor daughter has that phone on her all the time, where you get doctored Instagram shots that she's trying to match. It breaks my heart, her wanting to turn into some dull mindless beauty."

Skewed physical ideals have embedded deeper and deeper into our culture, impervious to the voices of parents and teachers shouting out, "This is unhealthy, and it's not real!" It is this environment that breeds anorexia and other eating disorders. While only 1 or 2 percent of the teenage population in the United States is diagnosed with an eating disorder,[4] it is estimated that 10 percent of girl teens have problems with diet and body image,[5] and a growing number of boys (estimates vary between 2 and 3 percent) use unhealthy means to control their weight; many more, equally driven by dissatisfaction with their body, overexercise or experiment with steroids to meet the muscular bodies they take as the ideal. Among teens who feel uncomfortable with their assigned gender, body dissatisfaction is even higher.[6]

The difference between the 1 or 2 percent of teens with a clinical diagnosis of an eating disorder and the larger 10 percent group is thought to be attributable to genes and metabolism.[7] The emotional burdens of negatively skewed body image and obsession about flaws in their appearance, however, are at their root, and these extend way beyond those with a clinical diagnosis of eating disorder or body dysmorphia.

For all the change there has been in teen girls' outlook and opportunities, the importance of looks and constraints on what looks good persist. Yet when I explore teens' own perspectives, they rarely ask, "How can I resist unhealthy cultural pressure?" They are more likely to ask, "How can I comply with the cultural ideals?" Teens suffering from anorexia and bulimia (90 percent of whom are girls) say, "What you call my eating disorder is not really a problem. It is a solution to my problem."

When fifteen-year-old Georgie looks at her body, whether her waist, legs, hips, or arms, she sees any fat, any *hint* of fat, as ugly. The curves, the shapeliness, the plump skin that others once admired are repulsive to her, and she is determined to excise fat from her body. As parents and passers-by alike shudder at the skeletal outlines of her ribs and her shrunken cheeks, Georgie sees her emaciated body as an "achievement."

A year before, at the age of fourteen, Georgie did not strike anyone as being at risk of anorexia. Compact and muscular, she showed less concern about her appearance than many of her friends. "She never pestered me for swish clothes or designer sneakers and seemed really happy in the kind of clothes she wore as a child," her mother, Laurel, tells me. "Something happened, and I just don't know what, when she turned fifteen, and suddenly she was eating cucumber and celery and nothing else. I wrack my brains to make sense of this. Georgie was always a relaxed eater. I never saw Georgie diet. I don't diet. Some of her friends—well, she has this friend who I'm sure is bulimic. My God, I get so mad when I think of her. She's a really sneaky eater. Any food that's out just disappears when she's around. And at parties, where there's cake and stuff, she just gorges. I sort of blame this Sian for a lot of Georgie's problems. I mean, these issues, they're contagious."

It sounds strange to talk about a mental problem as being "contagious." Contagion deals with the spread of germs from one person to another, and mental illness is not caused by any kind of germ. But Laurel touches on an important and puzzling feature: eating disorders, including anorexia, bulimia, and binge eating, often occur in clusters, just like a contagious illness. To explore what mindset underlies this particular cluster, I arrange to speak to Sian, the "unsuitable friend" with suspected bulimia.

I know this interview will not be easy. Bulimics binge-eat and then purge, usually by vomiting what they have just eaten. They know others will find this revolting, and therefore try to hide what often becomes a habit as compulsive as any addiction. However, Sian surprises me with her frankness.

When I ask her about her appetite and about weight, she tells me proudly that she does "gorge" just as Laurel described her doing, but she boasts that she is an expert at "getting rid of it." She can indulge her "gross" appetites, she explains, without facing any "consequences."

Neither Georgie nor Sian sees herself as having a problem. In Georgie's view, self-starvation is evidence of her "strength." She shrugs when I express concern. "Hunger can give you a high. I have more energy than ever. I'm, like, wired." I think about that word "wired." She looks now like she is made of wires, and she has the hectic energy and steely focus associated with broader meanings of "wired."

We sit together for some time, chatting about other, neutral things before Georgie returns to the topic of what she calls "controlled eating." Drawing a pattern on the carpet with the tip of her shoe, she speaks quietly. "I like staying this height, too. I used to be average. Now my friends have shot up, and I'm still little." She smiles and turns her head, still bent towards the floor, and watches me closely. I sense she is on the verge of disclosing something deeper. I return her gaze, trying to be neutral but interested. "I'm like an elf among people who have to live in the dirty real world, a kind of Ariel." After a beat she adds, "And I don't get my period. I don't have any of that mess. I'm escaping the system."

That "system" is normal physical development. Georgie, whose life-threatening condition is in clear sight, feels more physically confident than do the healthy teens who also feel uncertain and anxious about how others see their developing bodies. Although her condition weakens her immune system, stunts her growth, and shuts down her natural menstrual cycle, Georgie feels "strong." Sian, whose illness unbalances her metabolism, wrecks her teeth, and damages her esophagus, proudly declares that she has perfected a technique for remaining thin while accommodating a runaway appetite.

Parents, particularly mothers, feel guilty when they see their teen engaged in this kind of self-harm. There is a long history in psychology of blaming mothers for teens' eating disorders. The repudiation of appetite and desire has been seen by some psychologists as a teen's attempt to reject a mother's control. Others argue that eating disorders result from the mother's intolerance of her teen's appetites and desires. An anorexic girl, it was once thought, has a mother who does not respond to her needs; as a result, the teen is ashamed of her own needs, and shuts them down. A bulimic girl, it has been argued, wants to defy the mother who tries to control her appetites, but then she erases the "evidence" of her indulgence. Under the umbrella of these theories, eating disorders are means by which a teen tries either to comply with or defy her mother's wishes.[8]

In most cases, mother-blaming theories are wildly inaccurate. Parents tell me they themselves feel "heartache," that each day is "like walking on broken glass," that they would "do anything to help" their teen. The challenge they face is that teens like Georgie and Sian do not want to "get better." The prospect of "losing" their illness frightens them. Sian tells me, "There's nothing worse than eating a big meal and then finding there's no way to get rid of it. Like if it's a formal dinner, or in a restaurant and I can't get up. I feel trapped. It's awful." And Georgie says, "Sometimes there's a kind, proud voice inside me, telling me I'm wonderful. You can ride out any hunger pangs with that voice cooing at you. But if I eat something—boy!—the voice turns mean. It can be really vicious. I don't want to say the words. They're awful words. The voice wants to tear me to shreds. So when Mom kind of coaxes me to eat, or starts pressuring me about it, I freak out."

Each teen's eating disorder arises from a unique combination of personal need, desire, emotional history, and genetic makeup. The complex causation is neither "all the parent's fault" nor "all society's fault." Binge eating accompanied by rapid weight gain is sometimes activated by the wish to be repulsive and deter sexual approaches. In one tragic case, a thirteen-year-old who had been sexually abused by a stepbrother liked the way her enlarged stomach folded over her genitals. "If I can't see them, they're not part of me," she explained. Feminist author Roxane Gay recounted in her memoir *Hunger* how she used obesity to avoid being targeted as a sexual victim. After being gang-raped by some "school friends," she wanted to turn herself into someone who did not look like anything anyone would approach sexually.[9] "Fat is a feminist issue," Susie Orbach noted, as she discovered that many of her patients were using obesity to escape the brutal consequences of female sexuality.[10]

Though eating disorders are usually not caused by family dynamics, they complicate them. Teens resent a parent's focus on their illness. They label parental concern an "intrusion" and "control." Parental anxiety increases the teen's anxiety, thereby making the illness more likely to "stick."[11] As one highly experienced therapist explained, in families "intense feelings can escalate rapidly . . . resulting in more heat than light . . . the stage is set on a daily basis for interactions that potentially stimulate a loss of [balance and understanding] in one or more of the family."[12]

Teens who suffer from an eating disorder need intervention by a skilled mental health professional.[13] When a parent tries to "fix" the problem, the teen/parent relationship centers on the eating disorder. "It's all she talks about. It's all she cares about," Georgie says. While Sian reflects, "When my parents see me, all they see is a problem."

Yet teens, even when they need professional intervention, still need parents' engagement, appreciation, and curiosity. So the best advice is for the parent to leave the condition to the teen and the expert, while continuing to engage with other aspects of their teen's life. The parent can continue to ask, "What did you enjoy about today?" and "How are your friends?" and "Can we choose a color for your curtains?" and "Can we walk the dog together this evening?" A parent who laughs at the teen's jokes, delights in the teen's take on a film or news topic, and invites her to share ordinary activities reminds them both that there is far more to the teen than her eating disorder.

PANIC ATTACKS: WHEN MIND AND BODY SPIRAL DOWNWARD

Teens worry. They worry about how they look. They worry whether a friend likes them as much today as she did yesterday. They worry about appearing stupid or stuck up. They worry whether they said the right thing. For many teens, these daily worries come and go. The bicycle ride to school uses up the adrenaline that filled their bloodstream when they looked in the mirror and worried whether they were too fat or whether their clothes were right. A friend greets them enthusiastically, and the shadow voice murmuring "They don't like you anymore" disperses. They sit in math class, and suddenly figure out how to solve an equation, and their mood lifts. By the time they enter the school cafeteria they confidently join their friends. The conversation flows. Laughter ripples among the group. The morning's woes are forgotten.

But sometimes the common worries of a teen's day do not go away. Kevin, fifteen, looks in the mirror and notes that his ears stick out, his chest seems concave, and his feet look too big in the new shoes his mother bought him. By the time he reaches school, the worry about his appearance sits at the center of his mind. That distinctive looking-glass self, driven by self-doubt, absorbs all his attention. He walks towards the school entrance, past groups of teens lingering to enjoy the last few minutes of reprieve before the start of school, and he is convinced that other people are critically eyeing his appearance, just as he did. When a friend greets him with a smile, Kevin wonders, "Is she laughing at me? Have others been talking about me behind my back?" He sits in geography class, or chemistry, or English, and the teacher's words make no sense. Individually, he knows the meaning of each word, but he cannot follow the instruction or explanation or argument. When classmates raise their hand and speak, he is puzzled by their ability to make sense of the class and contribute to it. "I am so different from them," he thinks. "They live in a carefree world. They don't have to worry about their ears or the shape of their chest or the size of their feet. They can think about other things. They're smart. They feel confident about their future. I'm the only one here who isn't getting straight As."

Kevin concludes, "There's something wrong with me. I'm going to fail. My parents will be devastated. They'll make my life even more miserable. I won't get into college. I won't get a job. I'll be stuck at home forever. Every day I'll be reminded what a loser I am."

As he enters the school cafeteria and picks up his lunch tray, he freezes. There is no place at any table that feels safe. He knows he looks ridiculous, standing stock still with his lunch tray while the other kids are already stacking theirs up, having finished lunch. He cannot eat anyway. His stomach is doing somersaults. He is sweating. His heart is pumping. He knows his face must be red. He can't get enough air in his lungs. The sound of shared laughter rings somewhere in the hall, and he is sure it is directed at him. He cries out, and crouches on the floor.

Teens' ability to mentalize—to explore their own and others' internal worlds—normally enhances their communication and connection, but when teens hypermentalize, overanalyzing every facial expression or comment, they feel as though they are isolated in a hostile land. Kevin makes a series of assumptions about what other people are thinking and concludes that everyone is harboring negative, derisory thoughts about him. Behind every word and every glance he perceives a threat. His body responds just as the body should respond to a real threat, priming his muscles to fight or flee.

But the danger Kevin perceives is not something he can address, because it is not real. The adrenaline released by his nervous system is not used up, as it would be if he faced real physical danger, by either running away or fighting. Instead, the adrenaline remains in his system, signaling the presence of a threat that he cannot name or escape. So he panics.

Panic is a physiological response to the mind's perception of danger. The physiological responses—the trembling, sweating, stomach clenching, and inability to breathe normally—signal to the mind: "You are under threat. You are not in control. Something awful is about to happen."

Feelings related to panic, such as anxiety, are common, but normally we learn to calm the body's distress signals just enough for the mind to reassess the situation. As we realize, "The people looking at me are not going to kill me" and "Failing one test won't be the end of the world," our heart rate slows, our breath steadies, and the sweating stops. The moderated physiological tempo confirms the mind's assessment that there is no imminent danger.

But sometimes, as with Kevin, body and mind get caught in a downward spiral. When anything goes wrong—when someone snubs him, or when he struggles with a reading comprehension exercise—Kevin "catastrophizes." This means that he imagines the worst possible outcome. He believes one unfriendly glance proves that no one likes him. He believes that the difficulty he has with one set of questions not only means he will fail the class but that he will ruin his entire life. When he enters the cafeteria and wonders where to sit, the minor decision seems like a life-or-death issue. However objectively safe his surroundings, he sees danger everywhere. When he is unable to reduce the physiological side of anxiety, his mind remains on high alert, "reasoning" that "if my body is so frightened, there must be real danger."

The school nurse helps Kevin calm his breathing, and his panic attack eases. But later that evening, he feels the dry mouth, the churning stomach, the breathlessness and terror that he interprets as life threatening. He calls out to his parents for help. "There's something wrong with my body!" he insists. "I need to go to the hospital."

"No," his mother Rosa says. "You are okay. Try to calm yourself down. Take deep breaths, like the nurse showed you."

"You're not listening to me," he insists. "You don't care about me. I feel like I'm going to die, and you don't care!"

And so a mind/body puzzle becomes a teen/parent rupture that can only be healed (as shown in the final section of this chapter) by listening to the body's speech.

MEDICALLY UNEXPLAINED SYMPTOMS: WHEN "THERE'S NOTHING WRONG" IS DISTURBING

Sandy, age sixteen, is a dedicated mathematician. As she walks through the corridors of school, she focuses on the recent calculus lesson where she's just learned how to produce a derivative function. She imagines the numbers and graphs in colors, "like tender butterflies." These images protect her from social challenges, such as walking past other people, with their breezy smiles and easy manners. Sometimes she wonders what it is like to initiate conversation, confident you can follow the strange rules of talking. She puzzles over "that foreign country where they get dressed." She cannot fathom how other girls choose their clothes, how they know what store to enter, what site to open to gain access to their stylish tops and skirts.

Yet Sandy is clearly well liked. Other girls greet her and don't seem to mind that she responds with a timid wince, as though shying away from contact. Many of the boys she passes give a casual wave or nod, low-maintenance greetings that are friendly but only require minimal acknowledgment. When she approaches the heavy fire doors in the corridor, there is always someone who rushes ahead to open them for her.

Sandy has constant pain and weakness in her left arm. She used to play the piano and, I am told, showed the kind of promise that leads parents and teachers to suggest that she consider a professional career. When the pain started, her father, Manuel, took her to an emergency room, where she was quickly discharged. "Nothing broken. Not even a strain," they were told. "Then what is it?" Manuel demanded. The doctor shrugged. "Fatigue, maybe a pinched nerve. It should resolve itself. If it doesn't, take her to her primary physician."

Manuel took Sandy to the pediatrician who had looked after her from early childhood. She had shepherded the family through a diagnosis of autism spectrum disorder (ASD). "I can't tell you how relieved we were when we got that diagnosis," Manuel tells me. "It explained so much, and made things so much easier. She can be very stubborn, you know, and—wow—really picky about loud sounds and sudden changes. I used to get so angry. Not only me—the teachers, the neighbors, all our friends and relatives. They thought she was being perverse. They blamed us, as though we were, you know, allowing her to be difficult. So hearing what it was, with the name and a kind of explanation, that was really helpful."

Getting a helpful diagnosis for the pain and weakness in Sandy's arm was not as easy. The pediatrician found nothing and suggested that though her reflexes were "fine," there might be a damaged nerve that would "mend with time." She suggested Sandy take safe doses of over-the-counter pain relief tablets. When Sandy returned a month later in tears, saying, "It doesn't even *touch* the pain," the doctor prescribed opioid pain relief, "but only five days' worth." With no remission of pain, and no further prescriptions for pain medication, Manuel took Sandy through a lineup of specialists—rheumatologist, osteopath, internist. Joints and bones were given the all-clear, as were the muscles and, finally, the nerve pathways between the arm and brain. Sandy then tried physiotherapy. When that did not help, she tried acupuncture. The pain was sometimes more and sometimes less intense, but overall, after eighteen months of various treatments, there was no improvement.

Manuel then took Sandy back to her pediatrician. "I laid it out straight. 'There's something going on here,' I said. 'If you can't sort it out, then for crying out loud give us the name of someone who can. There's been all this messing around, and we're still at square one. You either care or don't care. Which is it?'"

The pediatrician's response was, "The neurologist [the specialist who explored the possibility of nerve damage or a neurological condition] advised that the next step is a referral to a psychiatrist. I'd be happy to refer you. We cannot find anything medically wrong."

"I thought, 'That's it. We're finished with this gal.' " Manuel pauses. His breathing is labored, and his eyes fill with tears. "We've gone to her for ten years, you know. And this is how she treats us. Useless!"

In most cases, the news "There is nothing physically wrong" is reassuring. Wouldn't a parent be relieved to be told that nothing is physically wrong with their teen? But outrage like Manuel's is very common, and understandable, given how most people understand pain—as a signal that something is physically wrong. Manuel and Sandy feel insulted, undermined, and abandoned. They hear the words of the pediatrician as "The pain isn't real. She's either imagining things, or she's pretending." But pain is far more complicated than most people realize.

So-called non–medically explained symptoms or somatic symptom disorders are very common and woefully understudied. The most recent report by the World Health Organization found that 20 percent of people experience at least six medically unexplained symptoms in their lifetime.[14] Teens, who are novices in interpreting interoceptive signals—the internal sensations that we constantly interpret as positive or negative—and who struggle to name and tame emotions, are particularly vulnerable to pain, immobility, nausea, or fatigue for which no medical explanation can be found.

Sometimes "non–medically explained" is taken to mean, "It's all in your head."[15] But what does that mean? All pain is generated within the brain. Nerve cells send messages to the brain to signal trouble—your skin is dangerously close to heat, your foot is trapped, your bone is broken, your stomach cannot cope with what you've eaten. Whatever the injury, without a brain, we would not experience pain. So, in some sense, pain is always "all in your head." The difference is that, in Sandy's case, it seems that there is no injury, no tissue or bone damage, no physiological malfunction to explain the arm weakness or the pain. But the brain experiences pain through many different routes.

Let's for a moment consider how stress or misery or loneliness sometimes generate pain as real as that from any broken bone. We saw in Chapter Three how emotions affect body functions and how bodily sensations also affect emotions. When we are stressed or miserable, we produce a hormone called cortisol. This normally reduces inflammation—the body's response to injury or illness (which is why people with swollen joints get cortisone injections and why hydrocortisone creams reduce itching and redness on our skin). But when we remain stressed or miserable or frightened, our body stays on alert, with high cortisol levels. After a time, these high cortisol levels lead to more, not less, inflammation (which is why cortisone is normally prescribed for only limited use). Persistent inflammation makes us feel tired. We have greater difficulty concentrating. We have trouble remembering things. We are also at much greater risk of getting sick because prolonged inflammation reduces the efficiency of our immune system.

Scientists now understand that the problems of inflammation don't stop there. About ten years ago the astonishing discovery was made that little proteins released by stress called proinflammatory cytokines can cross from the body to the brain.[16] These tiny proteins interfere with all those neural connections that are remodeling the teen brain. They induce feelings of fatigue or misery. The fatigue and misery then message the brain, "Something is wrong." The body's alarm system remains switched on, flushing the entire system with cortisol and cytokines, just as if the body were actually sick or injured.[17] The brain behaves as if the body is damaged, and the nerves, talking back and forth, produce pain. This is very different from malingering, or faking pain. Nor is this imagined pain. This pain is real.[18]

Like that of many teens, Sandy's daily environment is rife with stress, and hence with cortisol triggers. The stress from social encounters, self-doubt, and schoolwork can be problematic for any teen, but having ASD intensifies commonplace teen anxieties. Every social encounter is packed with uncertainty. While many teens are nervous about how others see them, Sandy feels at a special disadvantage in reading social cues. "Why," she wonders, "did that girl's facial expression suddenly change?" and "Is that sound [that others would immediately recognize as laughter] anger or derision?"

In addition, Sandy's exteroception—awareness of external stimuli such as sound, movement, and touch—is heightened. The bang of a door or a cough or a flash of light disorients her. "It's like her whole geography switches around, and she's gone from a familiar place to one she doesn't recognize," Manuel tells me.

Real-life interactions, Sandy explains to me, happen "too fast." Other people understand their rhythm and flow, but she experiences them as a series of unrelated snapshots, speeding by before she can process them. She is unsure how to greet people or join a group. A friendly smile alarms her if she thinks something—and she knows not what—might be expected of her in exchange. Yet, like most teens, Sandy also wants to be liked by others.

The school has a done good job in explaining ASD to her classmates. They enjoy telling me what social life is like for her. "You can't tell her jokes," sixteen-year-old Leilah explains. "She understands things literally. You have to say just what you mean. You have to be careful about sarcasm, because she won't get it." Sandy depends on close friends to navigate her day. They are, she tells me, "scouts who go ahead and show me the way." Without constant reassurance of people showing her the way, she feels lost—and stressed and alarmed.

These are issues that confront many teens with ASD, but most teens with ASD do not develop medically unexplained pain or paralysis. Like any mind/body puzzle in any teen, the explanation lies across the individual teen's needs, fears, and expectations. It may be that Sandy had an injury in her arm that established a pain circuit. Sandy feels the pain before she moves her arm to open the door. She winces and cradles her elbow when she simply sees the door ahead of her, just as she would if her arm were broken. As people respond to her as someone who feels pain, then pain and a weak arm become part of her "self-schema," or how she sees herself, both socially and physically.

The brain is a highly predictive organ. Everything we do

involves predictions, from waking in the morning and putting our feet on the ground to getting into bed at night. Every action, no matter how simple, involves predictions about what physical objects, including our bodies, do. The floor will provide a supportive base when we stand up; the spoon will hold cereal or stir a drink; the bed will offer a certain kind of comfort. Our bodily sensations, too, flow from the brain's rapid computation, based on predictions about what is out there in the world and what is happening within us. These are micropredictions computed as millions of neurons "talk" to one another. Lisa Feldman Barrett explains, in *How Emotions Are Made*, "These neural conversations try to anticipate every fragment of sight, sound, smell, taste and touch that you will experience, and every action that you will take. These predictions are your brain's best guesses of what's going on in the world around you, and how to deal with it to keep you alive."[19]

We feel the discomfort before the needle touches our skin. If we experience migraines, our head starts pounding even if the pain is initially slight. If we associate stress with nausea, one of these feelings predicts the other. We sometimes give meaning to the sensations associated with an emotion as pain or fatigue, and sometimes as paralysis or blindness. Psychology professor Tamar Pincus notes, "After a while, you see things coated with pain . . . you might experience more intense pain simply because you are expecting it."[20]

Feeling depressed also increases pain. When we are emotionally "down," pain areas of the brain are more active, so the pain seems more severe. Teens, who experience more social stress than either children or grown-ups, who are more likely to undergo mood swings, and whose body clock makes them particularly vulnerable to fatigue, are at greater risk of pain and fatigue that seems to have no physical cause.

A further mystery about pain arises from how, sometimes, it serves a special purpose. Perhaps pain or paralysis or illness brings the help we need. Perhaps pain provides space to rest. Perhaps our pain reminds others not to expect too much of us. If a teen like Sandy suffers daily social stress but finds that being in pain or being weak elicits responses that help her deal with very difficult emotions, then her pain, though real, is not from injury. This unconscious strategy is sometimes called functional neurological disorder, indicating that the nervous system is not functioning properly. The brain converts an emotional problem into pain or paralysis or fatigue. Though the physical symptoms might serve a purpose—by, for example, relieving the pressure of others' expectations or ensuring others' attention—they present problems of their own by limiting activities and opportunities. In addition, physical pain obscures the underlying psychological problems and prevents these from being addressed.

When a teen is referred to a psychiatrist rather than a rheumatologist or internist or neurologist for pain or paralysis or chronic fatigue, this does not mean that the teen is a "hypochondriac" or "malingerer." It means that emotion, sensation, and the body are intricately connected, and that sometimes the connections get tangled. It takes an expert to support the teen while he or she unravels the knots.

"All in the mind" is a phrase often used to dismiss pain. This is strange because there are many conditions that are in the mind but are very different from those that have the stigma of "only in the mind" or "psychosomatic." Depression, for example, is in the mind, but not psychosomatic; it is a real condition, for which there are effective treatments. If untreated, this condition of the mind alongside stress and anxiety result in persistent inflammation that turns negative feelings into physical illness. Schizophrenia is "in the mind," and though researchers have not yet finalized any physiological explanation of the illness, no one thinks of it as psychosomatic. The gap between medically unexplained and medically explained conditions is not as stark as supposed.[21]

The long journey to recovery involves a kind of supereducation in emotional granularity and new techniques in problem solving, often with professional support. This journey follows the course we have already seen, taking in the importance of emotional granularity and naming emotions to activate the prefrontal cortex, which then conducts a reality check and calms the body.[22] As the body's alarm system switches off, the underlying problem can be tackled and the mind/body puzzle can then be resolved.[23]

OVERVIEW AND EXERCISES

Mind/body puzzles cover a range of problems that are common in teens. These include eating disorders, panic attacks, and non–medically explained symptoms.

Fifty-three percent of thirteen-year-old girls are unhappy with their bodies, and this rises to 78 percent among seventeen-year-olds.[24] While body dissatisfaction is less common among boys, 30 percent say they would like to change their body shape.[25] Small but increasing numbers of teens (0.6 percent of females and 0.2 percent of boys) feel their gendered body is incongruent with who they really are, and want to remove or change their sex characteristics.[26]

One third of all teens, across genders, between the ages of thirteen and eighteen experience acute anxiety, including panic attacks.[27]

The incidence of medically unexplained symptoms is difficult to assess, but psychiatrists estimate that a quarter of people who see a primary care physician have at least one such symptom.[28]

These conditions often need professional support, but the hard work towards recovery has to be done by teens themselves. As always, parents' support is invaluable, and more effective when parents also understand some techniques for managing mind/body problems, particularly acute anxiety and panic attacks.

As we have seen, an important part of managing difficult emotions—including anxiety—is recognizing them and naming them. When, instead, teens fear and try to avoid an emotion, they perpetuate anxiety with a fear-adrenaline-fear cycle.[29] Fear (or anxiety or sadness or anger or shame) pumps adrenaline throughout the body. This influx of adrenaline is accompanied by rapid breathing and a racing heartbeat. If a teen comes to fear *that* response, then a secondary fear arises—fear of feeling fear. This secondary fear comes with its own powerful physiology, which the teen also fears, and which releases another fear response. This cycle, which seems endless to those in its grip, is what causes that "end of the world" panic.

Teens who suffer from panic attacks need a tool kit for self-management. Every time they ride out the panic themselves, they strengthen the neural connections that take them from panic to safety.

The first step in a panic attack is to calm the physiological onslaught—the beating heart and shallow breathing, the stress response—that locks down thought and diverts blood from the brain towards the muscles that are preparing to fight or flee from danger. Simple steps can be effective in calming the physiology, so that the mind can grow calmer, too.

Folding the arms across the chest and pressing them close, with one hand resting on the beating heart, is a useful technique. Strangely, some people find crossing the right arm over the left more effective, while for others, the left arm over the right is preferred. At the same time as people take this "barrier" pose—both arms folded across the chest—they need to regulate breathing.

When we panic, we tend to take quick, shallow breaths through our mouth, but what we need are slow deep breaths through our nose. When we do this, and oxygen is restored, the neurochemical storm signaling imminent danger ceases, and the teen is now ready to think. Then the conversation and problem solving can begin.

Sometimes a parent is so worried about a teen's problem that the parent's anxiety amplifies the teen's anxiety. Instead of focusing on the question, "What's wrong with my teen?" it can be more effective to ask, "How can I reassure, support, and understand my teen?"

The best way to answer this question is to ask the teen, "What do I do that makes you feel worse?" If a teen describes something "you do that makes me feel worse," you can suggest that the teen give that kind of interaction a special name. Georgie suggests to her mother, Laurel, that their conflicts about eating could be called "the 'Do that' scenario." Sandy feels like cowering when her father vents about the medical diagnosis, and she calls this "Dad's shout at the doctor time." When Kevin has a panic attack, he says his mother's face reveals the "There he goes again" routine.

Once the dynamic has a name and both teen and parent are able to recognize it, the parent can say to the teen, "Can you help me here? When I tell you to eat/complain about the doctors/tell you it's all in your head, I'm trying to help you. What's it like from your side? How do you see this? What are you feeling?"

Kevin might say, "I feel everyone is disappointed in me," or "I feel I'm bothering people," or "I feel I'm drowning and you're not paying attention."

In response a parent can pause and reflect. "I am worried about you and I sympathize with you. But I've been told not to take you into the hospital because this panic attack isn't dangerous. I know it feels awful, but you will get past it." After this explanation, the parent needs to refocus on the teen. "How does that make you feel?"

"It feels like I'm dying," Kevin might say. "And that you don't care."

"That must be terrible," his mother could say, focusing on what the teen is saying about his feelings, not on the implicit accusation ("You don't care"). "I want to help. Can you think of how I might help you—but not by taking you to the hospital?"

"Maybe just sit with me? Breathe with me? Until it's over."

"I would like that. It would help me feel close to you."

Rosa could then show gratitude to Kevin for explaining himself and offering her the chance to help him. It would also provide the opportunity for Rosa to prompt the simple calming techniques of folding his arms close to his chest and regulating his breathing. She could breathe alongside him, and suggest the 4-7-8 breathing technique, whereby first he exhales fully through the mouth, then breathes in through the nose, counting to 4, then holds his breath as he counts to 7. Then he exhales slowly as he counts to 8. Even five cycles of 4-7-8 breathing are enough to restore a state of "rest and digest" in which the body functions normally and the stomach is no longer "doing somersaults" or harboring "butterflies." Parents can help teens practice this method when they are calm, so they are familiar with the routine when they need it. In the grip of a panic attack, it is hard to learn new things.

Once Kevin "gets" that Rosa wants him to teach her how to help, he is more likely to welcome further conversation. Rosa could ask, "Are there some other times I don't listen to you?" or "What other things do I miss?"

Kevin might then say, "I don't think you get just how I struggle in school. I'm going to be a big disappointment."

Instead of saying, "How ridiculous!"—which would send the message, "What you feel/think/fear is ridiculous," Rosa could say, "I don't understand. How would your struggle with schoolwork disappoint me?"

This would give Kevin an opportunity to say, "I will fail this class. I might not even graduate. I'll never get a job. I'll never be able to amount to anything."

Once this disaster scenario is voiced, the irrationality can be addressed through a process called "decatastrophizing." Rosa could say, "Okay, maybe you do fail a test. Maybe you even fail the course. That would be a setback, for sure. We'd all be upset. But we'd get over it. Remember, everyone has setbacks. Your life doesn't end with one disappointment. We don't expect everything to be plain sailing."

The next step involves problem solving. "What can we do to help with the schoolwork? I'm sure it's hard. I struggled too, you know. Can we tell someone at the school? We all need extra help with some things."

And of course, reassurance and appreciation always help: "I'm sorry you have been struggling in class. We'll always be here for you. I'm so proud of you for thinking this through."

I am under no illusion that such conversations are easy. The parent has to shut down his or her own defensiveness and hurt at being so misunderstood by a teen who says, "I feel like I'm dying and you are ignoring me." The parent is being asked to be humble and patient, but that is what we sometimes need to be, as we interpret our teen's needs.

The challenges are greater, but not totally dissimilar, for parents of teens with ASD. In this case, the parent will already be in contact with professionals and support groups that provide guidance. Here I simply add that for people with ASD, the teen years require a special stamina. The need for friends, the longing for acceptance, and the pressure to read others' emotions that all teens feel can be particularly difficult for teens with ASD. Along with the advice you will get from experts, I offer the reminder that your teen benefits from the same interchanges that benefit other teens.

With ASD, a teen becomes anxious more quickly, partly because the interpersonal world is a constant puzzle. ASD teens are also highly sensitive to external stimuli, such as sounds, smells, movement, light, and touch, but may be slower to read internal physiological cues of anxiety until they are overwhelming. The breathing and body routines that normally ease a panic attack can also help a teen who is overwhelmed by background noise and sudden change, but more effort will be needed by a parent to help the teen lower anxiety to a point at which a soothing routine can be adopted.

The emotion-naming exercises that help a wide range of teens are particularly important to teens with ASD. The books they read, the programs they watch, the photos you look at together, all present opportunities for reflecting together on inner worlds—both theirs and others'. There is a common and very mistaken belief that teens with ASD are not interested in other people's minds. They are, but do not have the intuitive grasp many others have, so they need prompts, cues, and pointers. This does not apply only to negative feelings. It is helpful to emphasize the feelings and contexts associated with positive emotions, such as happiness and excitement and love. In this way you help normalize strong feelings and assure your teen that an emotion can be powerful without being negative.

What I have said elsewhere about coercive punishment being counterproductive in the teen years is especially important for teens with ASD. Most teens focus on emotional elements in the environment and are unable to process any rational argument if it is accompanied by shouting. Teens with ASD rapidly experience sensory overload and have particular difficulty with this.

What complicates any advice to parents about forgoing anger and shouting is that teens, whether or not they have ASD, are less compliant than they were as children and can be infuriatingly stubborn. Parents will sometimes lose their temper and may exhibit the lack of emotional control that is more typical of their teen. However, teens do not need perfect parents—as will be explored further in the next chapter—but they do need a parent willing, most of the time, to engage with their developmental challenges.

10

"You're not so perfect, either."

Parents Make Mistakes, Too

WHEN A PARENT looks into the eyes of the infant child, it is with a kind of moral prayer and promise: "I will look after you. I will do anything to give you what you need. I will always put you before anything else, including myself and my own needs."

But life takes unexpected routes. There are upheavals—social, financial, personal—that we cannot control, and that inflict unwelcome effects on the entire family. We lose our job, our savings, our home, and what we hoped to give our child is no longer ours to give. Sometimes we take a decision that, according to our teen, "messes up" his life. We accept a job in another city when, from a teen's point of view, leaving the familiar school and group of friends is a brutal displacement. We realize that our partner, who might still be a beloved parent, is no longer someone we can live alongside. The family unit that the teen takes for granted is ruptured. Then there are the mistakes we don't see. Unaware, we restrict our teen's horizons through our own biases. We try to boost a teen's confidence but find that we are sowing self-doubt. We try to celebrate our teen's identity but find that we are constraining it.

In this chapter, I look at common challenges parents unwittingly present to their teens. Some result from the unavoidable bad stuff that can happen to anyone, others arise from common myths about what teens need. This chapter explains how the former can be managed and the latter corrected.

DIVORCE

One of a parent's primary thoughts in considering divorce is "How will this affect my child?" Teens, however, seem so wrapped up in themselves and their friends that parents may believe their divorce will mean very little. "Tim never talks to us anyway. He doesn't seem to notice whether his dad is there or not. He's not into doing things with us. He seems to think that even sitting down to eat with us is a chore. Us splitting would have been hard for him ten years ago—and I think that's when I realized I would get out of this marriage at some stage, it was just a question of when. But how can you explain that to a six-year-old? Now I can explain things to him, if he wants to hear it. My guess is he'll just shrug it off. And my happiness matters too."

Jasmin shares with many parents the belief that when a son or daughter is old enough to understand divorce, it won't be so painful. She also shares with many parents the belief that her teen's sulky or hostile manner signals lack of need for family cohesion. And, like many parents, Jasmin believes her teen son is too self-absorbed to be overly concerned with his parents' breakup. Jasmin's decision to seek a divorce can be justified in many ways, but her decision will still greatly affect her teen.

The aim of this discussion is not to dissuade anyone from separating from an unsuitable partner, but to show what parental separation means to teens. Then a parent can offer support and empathy during the long process we call divorce.

Teens often hide their sadness under a cloak of irritability and indifference. For all their apparent lack of interest, they worry about their parents and want to help them. One way they sometimes try to help is by "not making a fuss" or "just going along with things." Sixteen-year-old Tim's apparent nonchalance at the news that his parents are separating disguises a deep sense of loss and confusion: "When I heard it, I thought, 'Yeah, I knew this was coming.' I guess my first thought was, 'What's it going to mean for me?' Mom said we'd still live here and everything would be the same, but that's a rotten lie. Yeah, I don't have to ship out to some weird place, but I have to spend time at my Dad's and keep track of my stuff, and every time I set up to see my friends or go to a meet, I have to figure out where I'll be heading from and where I'll be going. My Mom keeps asking me if I want to talk, and that's kind of stupid. Like she's so wise, but can't work this out with Dad? I say I'm okay, it's up to them. I just sort of pretend I'm not bothered."

A teen might "pretend I'm not bothered" in ways a young child never would. A child believes that her passionate wishes have power to change the world. The hope that "Daddy/Mommy will come back," shapes her expectations. Every footstep or knock on the door renews that hope. When wishes prove impotent, tantrums take over. A child's apparent "acceptance" is often mere exhaustion from upholding either fantasy or fury. By the time the child is a teen, the boundary between wish and reality is more firmly established. Teens grieve as a child does, but know, as a child does not, that their pain is powerless.

The unfounded reputation teens have for being totally self-absorbed leads many parents to believe that their own problems, their unhappiness, their own sense of loss will not really matter to their teen. Even when in late adolescence a teen may "leave home" for college or travel or employment, a parent's (or stepparent's) breakup is deeply disturbing.

Hard fact number one for parents is that divorce deeply affects teens. Teens have been shown to experience, in the wake of parental divorce, a greater challenge to their well-being than younger children.[1] However, the only advice that arises from this hard fact is "Be aware" and "Offer comfort."

Hard fact number two is that teens are highly sensitive to their parents' emotions. Most parents try to protect a teen from their own distress, but teens, with their heightened emotional focus, are supersensitive to parents' loneliness, bitterness, anger, and pain, and see through a cheerful façade. When a parent assumes a breezy manner and insists that everything is fine, teens may feel shut out rather than protected.

Teens hold strong moral codes about relationships and honesty. In a close relationship, not speaking seems as deceitful as speaking untruths. Like other researchers engaging with adolescents,[2] I hear teens like sixteen-year-old Mandy say, "My mom complains I don't tell her anything and she doesn't know what's going on with me. But what's the point of talking to her, when she says things with her are 'fine' and my dad is 'fine'? She pretends like nothing's really happened, and divorce is some kind of thing you do and forget all about the next day. It's like she's lying to me the whole time. So why should I tell her anything about me? She's slamming a door in my face all the time smiling and saying, 'Of course my door is always open.' All this talk about being honest and open is a scam."

Honesty, in the teen's moral lexicon, has to be mutual. If one person—whether parent or a friend—is not open, then there is no point in being open with the parent or friend. If, instead of trying to protect a teen by hiding real feelings, a parent manages to achieve that tricky balance between opening up about her situation, its context and its problems, and offering the teen assurance that the parents can manage their own pain, there are significant benefits. As one seventeen-year-old said to me, "The one good thing about my parents' awful divorce is that I now have real conversations with them."

A third hard fact about divorce is that this significant change in the parents' lives is unlikely *not* to change the way they treat their teen. Jasmin tries to assure Tim that "nothing will change," yet, in the heat of the moment, she tells Tim, "Oh, you're turning into your dad." At one time such a comment might have felt affectionate, warm, or funny. Now Tim believes that, from his mother's standpoint, it is hostile. "I know she's angry with dad, and it can spill over when she's angry with me. It's like she punched me when she said that. It was a mean thing to say, but I felt, 'Okay, I am like my dad. So what? Do you want to kind of cancel me out because you don't like Dad anymore and I'm like him?' There's lots of good things about my dad and I don't mind being like him." Tim pauses. His heavy breathing becomes more regular. "It's a complicated kind of arguing. It's not, you know, yelling at each other. It's slow, and there's time to think. I say: 'You can't use this against me. I have a right to be angry too. And I have a right to admire my dad.' And she's like, 'Really?' Like she's ready to hate me too."

Most parents resolve to be fair and reasonable, but stress takes its toll. Before, during, and after divorce, some teens witness fierce arguments, angry phone calls, and nasty texts. It is frightening to teens, who still need a parent as a collaborator in their own emotional regulation, to see parents out of control. "If I acted like that, they'd ground me for a month," Tim reflects.

Throughout this book I have focused on teens' limited self-control. The brain's prefrontal cortex in adolescence does not yet have adult robustness. Information and sensations and desires easily short-circuit, leaving the entire processing system without control switches. But short-circuiting of the brain's control centers can occur in the grown-up brain too. Parents can "lose it," and in this state their priority is no longer, "How can I be reasonable?" or even "How can I avoid hurting someone I love?" The priority is venting the chaos within.

A parent who lashes out at a teen and breaks his or her own rules of fair play usually then feels ashamed. A positive impact of shame is that we acknowledge the harm we have caused and try to make amends. A negative effect is that, ashamed of our behavior, we may become defensive. We deny we were in the wrong. We lash out at those who have witnessed our missteps. "You think you're so perfect? You think you never shout at me? You think it's okay to hurt me, but you condemn me if I say something you don't like?" Sometimes we try to justify our hurtful actions. "I had to tell you what your father is really like," Jasmin says to Tim. But twenty minutes later she buries her head in her hands and says to Tim, "I can't believe I said that. I'm so sorry."

Sometimes the best we can do is use our outbursts as an opportunity to say, "I can get things wrong." Sometimes admitting that you are not the parent you would have liked to be is enough to become the parent your teen needs.

COUNTERPRODUCTIVE PRAISE

If I ask parents what single trait is most important to instill in a teen, I often hear "self-esteem" or "confidence." Leah says of her son Jason, "I want him to know how great he is. I want him to be confident that he can do so much." Judy says of her daughter Kirsty, "It's not so much about how she treats me. It's how this irritability brings her down on herself, like she's worthless." And Pete, whose teenage daughter Luanne walked the dangerous snow dunes of Lake Michigan, says, "I want her to value her life, to see who she can be, and, you know, not lose all that on a stupid whim." But parents often miscalculate the impact of their efforts.

Many parents share the belief that to bolster confidence, teens should be fed a steady diet of praise.[3] Teens will then, it is supposed, "feel good about themselves," and if they feel good about themselves, they will believe they can succeed, and if they believe they can succeed, then they will. There are three significant problems with this approach.

The first problem is that in the teen years parental praise can seem stale, outdated, and patronizing. Teens value a parent's high opinion, but, as we have seen, they want to influence a parent's view of them, to make sure it is adjusted to who they want to be. Often they reject parental praise (such as looking "sweet" or "neat"), complaining it is "useless" or "dumb."

The second problem is that constant praise is confusing, especially when it is unfocused. "You are wonderful" and "You are clever" and "You can do anything" and "You are terrific" are spoken with the good intention of boosting confidence. But when teens are used to being told that everything they do is "wonderful," then they are unclear as to what is being praised. Are they always wonderful, regardless of what they do? And what if they see that their efforts have fallen short? Is it then unacceptable to admit they haven't done well? As parents press on with "You're great" and "You're so smart," teens feel unsupported in dealing with their inevitable failures. Is a parent blind to these? Are they being brushed aside because they don't matter, or because the parent doesn't want to acknowledge them? Is the teen hiding behind a front, like an impostor? What will happen when they are revealed as not always being smart or talented or wonderful?

The third problem with constant praise is that it does not achieve its goal of building self-confidence. New research has blown out of the water old assumptions about what kind of praise boosts confidence. A young person who believes that intelligence and talents are qualities they own is less likely to maintain confidence than young people who view their intelligence and talents and overall abilities as qualities they can grow.[4] When young people see intelligence and talent as traits that gradually develop by means of their efforts—rather than traits they either have or don't have—they demonstrate more confidence, particularly when they confront difficult, challenging tasks. If they initially fail, instead of concluding, "I'm not smart after all," they are more likely to say, "I have to work hard to get better at this."[5]

Suppose we ask teens to assess their math ability. Those who say, "I'm really good at math" or "I have a talent for math" are the ones who founder when the subject gets more difficult. Those who say, "I have to work hard to learn this stuff" are more likely to stick with a difficult problem until they solve it. The teen who believes she has an inborn talent for art or writing or swimming or singing may conclude, when the work becomes more difficult, "I was wrong. I'm not so talented, after all." The teen who believes that talent and ability are qualities that can be achieved over time will not be so disheartened when tasks become more demanding.

Suppose now that a different set of teens is struggling at school. Some may conclude, "I'm stupid" or "I'm no good at school." How can we help them grow confidence? Should we feed them a steady diet of praise and tell them everything they do is great? Should we convince them that they have ability by limiting what we ask of them?

This approach—allowing them to experience success by limiting them to very easy tasks—may initially encourage them and boost their mood. However, this boost lasts only as long as the tasks they work on remain easy. As soon as the tasks become more difficult, teens revert to their demoralized mindset, where they conclude, "I'm no good at this."

If, however, struggling, demotivated teens are given increasingly hard tasks and offered support and detailed feedback while they work on them, their motivation is sustained. This process is called scaffolding—for a period of time, teens are shown how to do something, and each step in the process is explained. Then, when the teens tackle the task themselves, they are given step-by-step feedback, until they show they can move ahead themselves. Finally, they are prompted to reflect on how, through persistence, their skills improved. These are the experiences that sustain their confidence.[6]

Parents mean well when they praise inborn intelligence or natural ability, but praise can easily backfire. "You're so smart" all too often sends the message, "You will be able to do anything without having to struggle." Expecting that hard work is necessary, on the other hand, makes a challenge less daunting. It suggests that through your efforts you can *grow* ability in math or language or football. Hard work and occasional failures are part of a long learning process.

What teens need is not protection from failure, but guidance in critically assessing their work and developing strategies for improvement. A better message is "Everyone finds some things difficult. Don't be afraid when things are hard. Learn to relish a challenge."

The model of praise that includes persistence and scaffolding has ramifications well beyond the classroom. Parents can use this model as teens grow other qualities, such as responsibility, conscientiousness, and consideration for others. Teens require a special kind of praise-in-waiting that, for many traits, embraces who they might become, rather than who they are now. They are not yet equipped to be as responsible, conscientious, or considerate as parents would like them to be, or as teens sometimes think they already are. They need a parental scaffold that keeps them together even when they mess up,[7] that tracks their ability to take the next step forward, and that gives them feedback, sometimes in the form of praise and sometimes in the form of correction, as they move forward.

UNCONSCIOUS BIAS

From birth, the announcement "It's a girl!" or "It's a boy!" shapes a parent's expectations of a child. In previous generations, these expectations were clear and unquestioned. Boys, it was thought, liked playing rough, and they did not show "weakness" by being "emotional." Girls, it was thought, were obedient, quiet, and caring. Ambition could be fostered in boys, but ambition in girls was by proxy—on behalf of their brothers or husbands or sons. Boys were more intelligent than girls, though they did not always seem so, and girls were good at homemaking but not at science or math or physics or engineering or navigational skills. Girls' realm was home and family; the boys went out into the world. In the past, many parents enforced these gender roles because they believed their girls and boys needed to comply with these in order to have a good life as adults.

Most parents no longer sign on to this division of roles and talents. Girls' intelligence is celebrated and girls' ambition is encouraged just as with boys. I hear parents protest about gender stereotypes they see in teens' music, social idols, and fashions. I also hear them say to their teens, whether male or female, "You can reach any worthy goal. It doesn't matter whether you are a girl or boy."

But biases linger unseen, covertly shaping our words and expectations. While the overt biases of yesterday are greatly reduced in many cultures, implicit biases escape scrutiny. Implicit biases arise from associations that we make, often unconsciously, about what kind of thing a person in a certain group (such as male or female) can do, or be, or achieve. A parent says, in all sincerity, "I believe my teen girl can succeed in anything she wants to do" or "I wouldn't dream of discouraging my teen girl. For her, the sky's the limit." Yet when fifteen-year-old Rachel hears this, she scoffs, "My brother doesn't do as well as me in tests, but my parents are sure he's the one with real talent."[8]

Listen carefully to how you, or any parent, speak with a son and with a daughter, and you may well hear more "achievement words" with a son, such as "proud," "top," "ace," and "win."[9] As Rachel notes, her parents need very little evidence before they declare that her brother is an "ace in science." Before they applaud her ability, however, they need to see prizes and commendations. Teens, quick to spot parental inconsistency, bristle at the injustice. When parents are lucky, their confident outspoken teen will call them to account over such slipups. But parents in this position do not feel lucky. Instead, they feel yet another dreadful battle looming.

One of the hardest things about teens' criticism is that it is often right. But since there is more emotional heft than articulacy in their criticism, it feels wrong. "Rachel gets on her high horse about stuff," her father Paul explains. "As though we've ever treated her as lesser than her brother!" But then I show him the results of the word analysis that—with his blessing—we've done over the past week. He sees, highlighted in the transcripts of their conversations, the number of achievement words—"masterly," "aced," "won," "triumph," "success," "tour de force"—he used when he was with his teenage son, and compares it to the less punchy praise he offers ("great," "lovely," "wonderful," "nice," "cool") to his teenage daughter. He is abashed, but also gracious. "Gosh, that's an eye opener."

Paul is eager to correct his bias, but sometimes parents insist that they are right even when they are biased. While Kirsty's brother is given more freedom to go out "because he is now fifteen," but when she turns fifteen, Kirsty is warned about dangers "out there" and subject to greater constraints. At fifteen she is required to have at least two friends with her when she goes out at night, and her wardrobe is carefully policed.

"That's just how it is," Judy protests when Kirsty points out what to her seems unfair. "It's not safe to walk around dressed like that. I'm protecting you, not punishing you."

Kirsty rebels against her mother's fear because she herself does not want to be afraid. She enjoys a teen's sense of invulnerability. She relishes her indifference to danger. Her mother's caution irritates her, and she wants to prove her wrong. "See, nothing happened. There was no disaster. I defied you and I'm fine!" she wants to say when she breaks her mother's rules. Judy, in an effort to regain control, itemizes the dangers of Kirsty's defiance. "Go out like that, and you'll get raped!"

Kirsty retorts that her mother is "sexist and a hypocrite." She insists that her brother Mike "gets away with so much. He stays out late, and he doesn't get this grief."

Judy shrugs. "Well, you have to make allowances for boys. All that testosterone and stuff."

The testosterone bias that seems to grant more privileges to boy teens actually sells them short in the long run. There is no good evidence that testosterone really does require teens to let off steam or to take more risks.[10] So when parents believe a teen son is, by nature, aggressive, impulsive, or prone to risk taking, parents not only send the message that such behavior is okay, they also forgo the scaffolding that would help teen boys practice restraint and respect.

Many teens express impatience with "dinosaur parents" who are uncomfortable with the idea that their gender identity—their internal sense of whether female, male, or neither—is different from how others see them. "Oh, it's just a phase!" Caroline insists as she hears her fifteen-year-old daughter Alice say she wants to change her name to Ali, and be referred to as "they," rather than "he" or "she." "Why should I go along with some fad? She's doing it just to provoke me." But as she speaks, she appears more distressed than provoked. She sighs, "She's my darling girl. How can she take that away from me?" We sit together for several moments, not speaking. Then she reflects, "Okay, let me get my head around this. I don't want this to be a great big argument. 'They'—well, maybe that's not so bad. She's a good kid. We'll work it out."

As uncomfortable as it may be to learn that your teen embraces a new gender identity, as much as this seems to devalue your own sense of who they are, parental acceptance remains important to teens. In a recent study of young people who identify across a range of genders, the sense of acceptance they had from their parents was crucial to their overall well-being, even into their twenties.[11]

Getting our heads around our own gender biases is a difficult, demanding, and important task. It may help parents to know that everyone, including the most well-meaning promoters of equality, struggle with implicit gender bias.[12] It is not surprising that for parent and teen alike this is work in progress. It means we have to listen to our teen's self-righteous rant as she points to our lapses. It means admitting that we too are infected by biases that embed themselves in our language and culture.

Sometimes, as we have seen, the best we can do is assure our teens we want to learn to do better. We can encourage our teens to voice their challenges when they think we, unaware, reveal bias. We can remind them that everyone, sometimes, shows the effects of these biases. We can invite them to consider whether biases emerge in school and in TV shows and in conversations with friends. Rachel, when she saw her father's humble response, "That was an eye-opener for me, too," appreciates his admission. "Seeing him admit he doesn't know it all, and being willing to, you know, learn? There was like, well, you know that 'Grrgh feeling'? Well that just switched off, and I wanted to hug him."

Teens show us that our missteps can be opportunities for re-engagement, to the benefit of both teen and parent.

SELF-SERVING BIAS

Parental love is sometimes described as "selfless." "I would do anything for my child," parents often say, and it is a sentiment that describes how they usually feel. At the same time, parents are people and, like all people, become defensive when someone criticizes them. In Chapter Seven, I explained how teens' criticism is generally an effort to correct a parent's views and re-engage a parent's attention. But sometimes teens' criticism is just what it seems. It highlights a parent's real flaw or deficit. When we are criticized, the default response is to defend ourselves. "No I'm not!" we insist, wholeheartedly convinced that the charge is untrue. We may counterattack with, for example, "You're the one who's irresponsible/disrespectful/inconsiderate." This default response kicks in even when the criticism comes from someone we love "selflessly."

Our clever teens are adept at picking up on this default response and using it against us. "Put your phone away. We're eating. Don't look at your phone. Put it away *now*." Fifteen-year-old Tracey mimics her mother's words. "She tells *me* not to look at my phone, but *she's* on hers the whole time. What really gets me is that she *pretends* she's listening to me when what she's really doing is reading texts or looking something up. 'Mmmh' "—again Tracey imitates her mother. "She goes, 'Yes, yes?' But it's obvious her mind is somewhere else altogether. She might as well carry a sign that says, 'My phone is much more important than you.' "

I can match each parent's complaint of a teen, "She doesn't listen" and "She lives in her own world," with a teen's complaint of a parent, "She's not interested" or "He never listens" or "They're always on their phones."

Many teens' complaints are of the moment, the teenage moment, part of a struggle to manage their own altered attachment to a parent. But sometimes teens need parents to acknowledge their own deficits, not dismiss the complaint with, "I'm human, so sue me," or "Yeah, put it on the list," or counterattack with, "You're one to talk." Sometimes teens need parents to admit that they can be thoughtless or inconsiderate. We can put our imperfections to good use by giving our teen insight into what it's like to parent a teen.

One of the most important principles of good parenting is Donald Winnicott's concept of the "good enough" parent. This is often taken to mean that parents do not have to do everything right, that they simply have to get things right often enough, which means getting right about one in every three interactions.[13]

But Winnicott's "good enough" principle goes beyond assuring parents they do not need to be perfect. The principle includes the message that a perfect parent would not be a good parent. With a perfect parent—one who is always reasonable and measured, consistent and proportionate (who never loses it) and is always right—a child would miss out on important experiences. These include experiences of rupture and repair, when relationships seem to break apart in the heat of the moment and then repair, without leaving any scar. "Perfection" would rule out the important lessons learned by teens and their parents when mismatched feelings, needs, and responses prompt each to update their views of the other.

Teens need to learn that people, and relationships with people, are not perfect. They are often thrilled to note flaws in their parents. But their own discoveries are not enough. They need their parent to confirm what they see. However sure they *seem*, they do not yet *feel* sure of their criticism unless the parent sees it, too. Therefore, teens' complaints intensify in face of a parent's denial. "I never did that" or "You're talking nonsense" might, in the moment, protect a parent's pride, but ultimately ramps up the teen's grievance: "You don't listen to me" and "You don't respect my view or my feelings," they think. Conversely, when a parent shifts in response to the teen's perspective and acknowledges the legitimate complaint, resentment dissolves. Parents never should underestimate the comforting power of their understanding and willingness to share the teen's perspective.

OVERVIEW AND EXERCISES

Teens do not need perfect parents. In fact, they need parents who show them what it is to be a human who makes mistakes, who sometimes misunderstands, and who sometimes misjudges the effects of their actions. A parent's mistakes allow a teen to see that the life ahead requires resilience—capacities to pick oneself up after falling down, to repair a damaged relationship, and to correct a mistaken view.

A teen's pain in the wake of a parent's divorce should be acknowledged. At the same time, parents should leave space for a teen to articulate their feelings. One approach could be, "I know this is hard for you. But I don't know what you feel. It would help to know what's the hardest part. Maybe we can brainstorm to find ways to make things just a little easier."

Some teens feel anxious about showing loyalty to both parents. They may insist on spending the exact same amount of time with each parent and obsessively measure each hour. Some find moving from one home to the other highly disruptive, burdened by keeping track of their things and their schedules. (Some parents address this by changing homes themselves, while the teens stay put.)

Bad-mouthing a former partner is very hard on the teen. Most parents try to show respect for their ex-partner, or at least try to avoid being rude about them, but they do not always succeed. When you realize you have been criticizing the teen's other parent, admit it, and explain that the criticism comes from your feelings. "I get angry and hurt sometimes. And then I can be unfair. I'm glad you love and respect your [other parent]." Then, try to do better and find good things to say about your ex.

At the same time that you explain your feelings, assure your teen that you can manage them. "I get angry/sad/scared sometimes, but it passes, and I'll get on with things." The best balance is allowing the teen to be cognizant of some of your feelings without being burdened by them.

Most parents today want to avoid gender bias, yet unconscious biases in parents are more likely to emerge during the teen years than during childhood. It is difficult to eradicate biases embedded in expectations, hopes, and fears. However, if we are willing to call them out, we have a much better chance of protecting our teens from them.

The first step is to admit that you, like all people, harbor some bias. The next step is to explain to your teen that you want to counteract your biases. You might seek their help in this. Do they think that the language you use or your behavior or the rules you set reveal bias? Do they think family chores and roles are fairly distributed, or do these reflect bias? How would they change your behavior or your language to make it more neutral? Watch films or TV shows with your teen and, together, point out stereotypes or biased assumptions about how girls will behave and how boys will behave and who will love whom.

You could collaborate with your teen or your partner to track the language you use over the course of a few weeks, as Paul, Rachel, and I did. The point is not to call anyone out or assign blame, but to be aware of how everyday speech reinforces assumptions about boy teens' behavior and achievements, versus those of girl teens. Are you using strong achievement words for your teen girl, such as "proud," "ace," "top," and "win"? Are you acknowledging your teen son's emotional side with words such as "thoughtful," "sympathetic," "considerate," "loving"?

Share stories with your teen about your own experiences of bias. In many families, experiences of bias form an important part of the core family stories. Your teen may know, for example, that their grandfather was murdered because of his race or religion, or their grandmother was not allowed to go to college, or perhaps even to finish school, because she was female. But your teen might not know about your own experiences where you were treated as "less than" by other people because of your gender, sexual orientation, religion, or race. Tell your teen how you felt and how you handled cases of bias you experienced. Then ask your teen if they have witnessed cases of injustice and bias in school or among their friends or their friends' families. Ask them how they might confront bias, whether it is directed at them or someone else. Together you could think of examples of effective responses to others' biases and to your own biases. It is helpful to signal to a teen that this is a hugely complex issue and that you, like everyone else, are still learning, too.

Beware of accepting that "boys will be boys" or that "guys behave badly." You forgo your ability to scaffold their behavior when you do. Instead, challenge any speech that demeans girls. This may be for being weak (by calling a football player who plays badly a "girl") or for being sexual (and this includes words like "slut" or "slag"). But be prepared to welcome such corrections from your teen, too. Rooting out embedded bias requires collaborative effort. Once one person in a group becomes alert to implicit bias, awareness and intolerance for bias spreads through the entire group.

Encourage both your boy teen and girl teen to express their full range of feelings. Remember how, in Chapters Four and Five discussing teen friendships, we saw how boy teens restricted intimacy in friendships because they worried they might seem weak or unmanly? If you accept your boy teen's attachment to a close friend, and show that you understand it, and welcome conversations about the importance of friends, you have a better chance of protecting him against the guy code.

If a teen talks about shifting or changing gender identity or sexual orientation, a parent should feel rewarded rather than alarmed. Feeling able to "come out" to a parent makes a huge difference to a teen's self-comfort. In fact, wide-ranging conversations about gender invite your teen to teach you how they see it, and whether they see you as biased.

Working alongside your teen, you can explain that understanding and counteracting biases are lifelong activities. Demonstrating your willingness to learn from teens, you not only protect them from your own bias but also strengthen the bonds between you.

11

"I'm grown up now (and it's scary)."

When Does Adolescence Really End?

People often say, "Children grow up so fast these days." What do they mean? Every previous generation has had to accept adult responsibilities at a younger age than teens today who, in many cultures, are encouraged to pursue education and training well into their twenties. So why do we so often hear that "children grow up so fast these days"?

By the age of eleven or twelve, young teens have an air of "knowing everything." They dress and act with savvy and sophistication, as though they have left childhood far behind. But while children seem to "grow up quickly" by speeding into adolescence, teens take longer and longer to leave adolescence behind.

Thirty years ago, parents saw the age of eighteen as the age of maturity. As they went to college or married or took a job, these teens crossed the threshold from teen to adult. Some parents delighted in their new freedom from parental responsibilities. Some bemoaned the loneliness of their empty nest. But any parent expecting a teen today to be independent by the age of eighteen is in for a shock. This is the legal age of adulthood in many Western countries, yet it is not the age at which, in today's world, a teen can enter the grown-up world.

Today, "leaving home" is a prolonged phase, lasting between five and ten years. More and more young people return home after they finish college to live with parents again. Any step away from the childhood home, many parents discover, is more a revolving door than an exit. Nearly 60 percent of twenty-two- to twenty-four-year-olds still live with their parents. To understand our adolescent sons and daughters, we need to understand the underlying reasons for this dramatic change.

THE "SNOWFLAKE" MYTH

Many parents worry that the slow pace to adult independence is unhealthy. These concerns are fueled by some pundits' claims that parents, by offering teens continued support and care, turn young people into "lost boys and girls hanging out on the edge of adulthood like a posse of Peter Pans."[1] "Overprotective" parents are blamed for weakening the emotional backbone of a generation that has earned the label "snowflake." Today's teens, according to this view, melt in the heat of real life.[2]

Across the globe, teens' delayed entry into the adult world attracts pejorative labels. In Japan, older adolescents still living in the family home are called "parasite singles." In Italy, a common label is *bamboccioni* or "big dummy boys"—presumably because there is a particularly low tolerance of dependence in boys. Underlying these derogatory labels is the assumption that adolescence ends before the beginning of life's third decade and that continued dependence on others is unhealthy.

This perspective contains a number of dangerous myths about what teens need to become adults. These myths are demoralizing for both teens and their parents. They ignore the challenges older teens confront in today's adulthood[3] and disregard basic facts about the teenage brain.

WHEN DOES THE TEENAGE BRAIN GROW UP?

Throughout this book I have referred to adolescents as "teens" or "teenagers" but, as I flagged in the introduction, adolescence is not strictly bound within the "teen" years of thirteen to nineteen. The age of puberty, often seen as the start of adolescence (and indicated in girls by the first menstrual cycle) was seventeen years at the middle of the nineteenth century. By the middle of the twentieth century it was thirteen years, and now, in the twenty-first century, it is twelve years. Improved diet and health play a part, as does stress.[4] Psychological, physiological, and social forces activate puberty at an age that was once considered childhood.

The changing environment that kick-starts adolescence early also presents hurdles that delay adulthood. These hurdles include prolonged education, low-paying entry jobs, and the high cost of independent living. But the social story is not the full story. Young people between the ages of eighteen and twenty-one often seem more like teens than grown-ups because, in terms of brain development, they are still adolescents.

In Chapter Two I described various ways the teenage brain is remodeled by hormones and by genes, but above all by experiences. Brain cells, or neurons, multiply rapidly, and as young people start adolescence, their brains' gray matter is a dense, bulky tangle of neurons. This excess of neurons reduces the efficiency of the brain's signaling systems but offers huge opportunity. Rich with possibilities, the brain mass can be shaped in any number of ways, according to what that individual teen's brain does. What teens focus on, what interests they pursue, and what fills them with passion determine how the brain is modeled and remodeled. As teens talk to their friends, quarrel and converse with their parents, play hockey, listen to music, read, do homework, play chess, or program a computer, some neural connections are formed and strengthened while others, unused, are pared away.

By the time a teen reaches the age of eighteen, the mass of neurons has undergone substantial pruning. But the neural networks for impulse and emotion control are not yet at full adult strength. It will be six years—at about the age of twenty-four—before the eighteen-year-old teen's brain functions as an adult brain.

Teens know in their hearts that their heads are not quite ready to function well without a parent's support. Because of unrealistic expectations—that by the end of the teen years, they should be fully grown—teens worry that there is something wrong with them for being less than grown up. Parents, too, see that their twenty-one-year-old is still really a teen, and confront a familiar package of parental guilt ("What did I do wrong?") and anxiety ("Is something wrong with my son or daughter?").

When we need to understand something, it is often helpful to give it a name. A word can normalize what might otherwise seem problematic or unhealthy. I use the word "thresholder" to mark the phase during which teens stand on the doorway to adulthood but are not yet ready to step across.[5] Thresholders are in the later stages of adolescence and still engaged in the hard work of "inventing themselves."[6]

This period of continued brain refinement offers crucial positive features. Thresholders enjoy a heightened sensitivity to new people and new places and new ideas. Each new person they meet, each new task they face, each skill they practice, each lecture they attend, each paper they write or project they complete provides opportunities for discovery, sometimes exciting, sometimes scary. Their still-adolescent brains absorb new information, explore new meaning in familiar words, and invest importance in everything they learn. This hardworking brain that continues to shape them still benefits from parents' attentive understanding.

BACKSLIDING IN LATE ADOLESCENCE

Many parents say that the heated irritability, endless criticisms, restlessness, and risk taking subside by the age of seventeen or eighteen but then recur as the teen prepares to leave home. Joshri, mother of eighteen-year-old Nema, says, "Her last summer at home [before going to college] was a joy. She was cheerful with that summer job, even though I worried it would bore her silly. She came home after work and, you know, was a real person in the house. She helped me prepare dinner. She'd even eat with us and talk to us. My word, it was like all the teenage hustle and bustle just went out the door. This week she's off to college. But what a week! I do everything wrong, she tells me. She's more like fourteen than almost nineteen."

Eighteen months before, when Nema was seventeen, I found her easy to talk to. She reflected on "the awful stuff that used to go on between me and Mom," as though it were a closed chapter. "Mom gets that I'm a whole different person now. She knows she can't second-guess me, and asks real questions about what I think, and was really okay with me making decisions about college and stuff. We're in a totally different place than [we were] a few years back." But today, as I knock on her bedroom door, she utters what sounds like an unwelcoming "What?" I wait until she opens the door herself. She manages a social smile, but her face is still flushed with anger, like a petulant kid. "I'm sorry," she begins, and then bursts into tears. "Oh, I hate crying like this," she says.

After a few sharp intakes of breath, her tears ease and we are able to talk. "Mom's so excited about this thing, you know, going to college. I mean, I'm excited too, but it's also a lot . . . Yeah, well, I can't wait to leave . . . But it's still a lot. You know, a lot to take on."

As leave-taking approaches, she realizes that life on her own is "a lot to take." She wonders what will it be like, living apart from her family? The "regressive" behavior reveals Nema's anxiety about leave-taking, along with her belief that it is wrong to feel as she does. She does not want to need her parents, but the prospect of life without them is daunting. As with younger teens, her ambivalence is expressed through moodiness and irritability. With her still-teenage brain, ambivalence—along with anxiety—is hard to manage. And so the teenage eye-roll returns, as do the "porcupine coat" and "teenage lip thrust" signaling, "*Leave me alone but don't leave me.*"

Teens seem to regress at the point of leave-taking because they know they are unprepared for adulthood. They value self-sufficiency and independence and autonomy, but for today's young people, these goals hover in the distance. Setting up an independent home, for example, was once attainable for employed young people, even in their early twenties. The financial independence of the kind many teens' grandparents and parents achieved by this age is not within the grasp of most young people today—not until they are in their thirties. Their first good job will not be a lifetime job, but one of many they will hold between the age of twenty and thirty. When they leave their family home, fewer formal or informal support networks are at hand to support them. Religious groups, social clubs, unions, close-knit neighborhoods with a stable group of relatives and friends (outside social media) are, for many teens, far less prevalent than they were in their grandparents' generation.[7]

While parents often say teens and young adults have a much easier life, with fabulous opportunities, most teens face far more competition than their parents did for every student place, every job, every home. As teens ask themselves "Am I on track?" and "Am I where I should be at this age?" they compare themselves against a global field of talent. Compared to idealized snapshots they see on social media, their own achievements seem small. The heightened ambition many teens now have, along with the general expectation that life and work should be enjoyable and satisfying is encouraged by parents but difficult to secure.

Maturity during this stage is patchy. For some older teens, the management of day-to-day living eludes them. Some will be adept at handling their bank account but hopeless at making a necessary appointment for a dentist. Some will be savvy in writing an application for a course or a job but will forget to submit that well-polished application on time. Some will set up a job interview but be at a loss when it comes to planning travel to the interview. Some can regulate the pain of a romantic breakup, but not a bad grade on a test or a quarrel with a friend.

Parents can feel let down, even betrayed by an older teen's very patchy maturity. "You're nearly twenty. You should be able to manage these things," they insist. Sometimes parents despair of their teen's organizational skills, but thresholders who fail to make a dentist appointment or submit a job application on time are not "totally disorganized" or "hopelessly irresponsible." They simply find some specific things too confusing or anxiety-provoking to manage.

Until they reach the age of twenty-four, young people occasionally require a parental scaffold. Scaffolding begins with focus on the specific problem or deficit. Parents can then suggest how the issue might be solved and be on hand to give feedback as a thresholder works on the solution. It is feedback, specific and forward-looking, that is needed, rather than a "tough love" approach, with its message, "You're now completely on your own." While thresholders may seem more robust than younger teens, they remain highly sensitive to their parents' good opinion. They wish, even more than their parents, that they did not need support—but need it they do.

RETURN OF THE FRAGILE LOOKING-GLASS

Teens, we have seen, inhabit a looking-glass self, anxious about how others see them and puzzled about how they themselves want to be seen. Their days are punctuated with questions such as "Who am I?" and "What's happening to my body?" and "Should I be proud, or ashamed?"

Older teens are more relaxed, more comfortable in their bodies and their minds. They have put together a sense of who they are, which friends suit them, and what interests and goals they want to pursue. But as they move from home to college or a grown-up job, the looking-glass self returns. "How will I measure up in the wide, wide world outside familiar family bounds?" they wonder. "Will I be able to learn what I need to know?" and "Will I find friends to protect and comfort me?" they worry.

Deeper still are the questions: "Who am I among these new people? Where do I fit in? How do I compare?" The cruel self-consciousness that afflicted them at fourteen reemerges with vengeance in the first weeks and months of college. Suddenly teens are being seen and assessed by an entirely new group of people. They lose the familiar gauge for who might be an approving friend and who might freeze them out. But social learning is only one of their many new challenges.

Teens who learn easily and quickly in high school often find college difficult. They need more time to absorb what they are taught and more time to reflect on their experiences. Some think mistakenly that in being slower they are being "stupid," but this change of pace is a result of deeper learning—both in terms of what they are taught in college as opposed to high school, and also what they are learning about themselves. In this phase of slower, deeper development, some thresholders see their former confidence as a sign that they were duped, or were duping others as to their abilities. They conclude that if they seem smart to others, then they are putting on a false show. They then worry that at any moment their deficiencies will be exposed.

The fear that your abilities are subpar, that any apparent success is a mirage, and that at any moment you will be exposed as a fraud is known as *impostor syndrome*. This syndrome is not confined to adolescents. In a new job, with new demands and high expectations, even generally confident adults can feel anxious about their capabilities, and fear that they were appointed because others were fooled into believing in them. But grown-ups are better equipped to conduct a reality check, to work to their strengths and, in the meantime, up-skill their deficits.[8] During the threshold years, when the adolescent brain places enormous weight on how they are seen and what others think of them, and when their abilities are being tested in brand-new environments, teens are especially vulnerable to impostor syndrome and not always equipped to give it a reality check.

Teens have high expectations of their newly emerging self, the one that they aspire to but have not yet realized. They want to be more interesting, have more fun, and contribute more to society than their parents. They are eager to thrive and shine. In a new setting, with new challenges and new people, an empty space opens between their great expectations and where they are now. This is a chasm in which self-doubt is magnified.

The match or mismatch between self-expectation and reality is key to self-esteem. When what we expect of ourselves and what (we think) we have achieved are in alignment, then we are generally comfortable with ourselves. When we fall short of what we expect of ourselves, then our self-esteem is low. Young people, living at home, are surrounded by microsignals of love and support. There may be storms caused by teen behavior, cross and cold looks, angry postures, but within a family there is also a myriad of messages that signal, "You are lovable and important." The automatic smile that brightens a parent's face at the first morning sighting of a son or daughter, the welcome given when the teen returns home, the pleasure on hearing about ordinary successes of an ordinary day, whether that is getting to an appointment on time, finding some lost keys, or doing well on a school exam all convey, "You matter and you're lovable."

This support fades into the background, barely noticed—until it is no longer there. Its absence removes the protective layering, a second skin, between the thresholder and an apparently indifferent and competitive world. The clever things they say no longer get an appreciative laugh among their friends or a glow of recognition from a teacher. "I'm not the smart and funny person my family thinks I am. I am a fraud, just pretending I belong here," some teens conclude.

High-achieving thresholders are at particular risk of impostor syndrome. This might seem counterintuitive. After all, why should high-achieving teens worry more about being found out? It all has to do with expectations—what you think you should be and what you think you are. At eighteen, Christa has a stellar high school record. She is used to being among the smartest in her class. She has been told that she can "do anything" or "be anything" as long as she believes in herself. But as she navigates her freshman year in college, her self-belief evaporates.

She tells her parents that she is dazed by "how smart all the other guys here are. They talk in ways that would never occur to me. I mean, they're really deep thinkers." Christa's father says, "You're as smart as anyone," but she replies, "That just proves what a great big fraud I am, parading as someone who's such hot stuff."

Her father wants to raise his daughter's spirits, but instead she feels overwhelmed. "Please," she begs, "stop telling me how great I am. I feel I'm lying just by being here, pretending that I belong here."[9] Christa mistakes the normal challenge of college courses for a sign that she is "not as smart as everyone thought." She remains confused by the mantra, "You can be anything." At the same time, she explains, roughly and awkwardly, to her father, how his high expectations play a part in her self-doubt.

Christa's confusion arises partly from the good things we teach our teens—that they matter to us, that they have great potential, that in some sense they are always a "star." It arises from the misguided efforts of parents to offer constant praise and protect teens from experiences of failure. As we saw in the previous chapter, praise does not always boost morale. Praise for fixed qualities, such as "being smart" or "intelligent," often suggests "You learn quickly" or "You get things right away" or "You'll always do well." What happens then when learning is not easy?

Christa believes she is not "really smart at all" because—so she believes—a smart person would not struggle. Exposed as someone who does not effortlessly shine, she feels exposed as being "not smart, but lousy." Her plea to her father, "Stop telling me how great I am," presents an opportunity for him to grasp his own misunderstanding and ask the all-important question, "What worries you? What am I missing here? Help me out, so I can understand."

If Christa's parents understood that she felt discouraged, puzzled, anxious, and even ashamed of her academic struggle, they could help her decatastrophize her response ("I'm brain deficient, and won't get anywhere"). If Christa's father saw that his daughter felt more pressure than pride in being told she is inherently "smart," he could boost her morale with the assurance that she is capable of learning and growing. (See Chapter Ten for a discussion about counterproductive forms of praise.) But her father closes the conversation, using praise to silence her when she says, "I feel like a fake." Instead of offering comfort, he unwittingly indicates that self-doubt is not acceptable.

It is often said that impostor syndrome affects girls and young women more than boys and men. But among the older teens who participated in my research, I did not find any difference in this respect between teen boys and teen girls. There were, however, differences in the ways boy teens and girl teens dealt with impostor syndrome. While girls are more likely to believe that other people's confidence is genuine and well-deserved, Nick, nineteen, believes everyone presents a façade. "These other guys, I know they're pretending too. You can sort of feel them squirming inwardly when they speak out in a class. Like they're putting on the show and hoping for the best. They're expecting applause for their show-off talk, and don't even see how lame they are." Nick struggles with his own sense that he is "being unreal" and "pretending to be someone I'm not." Like Holden Caulfield, he concludes, "Everyone is phony."

Parents are quick to applaud and encourage their teen's confidence, but as we learn more about teens' experience, we see the importance of picking up signals of deep self-doubt. When teens flag their struggles with impostor syndrome, parents need to attend to the meanings behind "I feel like a fake" or "everything's phony" or "I'm not what you guys at home think I am." Instead of insisting, "That's not true" or "That's nonsense" or "Stop doubting yourself," we can take the opportunity to acknowledge the self-doubting thresholder.

Then we can help broaden the perspective by asking, "Help me understand what it is you doubt." Sometimes simply speaking aloud the doubt ("I'm having trouble in this course" or "I'm not as quick as I'm supposed to be") reduces its magnitude. Sometimes the discovery, "I can't be *anything*. There are limits to what I can do," opens deeper questions such as "What do you want to be? What do you value? Let's think of ways you can get there—because there are lots of different routes to what you want to be."

Thresholders, as we have seen, still need a parent to scaffold the path to adulthood, and parents can do this by suggesting, "Let's look at different ways of gaining skills you don't yet have." Whether or not you and your teen find a solution, you can reassure her that you are still "there"—curious, engaged, and ready to flex your views to her realities.

NEW CHALLENGES TO MANAGING EMOTIONS

Whatever our age, the presence of others helps us manage our emotions. Our breathing synchronizes with others' breathing, as do our posture, gestures, and even our heartbeat. Through the many ways emotions affect how our bodies function, we share feelings with others, and other people help us manage our feelings. Teens, as they leave home, lose the emotional thermostat families and close friends provide. They struggle anew with emotional spikes and troughs.

At the beginning of the summer, Peggy told me she wanted to "be free" from having to "tell Mom where I'm going and when I'll be back." She looked forward to "not worrying that they're worrying about me, what they call 'stewing,' and then giving me all this flak when I come home because when they stew, they blame me." She mimics her mother, " 'You got me so worried. I couldn't sleep,' you know, that sort of thing." But she discovers "freedom" is "like I'm walking in a vacuum." The parents and brother and long-term friends that boosted her oxygen supply are gone. In their absence, she is drained of mental energy and confidence. Anxiety and self-doubt tax her brain and reduce her ability to learn.

Peggy explains, "College is supposed to be challenging, but I don't feel challenged. I feel totally lost. . . . I sit reading a chapter for one hour, and for the life of me I couldn't tell you a minute later what I read. . . . My mind's emptier than anyone else's. . . . I don't think I'm stupid, but my head's empty."[10]

Peggy fills her emptiness by eating. She admits to gaining "about fifteen pounds" and she wears "these baggy clothes because nothing else fits. But they're really comforting." She pulls at her overlarge fleece. The sleeves hang below her wrists, but from time to time I see the raw skin around her unkempt nails. Her red-brown hair, which was long when she left for college, is now short and unevenly cut. "I chopped it off. I did it myself. I didn't feel real. It didn't seem I was really doing it. Not that it matters."

Eating, associated as it is with love and care and indulgence, provides comfort. But it is also a reminder to Peggy that no one is there for her, watching her diet. No one is there for her to help with self-control. She eats to gain comfort, yet in overeating she sees proof that no one cares enough to stop her.

The mix of unhappiness and anxiety absorbs her mental energies. She is no longer curious, no longer able to absorb new information. Meeting new people—something she was so looking forward to—turns out to be terrifying. Peggy becomes increasingly withdrawn over the course of her first year. She fails her end-of-year exams.

Peggy's mother, Ruth, "can't for the life of me understand what happened." She blames the teaching, both at college and in high school. She blames the lack of support offered by the college. And sometimes she blames Peggy for being "still too much like a little girl, when she should be ready to stand on her own two feet." Her stepfather says, "Ten months ago we thought we were saying goodbye to our girl. We thought she'd flown the nest. Now Ruth is up with her more times in the night than when she was a baby, just holding her, trying to keep her together."

Such setbacks are common. Thresholders—young adults aged between eighteen and twenty-four—have the highest prevalence (at nearly 30 percent) of mental illness.[11] Thirty-five percent of college freshman struggle with some level of depression or anxiety.[12] The mismatch of expectations that outstrip their realities leave both thresholders and parents unprepared for the slow transition to adulthood. As a result, parents miss opportunities to provide necessary support.[13]

Without a parent's continued engagement, the thresholder's transition to adulthood is more difficult than it need be. Without parents' support, teens' confidence can ebb, along with their ambitions and their goals. A five-year study that tracked six hundred young people between the ages of eighteen and twenty-four found that 28 percent of thresholders downsize their career plans; discouraged and disheartened, 50 percent do not believe they will ever achieve their aims.[14] More than one in three of the young people in the study judged their abilities to be significantly lower at twenty-one years than at the age of seventeen.

The thresholders who did thrive had one simple explanation: they described their parents as "being there" for them.[15] "Being there" includes comfort and advice and support, but above all, it means "knowing they'll listen," "being patient," "not lecturing or judging me, but helping me think things through."

This is not an easy task for parents. Thresholders do not always express their need for love in the most positive way. Peggy insists on answering the question, "How are you?" with an abrupt, "Fine." She tells me, "There's no point in saying more. I feel so messed up now. It's all on me. What can they do anyway?" The long phone calls to home that she made during her first months in college soon dry up. "I tell them stuff, and I wait for them to see what I'm really saying, but there's just this bland, 'Sounds great!' when that's not what I'm saying at all. Don't they really know me, after all this time?"

Peggy has tried to communicate her thoughts, but her parents do not hear her. "I tell them it's really hard here, and they say, 'Sounds like you're doing great.' What kind of deafness is that?" The parental "deafness" results from hope and high expectations that do not match thresholders' realities. New demands, new anxieties, new uncertainties engulf the nineteen-year-old who seemed so confident at seventeen. Even at twenty Peggy is still a teen, daunted by the adulthood that is rushing towards her. She is still dependent on a parent's responsive focus that helps organize her own mind.

Understanding our teen during the threshold years comes up against many expectations about who young people are and what they should be. The self-control a thresholder has learned by this point is sometimes just enough to hide her need, her fear, and her anxiety but not reduce them. And for parents to respond appropriately, they need to fine-tune their antennae. Checking in with a teen is not a simple process of hearing their voice or getting the headline news of the day, but exercising warm, respectful curiosity and a willingness to correct misunderstandings.

"It sounds to me like things are going well. Is that what it's like for you?" is one possible signal of willingness to listen. Or "It sounds as though you might be feeling a little low. Is that right? Can you fill me in?"

Sometimes it is only after a conversation ends that a parent reflects on a tone of voice or hesitation she didn't pick up on at the time. A parent can loop back to this next time they talk. "Can you let us know how you're dealing with the hard stuff?" is another possible opening that indicates it is safe for the teen to be having problems.

Remember, misunderstandings offer opportunities to show the teen you want to understand. You might say, "I sometimes miss the boat when it comes to how you're feeling. So I want to check in with you. I know you are able to deal with a lot yourself. But I don't want to miss things. It's easy to miss things when you're growing up so fast, and you're not at home."

Like any approach, this might not be right for this teen at this time. Interpreting a teen often requires trial and error. Getting our teen wrong, sometimes, and then understanding how we have misunderstood, is part of the positive process whereby an adolescent shapes and refines a parent's way of seeing.

The challenges of crossing the threshold from adolescence to adulthood are not new. But this transition is now increasingly unpredictable and unsupported. Teens' futures appear before them as a maze rather than a path, and those who navigate this transition well do so with parents' continued engagement.

CONCLUSION

MANY THEORIES of parenting suggest that *childhood* attachment is the magic key to successful outcomes. The familiar message is that as long as a parent "holds the baby in mind" and is attuned to the child, the child's future is in good hands. In this book I have argued that childhood is only one phase during which young people grow their brains, minds, and emotions with the help of attuned, curious, and engaged parents.

As the adolescent brain presents new challenges to both teen and parent, there are opportunities for a deeper attachment. The early basic learning, when children come to understand themselves and others as thinking, believing, wishing, and desiring beings, is the beginning of a prolonged process that continues throughout the teen years.

Teens need parents' continued mirroring, not to tell them who they are nor to instruct them on who they should be. They seek the parent as collaborator in organizing their minds and emotions. Though not always a positive contributor themselves, teens demonstrate their need, their appreciation, and their willingness to offer their parents direction, as long as parents show a willingness to interpret the signals. These signals include "identity reminders" alerting parents who cease to track their changing interests, beliefs, emotions, goals. They included frequent criticisms about what a parent says or does. These criticisms are efforts to correct the parent in the hope that, this time, they'll get the response they need.

Teens have high expectations of a parent's attunement. They want a parent to resonate with their inner life. These high expectations are based on past experiences, such as the warm curiosity the parent displayed during infancy and childhood. But as teens, they know far more about themselves, and what they feel and think, than they did in childhood. They now want to take the lead. They pester a parent to "get" them, and to correct any misunderstandings that arise within their relationship. At the same time, they want a parent to show respect by giving them some space and privacy, as they work out what identity they are trying to achieve.

The new complexity of teens' needs can make things difficult for parents. Commonplace problems can escalate, and sometimes a teen's mental life reveals unexpected frailties. Even in times of apparent chaos, however, teens' capacity to mend and grow should never be underestimated. This is an age of enormous potential, with teens' brains eager to learn and to explore, to think creatively, and to make a positive impact on the world. Throughout this long phase, adolescents—from teen to thresholder—want parents' guidance sometimes, their support sometimes, and their appreciative understanding always. This tricky balance between connection and independence, engagement and privacy will not be maintained in every exchange, but it will function well enough as long as parents are able to interpret their teen as positively and warmly as they interpreted their child.

ACKNOWLEDGMENTS

THIS BOOK ABOUT teens and parents could only be written with the contributions of people willing to reveal their love, confusion, and frustration with one another. Many participating parents began their collaboration in this research when they themselves were teens, but all participants became committed partners in the studies on which this book is based. My enormous debt to them should be a matter of public record.

The Leverhulme Trust supported my research on teens' engagement with social media. Edwina Dunn, Founder and CEO of The Female Lead, championed my proposal to trial an intervention to improve teens' social media health and provided the infrastructure to make it possible. The Female Lead team was a joy to work with, and very special thanks go to Veryan Dexter, research strategist, and Becky Small for their input, organization, and analysis. Newnham College, with its generous research support for Senior Members, provided essential personal and financial support that covered travel to the World Economic Forum in Davos as well as to the homes and schools of many teens and families participating in my research.

Conversations with Carol Gilligan provided inspiration and supportive excitement about this project. Ruthellen Josselson has over the years offered guidance, depth, and nuance to qualitative methodologies, and the work on girls' friendships I was fortunate to do alongside her remains a rich data source. Melissa Hines, Michelle Spring, and Maria Tippett offered encouragement and a useful sounding board. Julia Newbery, pediatric psychologist at St George's Hospital in London, talked me through the complex issues of medically unexplained symptoms in young people. The clinical conversations hosted by PESI UK provided access to experts in child and adolescent development, family dynamics, and the crises young people confront today. The Zangwill Club Lecture series at Cambridge, with its openness and breadth, provided opportunities to keep up to date with the rapidly changing field of adolescent neurobiology.

Throughout many years I have had the good fortune to be published by W.W. Norton, with Jill Bialosky as my editor. Her enduring engagement with my work has been of enormous value. For *The Teen Interpreter* I had the advantage of additional input from Drew Weitman, whose enthusiasm and guidance and attention to detail played a crucial part in shaping this book.

NOTES

Introduction

1. This exchange is also discussed in Terri Apter (2004), chapter 6, Portraits of mother/daughter meltdown, in *You don't really know me*, New York: W. W. Norton, pp. 128–129.
2. S. J. Crowley et al. (2015), Increased sensitivity of the circadian system to light in early/mid-puberty, *Journal of Clinical Endocrinology & Metabolism*, *100*(11), pp. 4067–4073; M. H. Hagenauer et al. (2009), Adolescent changes in the homeostatic and circadian regulation of sleep, *Developmental Neuroscience*, *31*(4), pp. 276–284.
3. Anna Freud (1958), Adolescence, in *The psychoanalytic study of the child*, *13*(1), pp. 255–278.
4. I use the term "Copernican revolution" in the broad sense of the revolution that largely began with Nicolaus Copernicus. While the revolutionary Copernican model began with the shift from earth to a sun-centered movement, the discovery that the orbits were ellipses, not circles, took place a hundred years later, and it was Newton who then explained how the ellipses are effects of gravity.

Chapter 1

1. Leah Somerville (2013), Sensitivity to social evaluation, *Current Directions in Psychological Science*, *22*(2), pp. 121–127.

2. The concept of looking-glass self was developed in 1902 by Charles Horton Cooley, who argued that a sense of self grows from others' perception of us. It is also used by Sarah-Jayne Blakemore in *Inventing ourselves* to elaborate distinctive teen experiences of their social worlds. See Blakemore (2018). S-J. Blakemore (2008), The social brain in adolescence, *Nature Reviews, 9,* pp. 267–77.
3. David Elkind coined this term in his writings on teens. See D. Elkind & R. Bowen (1979), Imaginary audience behavior in children and adolescents, *Developmental Psychology, 15(*1), pp. 38–44.
4. Carson McCullers (1962), *The member of the wedding*. London: Penguin, p. 16.
5. Niobe Way (2011). *Deep secrets: boys' friendships and the crisis of connection*, Cambridge, MA: Harvard.
6. UMass (2009, November 30), Still face experiment: Dr. Edward Tronick [video], retrieved from See also E. Tronick, Why is connection with others so critical? The formation of dyadic states of consciousness and the expansion of individuals' states of consciousness: Coherence governed selection and the co-creation of meaning out of messy meaning making, in J. Nadel and D. Muir (Eds.), *Emotional development: Recent research advances*, Oxford: Oxford University Press, pp. 293–315.
7. Peter Fonagy (2019, February 8), New understanding of the development of mental health disorders, presented at the Developing Minds Conference, London.
8. See Trudi Rossouw (2019, November 8), Self harm in young people and evidence for effective treatment, presented at the ACAMH Conference, London.
9. Peter Fonagy (2012), What is mentalization? the concept and its foundations in development, in Nick Midgley & Ioanna Vrouva (Eds.), *Minding the child: Mentalization-based interventions with children, young people and their families*, New York: Routledge; Peter Fonagy (2006, October 6), The growth of development of personality from childhood to adult years: Psychology and psychopathology, presented at the Copenhagen Seminar.
10. John Protzko & Jonathan Schooler (2019, October 16), Kids these days: Why the youth of today seem lacking, *Sciences Advances, 5*(10).
11. Lynn Schofield Clark (2014), *The parent app: Understanding families in the new age,* Oxford: Oxford University Press.

12. Erik Erikson (1950), *Childhood and society*, New York: Norton.
13. Anna Freud (1958), Adolescence, *The psychoanalytic study of the child 13*(1), pp. 255–278.
14. Sarah Jayne Blakemore (2018), *Inventing ourselves: The secret life of the teenage brain*. New York: Doubleday.

Chapter 2

1. In the 1960s and 1970s, Peter Huttenlocher studied brains of cadavers and noted that the number of synapses—the communicating and connecting junctions between brain cells—varied in different parts of the brain and across adult and adolescent brains. Christopher A. Walsh (2013), Peter Huttenlocher (1931–2013), *Nature, 502*(7470), p. 172.
2. William Shakespeare, *The winter's tale*. Act 3, scene 3.
3. N. Gogtay, J. N. Giedd, et al. (2004), Dynamic mapping of human cortical development during childhood through early adulthood, *Proceedings of the National Academy of Sciences, 101*(21), pp. 8174–8179.
4. Laurence Steinberg (2015), *Age of opportunity: Lessons from the new science of adolescence*, Boston: Houghton Mifflin.
5. Daniel J. Siegel (2014), *Brainstorm: The power and purpose of the teenage brain*, New York: Tarcher/Perigee, p. 67.
6. Adolescence as a period of brain growth and adventure seeking occurs in a range of animals. See Barbara Natterson-Horowitz & Kathryn Bowers (2020), *Wildhood: The astounding connections between human and animal adolescents*, New York: Scribner.
7. Blakemore (2018), p. 26.
8. David Elkind (1967), Egocentrism in adolescence, *Child Development, 38*(4), pp. 1025–1034.
9. K. L. Mills, I. Dumontheil, M. Speekenbrink & S-J. Blakemore (2015), Multitasking during social interactions in adolescence and early adulthood, *Royal Society Open Science, 2*(11), http://dx.doi.org/10.1098/rsos.150117.
10. Steinberg (2015), p. 37.
11. See D. W. Winnicott (1992) on the good-enough mother, *The child, the family and the outside world* (Classics in Child Development), New York: Perseus Publishing.
12. Sarah Whittle et al. (2014), Positive parenting predicts the develop-

ment of adolescent brain structure: A longitudinal study, *Developmental Cognitive Neuroscience, 8*, pp. 7–17.

13. Mary A. Carskadon (2011), Sleep in adolescents: The perfect storm, *Pediatric Clinics of North America, 58*(3), pp. 637–647.
14. Samantha Cole (2018, June 21), Study of 800 million tweets shows we get really emo late at night, Motherboard, *Vice*, https://www.vice.com/en/article/vbq8qy/study-twitter-emotions-university-of-bristol
15. Marion Forgatch & Gerald Patterson (1989), *Parents and adolescents living together*, Part 2, Family problem solving, Eugene, OR: Castalia; Laurence Steinberg (2015).

Chapter 3

1. R. Plutchik (1980), A general psychoevolutionary theory of emotion, in R. Plutchik & H. Kellerman (Eds.), *Emotion: Theory, research and experience*, Vol.1, Theories of emotion, New York: Academic Press, pp. 3–33.
2. Lisa Feldman Barrett (2017), *How emotions are made: The secret life of the brain*, Boston: Houghton Mifflin, p. 105.
3. Trudie Rossouw (2019, November 8), Self harm in young people and evidence for effective treatment, presented at the AMIH conference, Goldsmiths College, London.
4. Siegel (2014), p. 77.
5. R. Huntsinger, Linda M. Isabell, and Gerald L. Clore (2014), The affective control of thought: Malleable, not fixed. *Psychological Review,* 121 (4), pp. 600–618.
6. Barrett (2017), pp. 80–83.
7. Laura Spinney (2020, June), Body consciousness, *New Scientist 27*, pp. 29–32.
8. Juliana Menasce Horowitz & Nikki Graf (2019, Febraury 20), Most US teens see anxiety and depression as a major problem among their peers. Pew Research Center.
9. Larson Reed & Linda Asmussen (1991), Anger, worry and hurt in early adolescence: An enlarging world of negative emotions. Human Development and Family Studies, in M. E. Colten & S. Gore (Eds.), Adolescent stress, London: Taylor & Francis, pp. 21–41.
10. Reed & Asmussen (1991), pp. 21–42.

11. J. M. Spielberg, T. M. Olino, E. E. Forbes, R. E. Dahl (2014), Exciting fear in adolescence: Does pubertal development alter threat processing? *Developmental Cognitive Neuroscience*, *8*, pp. 86–95.
12. Claudia Gold (2017), *The developmental science of early childhood: clinical application of infant mental health from infancy through adolescence*, New York: W. W. Norton. See also Claudia Gold (2011), *Keeping your child in mind*. Boston: Da Capo Lifelong Books, pp. 5–10.
13. Claire Weekes (2015), *Self help for your nerves*, New York: Harper Collins. See also Steven Hayes et al. (2016), *Acceptance and commitment therapy: The process and practice of mindful change* (2nd ed.), New York: Guilford Press.
14. See Caroline Williams (2020, January 8), How to breathe your way to better memory and sleep, *New Scientist*, https://www.newscientist.com/article/mg24532640-600-how-to-breathe-your-way-to-better-memory-and-sleep/
15. See the useful article for teens: Karen Young (2019), Anxiety in children: A metaphor to put you in their shoes (and right beside them), Hey Sigmund, https://www.heysigmund.com/anxiety-children-metaphor-put-shoes-right-beside/
16. Siegel (2014), pp. 107–108. See also, Jared B. Tore and Matthew D. Lieberman (2018, April), Putting feelings into words: Affect labeling as implicit emotion regulation. *Emotion Review, 10*(2), pp. 116–124, and J. A. Brooks, H. Shablack et al. (2017), The role of language in the experience and perception of emotion: A neuroimaging meta-analysis, *Social Cognitive and Neuroscience*, 12 (2), pp. 169–183.
17. Weekes (2015). See also T. Apter (2020, September), Anxiety management and the paradox of trigger warnings, Domestic Intelligence, *Psychology Today*, https://www.psychologytoday.com/us/blog/domestic-intelligence/202009/anxiety-management-and-the-paradox-trigger-warnings
18. L. R. Starr, R. Hershenberg, Z. A. Shaw, Y.I Li & A. C. Santee (2020), The perils of murky emotions: Emotion differentiation moderates the prospective relationship between naturalistic stress exposure and adolescent depression, *Emotion, 20*(6), pp. 927–938.
19. Siegel (2014), p. 108.
20. M. R. Weierich et al. (2010), Novelty as a dimension in the affective brain, *Neuroimage, 49*(3), 2871–2878; Y. Moriguchi et al. (2011), Differential hemodynamic response in affective circuitry with

aging: An fMRI study of novelty, valence and arousal, *Journal of Cognitive Neuroscience, 23*(5), pp. 1027–1041.

21. S. Whittle et al. (2014), Positive parenting predicts the development of adolescent brain structure: A longitudinal study, *Developmental Cognitive Neuroscience 8*, pp. 7–17.

Chapter 4

1. For example, James S. Coleman (1961), *The adolescent society: The social life of the teenager and its impact on education*, New York: Free Press.
2. Fonagy (2019).
3. Roy Baumeister & M. R. Leary (1995), The need to belong: Desire for interpersonal attachments as fundamental human motivation, *Psychological Bulletin 117*(3), pp. 497–529.
4. Blakemore (2018), p. 38.
5. T. Apter (2001), *The myth of maturity: What teenagers need from parents to become adults*, New York: W. W. Norton.
6. Stephanie Cacioppo, John Capitano & John Cacioppo (2014, November), Toward a neurology of loneliness, *Psychological Bulletin*, *140*(6), pp. 1464–1504.
7. Brett Laursen et al. (2007), Friendship moderates perspective associations between social isolation and adjustment problems in young children, *Child Development*, *78*(4), pp. 1395–1404.
8. Sarah-Jayne Blakemore, H.E.M. den Ouden, S. Choudry & C. Frith (2007, June), Adolescent development of the *neural circuitry* for thinking about intentions, *Social Cognitive and Affective Neuroscience*, *2*(2), pp. 130–139.
9. The term used by Sarah-Jayne Blakemore in *Inventing ourselves* (2018).
10. Erik Erikson (1968), *Identity, you and crisis*, New York: W. W. Norton.
11. This was Holden Caulfield's repeated complaint in J. D. Salinger's *Catcher in the Rye*.
12. T. Apter & R. Josselson (1998), *Best friends: The pleasures and perils of girls' and women's friendships,* New York: Crown, p. 81.
13. Siegel (2014), pp. 107–108.
14. Siegel (2014), p. 57.
15. Whittle et. al. (2014), pp. 7–17.
16. A. Becht, L. Wierenga, K. Mills, R. Meuwese, A. van Duijvenvoorde, S-J. Blakemore, B. Güröglu & E. Crone (2020, December),

Beyond the average brain: Individual differences in social brain development are associated with friendship quality, *Social Cognition and Affective Neuroscience*. Corrected proof.

17. Apter & Josselson (1998), p. 95.
18. R. Dunbar, N. Duncan & A. Marriott (1997), Human conversational behavior, *Human Nature 8*(3), pp. 231–246.
19. Steinberg (2015).
20. Susan Greenfield (2015), *Mind change: How digital technologies are leaving their mark on our brains*, New York: Random House; Jean M. Twenge (2018), *iGen: Why today's super-connected kids are growing up less rebellious, more tolerant, less happy—and completely unprepared for adulthood—and what that means for the rest of us*, New York: Atria Books.
21. Bernadka Dubicka & Louise Theodosiou (2020), *Technology use and the mental health of children and young people*, London: Royal College of Psychiatrists.
22. Monica Anderson & Jingjing Jiang (2018, November 28), *Teens' social media habits and experiences*, Pew Research Center.
23. V. Rideout & M. Robb (2019), The common sense census: Media use by teens and tweens, San Francisco, CA: Common Sense Media, https://www.commonsensemedia.org/sites/default/files/uploads/research/2019-census-8-to-18-key-findings-updated.pdf
24. Pew Research Center (2018).
25. Greenfield (2015); Twenge (2018).
26. Amy Orben, Livia Tomova & Sarah-Jayne Blakemore (2020, June 12), The effects of social deprivation on adolescent development and mental health, *Lancet*, *4*(8), 634–640, https://doi.org/10.1016/S2352-4642(20)30186-3
27. I. Myklestad, E. Roysamb & K. Tamb (2012), Risk and protective factors for psychological distress among adolescents: A family study in the nord-trondelag health study, *Social Psychiatry and Psychiatric Epidemiology*, *47*(5), pp. 771–782.
28. Greenfield (2015).
29. D. Alkire, D. Levitas, K. R. Warnell & E. Redcay (2018), Social interaction recruits mentalizing and reward systems in middle childhood, *Human Brain Mapping*, *39*, pp. 3928–3942.
30. Marion Forgatch & Gerald R. Patterson (1989), *Parents and adolescents living together: Part 2, Family problem solving*, Eugene, OR: Castalia.

Chapter 5

1. T. Janssen, H. Treloar Padovano, J. E. Merrill & K. M. Jackson (2018), Developmental relations between alcohol expectancies and social norms in predicting alcohol onset, *Developmental Psychology, 54*(2), pp. 281–292.
2. B. Simons-Morton, N. Lener & J. Singer (2005, November), The observed effects of teenage passengers on the risky driving behavior of teenage drivers. *Accident Analysis & Prevention, 37*(6), pp. 973–982.
3. AAA data, cited by S-J Blakemore (2020, January 17), Zangwill Lecture.
4. Jason Chein, Dustin Albert, Lia O'Brien, Kaitlyn Uckhert & Laurence Steinberg (2011), Peers increase adolescent risk taking by enhancing activity in the brain's reward circuitry. *Developmental Science, 14*(2): pp. F1–F10.
5. Steinberg (2015).
6. Mentalizing as a teen requires the activity and coordination of four regions of the brain. The first of these (the dorsomedial prefrontal cortex) is active when we fix our attention on something and think about it. The second (the temporo-parietal junction) integrates information about the world we perceive and how we feel about it. The third (the posterior superior temporal sulcus) responds to social inputs, such as voices (as distinguished from other sounds), stories (as distinguished from a meaningless string of words), and moving faces (as distinguished from moving objects). The fourth (the anterior temporal cortex) works as a special kind of memory that stores social memories, so we can recognize common patterns of interaction.
7. E. J. Marshall (2014), Adolescents and alcohol use: Risks and consequences, *Alcohol and Alcoholism, 29*(2), pp. 160–164.
8. Girls indulge in some delinquent acts (such as vandalism and theft) to the same extent as boys; however, for so-called big crimes, such as murder, one is committed by a woman for nine committed by a man.
9. There has been considerable discussion about the relevance of adolescent neurobiology to the management of crimes committed by teens. In 2005 the Supreme Court ruled that the death penalty for children under the age of eighteen was unconstitutional because young people were not responsible for their actions in the same way as adults. In 2016 life sentences without the possibility of parole were, on the same reasoning,

ruled unconstitutional by the Supreme Court. However, in 2021 this ruling was reversed. The argument that prevailed was that states should have discretion in sentencing, and as long as judges had discretion in sentencing, no specific finding on the person's maturity or capacity to change was required. Many argue, however, that justice requires specific acknowledgment of teen brain development.

10. See T. Apter (2018), *Passing judgment: Praise and blame in everyday life*, New York: W. W. Norton, p. 115.
11. Apter & Josselson (1998).
12. Terri Apter (2019), The Female Lead Research Report, *Disrupting the feed: Teenage girls' use of social media—An intervention to improve social media health*, London: The Female Lead, https://www.thefemaleleadsociety.com/wp-content/uploads/2019/10/Research-Results-July-2019.pdf
13. Apter & Josselson (1998).
14. Dana Crowley Jack (1993), *Silencing the self: Women and depression*, New York: William Morrow.
15. William Pollack (2001), *Real boys' voices*, New York: Random House.
16. Niobe Way (2011), *Deep secrets: Boys' friendships and the crisis of connection*, Cambridge, MA: Harvard University Press.
17. Way (2011).
18. Sabina Datcu (2011, October 6), Cyber bullying, from name calling to gang harassment, affects most children, https://www.bitdefender.com/blog/hotforsecurity/cyber-bullying-from-name-calling-to-gang-harassment-affects-most-children. See also Pew Research Center (2015), Teens, technology and social media overview, Smartphones facilitate shifts in teens' communication and information landscape, https://www.pewresearch.org/internet/2015/04/09/teens-social-media-technology-2015/
19. Centers for Disease Control and Prevention (2019), High school youth risk behavior survey, www.cdc.gov/yrbs. See also Pew Research Center (2019, February 20), Most U.S. teens see anxiety and depression as a major problem among their peers, https://www.pewresearch.org/social-trends/2019/02/20/most-u-s-teens-see-anxiety-and-depression-as-a-major-problem-among-their-peers/
20. L. Gros, N. Debue, J. Lete & C. van de Leemput (2020, January 27), Video games addiction and emotional states: Possible con-

fusion between pleasure and happiness? *Frontiers in Psychology*, https://doi.org/10.3389/fp-syg.2019.02894

21. Nancy Jo Sales (2016), *American girls: Social media and the secret lives of teenagers*, New York: Alfred A. Knopf, p. 218.
22. Marian Keyes (2016, July 3), Mind your head, *Sunday Times*, Style section, p. 42.
23. Sales (2016), p. 138.
24. Lauren Sherman, et al. (2016, May 31), The power of the *Like* in adolescence: Effects of peer influence on neural and behavioral responses to social media, *Association for Psychological Science*, *27*(7), pp. 1027–1035.
25. Jeffrey A. Hall, Chong Xing, Elaina M. Ross & Rebecca M. Johnson (2019, November 5), Experimentally manipulating social media abstinence: Results of a four-week diary study, *Media Psychology*, *24*(2), pp. 259–275, https://doi.org/10.1080/15213269.2019.1688171
26. Apter (2019).
27. Apter (2019).
28. Our intervention is now being rolled out into schools across the UK. See Charlotte Edmond (2019, November), This UK scheme wants girls to fill their social media feeds with positive role models, World Economic Forum, https://www.weforum.org/agenda/2019/11/uk-girls-social-media-positive-role-models/
29. D. Murry et al. (2015), *Foundations for understanding self-regulation from an applied developmental perspective*, OPRE Report, p. 14.
30. S. Porges (2009, February), The polyvagal theory: New insights into adaptive reactions of the autonomic nervous system, *Cleveland Clinic Journal of Medicine 76*(4 suppl 2), pp. S86–S90.
31. T. S. Weisner (2014), The socialization of trust: Plural caregiving and diverse pathways in human development across cultures, *in* Hiltrud Otto & Heidi Keller (Eds.), *Different faces of attachment: Cultural variations on a universal human need*, New York: Cambridge University Press, pp. 263–277.
32. In childhood, girls and boys are equally risk avoidant and risk takers, but in early adolescence girls become more averse to risk than boys; though girls in adolescence are also greater thrill seekers than they were in childhood. James Andreoni et al. (2019, April), Risk preferences of children and adolescents in relation to gender,

cognitive skills, soft skills, and executive functions, NBER Working Paper No. 25723.

33. K. Rahman (2019, February), How risk-taking changes a teenager's brain, presented at TED Salon: US Air Force, https://www.ted.com/talks/kashfia_rahman_how_risk_taking_changes_a_teenager_s_brain
34. K. A. Maxwell (2002), Friends: The role of peer influence across adolescent risk behaviors, *Journal of Youth and Adolescence, 31*, pp. 267–277.
35. See for example the play by Ned Glasier, Emily Lin & Company Three (2016), *Brainstorm: The Original Playscript*, with a foreword by S-J Blakemore, London: Nick Hern Books.

Chapter 6

1. S. Wilson Shockley (1995), *Gender differences in adolescent depression: The contribution of negative affect* (Master's thesis, University of Illinois at Urbana-Champaign), cited in B. Bradford Brown, Candice Feiring & Wyndol Furman (1999), Missing the love boat: Why researchers have shied away from adolescent romance (p. 5), in Furman, Brown & Feiring (Eds.), *The development of romantic relationships in adolescence*, Cambridge, UK: Cambridge University Press.
2. See quotes from Peter Delany, Anthony Jack, and Eugenio Rothe in C. Dell'Amore (2013, July 16), Five surprising facts about daydreaming, *National Geographic*.
3. From a study by Laura Hawks et al. of 13,310 women in the US. See also Noam Shpancer (2020, March/April), Before and after, *Psychology Today*, pp. 82–85.
4. Deborah L. Tolman, Brian R. Davis, and Christin P. Bowman (2016), "That's just how it is": A gendered analysis of masculinity and femininity ideology in adolescent girls' and boys' heterosexual relationships. *Journal of Adolescent Research, 31*(1), pp. 3–31.
5. Sharon Thompson (1998), *Going all the way*, New York: Hill and Wang.
6. Thompson (1998). See also Jennifer F. Chimielewski, Christin P. Bowman, and Deborah L. Tolman (2020), Pathways to pleasure and protection: Exploring embodiment, desire and entitlement to pleasure as prediction of Black and White young women's sexual agency, *Psychology of Women Quarterly, 44*(3), pp. 307–322.

7. There are some hopeful signs that new approaches to reduce sexual entitlement in boys is having some effect. Reports of coercive sex in teens have declined from 2012 to 2017. However, evidence for teens' real experience requires very careful investigation and interpretation.
8. Tolman et al. (2020).
9. These guidelines are adapted from a piece I wrote for *O, The Oprah Magazine*, Terri Apter (2009, May), How to talk to your daughter about sex, https://www.oprah.com/relationships/how-to-talk-to-teen-girls-about-sex-dr-terri-apters-advice/all
10. J. Dunn & R. Layard (2009), *The good childhood report: Searching for values in competitive age*, London: The Children's Society.

Chapter 7

1. R. F. McGivern, J. Andersen, D. Byrd, K. L. Mutter & J. Reilly (2002), Cognitive efficiency on a match to sample task decreases at the onset of puberty in children, *Brain and Cognition*, *50*(1), pp. 73–89.
2. Blakemore (2018), p. 131.
3. As happens in a wonderful scene between father and seven-year-old son in the 1979 film *Kramer versus Kramer*.
4. I first presented this case in T. Apter (1990), *Altered loves: Mothers and daughters during adolescence*, New York: St. Martin's Press, pp. 141–144.
5. Shakespeare, *The winter's tale*.
6. See Siegel (2014).
7. Apter (1990), p. 80; Apter (2019).
8. Nassim Taleb (2014), *Antifragile: Things that gain from disorder*, New York: Random House.
9. A. Wolf & Suzanne Franks (2014), *Get out of my life: The bestselling guide to the 21st century teenager*, London: Profile Books.

Chapter 8

1. Laurence Steinberg explains, "It's as if memorizing the capitals of European countries . . . also made it easier to . . . remember the multiplication tables," Steinberg (2015), pp. 161–162.
2. This effect is referred to as metaplasticity because exercising the

adolescent's neural plasticity increases the plasticity of the adult brain. Steinberg (2015), p. 35.

3. This does not mean that 75 percent of teens have mental health problems. Seventy-five percent of those who have mental health problems as adults experienced the onset of those issues in the teen years.
4. C. Schmahl (2019, November 8), Neurobiology of self-harm in borderline personality disorder, ACAMH Conference, London. For an overview of the neurobiology of self-harm see also Paul L. Plener, Michael Kaess, Christian Schmahl, Stefan Pollak, Jörg M. Fegert & Rebecca C. Brown (2018, January), Nonsuicidal self-injury in adolescents, *Deutsches Ärzteblatt International*, *115*(3), pp. 23–30.
5. Forty to fifty percent of people who die as a result of suicide have a prior history of self-harm. K. Hawton, S. Hall, S. Simkin, E. Bale, A. Bond, S. Codd & A. Stewart (2003), Deliberate self-harm in adolescence: A study of characteristics and trends in Oxford, 1990–2000, *Journal of Child Psychology and Psychiatry and Allied Disciplines*, *44*, pp. 1191–1198.
6. C. Schmahl (2019, November 8), Neurobiology of self-harm in borderline personality disorder, ACAMH Conference, London. For an overview of the neurobiology of self-harm, see also T. Apter (2020, March–April), The pain paradox, *Psychology Today*, pp. 50–52.
7. T. Rossouw (2002), Self-harm in young people: Is MBT the answer?, in P. Fonagy, G. Gergely, E. Jurist & M. Target (Eds.), *Minding the child: Mentalization-based interventions with children, young people and teens*, New York: Other Press, pp. 131–144. See also P. Fonagy, G. Gergely, E. Jurist & M. Target (2002), *Affect regulation, mentalization and the development of the self*, New York: Other Press.
8. Rossouw (2002), pp. 134–135.
9. Schmahl (2019).
10. Fonagy, Gergely, Jurist & Target (2002).
11. Pew Research Center (2019, February 20), Most U.S. teens see anxiety and depression as a major problem among their peers, https://www.pewresearch.org/social-trends/2019/02/20/most-u-s-teens-see-anxiety-and-depression-as-a-major-problem-among-their-peers/
12. Angus Crawford (2019, January 22), Instagram 'helped kill my daughter,' BBC News, https://www.bbc.com/news/av/uk-46966009

13. R. Baumeister, E. Bratslasky & C. Finkenhaur (2001), Bad is stronger than good, *Review of General Psychology, 5*(4), pp. 323–370.
14. Twenge (2018).
15. Parliamentary Report: The best quality research is by Andrew Przysbylski & Netta Weinstein (2017), Large scale test of the goldilocks hypothesis: quantifying the relations between digital screen use and the mental well-being of adolescents, *Psychological Science, 28*, pp. 204–215.
16. Dennis Ougrin, Troy Hannah, Eleanor Leigh, Lucy Taylor & Joan Rosenbaum Asarnow (2012), Practioner review: Self-harm in adolescents, *Journal of Child Psychology and Psychiatry*, *53*(4), 337–350.
17. There is a new approach that replaces risk assessments with assessing implicit associations between self and death. Brian O'Shea, Jeffrey Glenn, Alexander Milner, Bethany Teachman & Matthew Nock (2020, July 20), Decomposing implicit associations about life and death improves our understanding of suicidal behavior, *Suicide and Life-Threatening Behavior, 50*(5), pp. 1065–1074.
18. Fonagy (2019).
19. The difference involves the length of alleles in the serotonin transporter gene (the 5-HTT gene). People with at least one short 5-HTT gene are more prone to depressive illness. This is thought to be related to the different-length genes' different receptivity, or take up, of serotonin. T. E. Moffitt (2003), Life-course-persistent and adolescence-limited antisocial behavior: A 10-year research review and a research agenda, in B. B. Lahey, T. E. Moffitt & A. Caspi (Eds.), *Causes of conduct disorder and juvenile delinquency*, New York: Guilford Press, pp. 49–75.
20. Moffitt (2003).
21. Michael Pluess, Elham Assary, Francesca Lionetti, Kathryn Lester, Eva Krapohl, Elaine N Aron & Arthur Aron (2018), Environmental sensitivity in children: Development of the highly sensitive child scale and identification of sensitivity groups, *Developmental Psychology, 54*(1), pp. 51–70.
22. Stuart Hauser, Joseph Allen & Eve Golden (2006), *Out of the woods: Tales of resilient teens*, Cambridge, MA: Harvard University Press.
23. Hauser, Allen & Golden (2006), pp. 120–160.
24. Hauser, Allen & Golden (2006), pp. 76–115.
25. Peter Fonagy & E. Allison (2014), The role of mentalizing and

epistemic trust in the therapeutic relationship, *Psychotherapy, 51*(3), pp. 372–380.

26. J. Fritz, J. Stochl, E. I. Fried et al. (2019), Unraveling the complex nature of resilience factors and their changes between early and later adolescence, *BMC Med, 17*, p. 203.
27. Fonagy & Allison (2014).
28. For cases where a teen gives up on the need to see a positive and responsive reflection in the parent, see T. Apter (2012), *Difficult mothers: Understanding and overcoming their power*, New York: W. W. Norton.
29. Mentalization-based intervention has been found to be more effective than other psychosocial therapies in preventing recurrence of self-harm. K. Hawton, K. Witt et al. (2015, December), Interventions for self-harm in children and adolescents, *Cochrane Database Systematic Review, 12,* https://doi.org/10.1002/14651858.CD012013.

Chapter 9

1. Parts of this televised workshop were broadcast on the Channel 4 show *Jo Frost: Extreme parental guidance,* on February 23, 2010.
2. Eating Disorders, Body Image and the Media (2000, June 5), UK Parliament.
3. Rachel Hoise (2017, December 13), Missguided launches unretouched campaign to champion body positivity, *Independent*, https://www.independent.co.uk/life-style/fashion/missguided-body-positivity-unretouched-photoshop-size-imperfections-fashion-shoot-a8107216.html
4. Other disorders (such as bulimia) have a little higher, but also low, incidence—about 2 percent, and binge eating affects about 3 percent of the population.
5. Cynthia Bulik (2012), *The woman in the mirror: How to stop confusing what you look like with who you are*, New York: Walker Books.
6. Stephen Feder, Leanna Isserlin, Emily Seale, Nicole Hammond & Mark L. Norris (2017), Exploring the association between eating disorders and gender dysphoria in youth, *Eating Disorders, 25*(4), pp. 310–317.
7. Bulik (2012).
8. Theories of eating disorders are discussed in Apter (1990), pp. 43–50.

9. Roxane Gay (2018), *Hunger: a memoir of (my) body*, New York: Corsair.
10. Susie Orbach (2016, reprint), *Fat is a feminist issue*, London: Arrow.
11. Professor Janet Treasure, director of the Eating Disorders Unit at the Bethlem Royal Hospital, the South London and Maudsley NHS Foundation Trust, quoted in Charlotte Philby (2009, March 14), One milliion Britons suffer from eating disorders—so why is so little being done to help?, *Independent*, https://www.independent.co.uk/life-style/health-and-families/healthy-living/one-million-britons-suffer-from-eating-disorders-so-why-is-so-little-being-done-to-help-1642775.html
12. C. Grimes (2019, March 3), Mentalization-based family therapy with adolescents and family, *GAP Call-in Series on Youth, Early Prevention and Intervention of BPD* [podcast], NEABPD.
13. A very good place to start is with this advice from UK's NHS: https://www.nhs.uk/conditions/eating-disorders/advice-for-parents.
14. C. Nimnuan, M. Hotopf & S. Wessley (2001, July), Medically unexplained symptoms: an epidemiological study in seven specialties, *Journal of Psychosomatic Research, 51*(1), pp. 361–367.
15. This is the unfortunate and misleading title of Suzanne O'Sullivan's excellent book. Suzanne O'Sullivan (2015), *It's all in your head: Stories from the frontline of psychosomatic illness*, New York: Vintage.
16. Andrew Miller, Ebrahim Haroon, Charles Raison & Jennifer Felfer (2013), Cytokine targets in the brain: Impact on neurotransmitters and neurocircuits, *Depression and Anxiety, 30*(4), pp. 297–306.
17. Lisa Feldman Barrett (2018), *How emotions are made: The secret life of the brain*, New York: Pan Books, p. 202.
18. Barrett (2018), p. 207; Tor Wager & Lauren Atlas (2015), The neuroscience of placebo effects: Connecting context, learning and health, *Nature Reviews Neuroscience, 16*(7): pp. 403–418.
19. Barrett (2018).
20. Clare Wilson (2019, April 3), The illnesses caused by a disconnect between brain and mind, *New Scientist*, https://www.newscientist.com/article/mg24232240-100-the-illnesses-caused-by-a-disconnect-between-brain-and-mind/
21. See Richard Holton (2018), Illness and the social self, Uehiro Lectures, Oxford.

22. G. Tabibnia, M. D. Lieberman & M. G. Craske (2008), The lasting effect of words on feelings: Words may facilitate exposure effects to threatening images, *Emotion, 8*(3), pp. 307–317.
23. T. Hoyt & K. D. Renshaw (2014), Emotional disclosure and post-traumatic stress symptoms: Veteran and spouse reports, *International Journal of Stress Management, 21*(2), pp. 186–206, https://doi.org/10.1037/a0035162.
24. H. Gallivan (2014, May) Teens, social media and body image, Park Nicollet Melrose Center, https://www.macmh.org/wp-content/uploads/2014/05/18_Gallivan_Teens-social-media-body-image-presentation-H-Gallivan-Spring-2014.pdf
25. D. A. Hargreaves & M. Tiggemann (2004), Idealized media images and adolescent body image: "Comparing" boys and girls, *Body Image, 1*(4), pp. 351–361; M. Lawler & E. Nixon (2011), Body dissatisfaction among adolescent boys and girls: The effects of body mass, peer appearance culture, and internalization of appearance ideals, *Journal of Youth and Adolescence, 40*(1), pp. 59–71.
26. J. Arcelus, W. P. Bouman, w. Van Den Noortgate, L. Claes, G. Witcomb & F. Fernandez-Aranda (2015), Systematic review and meta-analysis of prevalence studies in transsexualism, *European Psychiatry, 30*(6), pp. 807–815; K. L. Zucker (2017), Epidemiology of gender dysphoria and transgender identity, *Sex Health, 14*(5), pp. 404–411.
27. National Survey of Children's Health (2018, October), Maternal and Child Health, Health Resources and Services Administration.
28. Medically Unexplained Symptoms (2015, November), London: Royal College of Psychiatrists. See also F. Creed, P. Hennisen & P. Fink, eds. (2011), *Medically unexplained symptoms, somatisation and bodily distress: Developing better clinical services,* Cambridge, UK: Cambridge University Press.
29. Claire Weekes (2015), *Self help for your nerves*, New York: HarperCollins. See also Hayes et al. (2016).

Chapter 10

1. Emla Fitzsimmons & Aase Villadsen (2019, February), Father departure and children's mental health: How does timing matter?, *Social Science & Medicine, 222*, pp. 349–358. See also A. O'Quigley (2000), *Listening to children's views: The findings and recommendations*

of recent research, Layerthorpe, York: York Publishing Services; M. J. Lawrence & S. Fife (2018), The impact of parental divorce: The relationship between social support and confident levels in young adults, *Journal of Divorce and Remarriage, 59*(2), pp. 123–140; R. Rosnati, et al. (2014), Adolescents and parental separation or divorce, *Procedia: Social and Behavioral Sciences, 140*, pp. 186–191.

2. See Lyn Mikel Brown & Carol Gilligan (1992), *Meeting at the crossroads: Women's psychology and girls' development*, Cambridge, MA: Harvard University Press.
3. For a comprehensive discussion of parental praise, see T. Apter (2007), *The confident child*, New York: W. W. Norton; T. Apter (2018), *Passing judgment: praise and blame in everyday life*, New York: W. W. Norton.
4. C. S. Dweck, C. Chiu & Y. Hong (1995), Implicit theories and their role on judgments and reasons: A world from two perspectives, *Psychological Inquiry, 6*, pp. 267–285.
5. C. S. Dweck (1999), *Self theories: Their role in motivation, personality and development*, Philadelphia: Psychology Press; C. S. Dweck (2006), *Mindset: the psychology of success*, New York: Random House.
6. C. S. Dweck (1986), Motivational processes affecting learning, *American Psychologist, 41*, pp. 1040–1048.
7. Steinberg (2015), p. 35.
8. See also R. S. Jessen & K. Roen (2019), Balancing the margins of gender, *Journal of Psychology and Sexuality, 10*(2), pp. 119–131.
9. See for example Jennifer Mascaro, Kelly Rentscher, Patrick Hackett, Matthias Mehl & James Rilling (2017), Child gender influences parental behavior, language and brain function, *Behavioral Neuroscience, 131*(3), pp. 262–273.
10. M. Gutmann (2019), *Are men animals?: How modern masculinity sells men short*, New York: Basic Books; R. Jordan-Young & K. Karkazis (2019), *Testosterone: An unauthorized biography*, Cambridge, MA: Harvard University Press.
11. S. Franklin & E. Sandler (2021), Out at Cambridge: A new report on LGBTQ+ experiences, Department of Sociology, University of Cambridge.
12. See for example Caroline Criado Perez (2019), *Invisible women: Exposing bias in a world designed for men*, London: Chatto and Windus; Gina Rippon (2019), *The gendered brain: The new neuroscience*

that shatters the myth of the female brain, London: Bodley Head; Cordelia Fine (2011), *Delusions of gender: the real science behind sex differences*, London: Icon Books.

13. Ed Tronick & Marjorie Beeghly (2011), Infants' meaning-making and the development of mental health problems, *American Psychologist, 66*(2), pp. 107–119.

Chapter 11

1. F. Furedi (2010), *Paranoid parenting: Why ignoring the experts may be best for your child*, New York: Continuum.
2. J. Haidt & G. Lukianoff (2018), *The coddling of the American mind: How good intentions and bad ideas are setting up a generation for failure*, New York: Penguin Random House. Here I address Haidt and Lukianoff's arguments about delayed adulthood. Other points made in *The coddling of the American mind* have my wholehearted agreement, particularly in regard to the damaging messages contained in the practice of trigger warnings.
3. Kim Parker & Ruth Igielnik (2020, May 14), On the cusp of adulthood and facing an uncertain future: What we know about Gen Z so far, Pew Research Center, https://www.pewresearch.org/social-trends/2020/05/14/on-the-cusp-of-adulthood-and-facing-an-uncertain-future-what-we-know-about-gen-z-so-far-2/
4. Julia Graberc, Jeannne Brooks-Gunn & Michelle Warren (1995, April), The antecedents of menarcheal age: heredity, family environment and stressful life events, *Child Development, 66*(2), pp. 346–359.
5. I first used this term in Terri Apter (2001), *The Myth of maturity: What teenagers need from parents to become adults*, New York: W. W. Norton.
6. Blakemore (2018).
7. R. Putnam (2020), *Bowling alone*, revised and updated, New York: Simon and Schuster.
8. For a discussion of adult management of impostor syndrome, see T. Apter (2021), *Women at work: Breaking free of the 'unentitled mindset.'* London: The Female Lead, https://34062f6f-6645-47e1-ada9-901d93ecf266.filesusr.com/ugd/05606b_2c06ec00b1d84c2da686cbdc4232b9cd.pdf

9. Christa is also discussed in Apter (2001), pp. 158–160.
10. Peggy was also discussed in Apter (2001), pp. 44–48.
11. National Institute of Mental Health (2021), Statistics: Mental illness, https://www.nimh.nih.gov/health/statistics/mental-illness
12. R. Auerbach, C. Benjet, J. Cuipers, K. Demyttenaere, D. Ebert et al. (2018), WHO world mental surveys international college student project: Prevalence and distribution of mental disorders, *Journal of Abnormal Psychology, 127*(7), pp. 623–638.
13. Apter (2001); Liza Catan, (1998–2003), Becoming adult: changing youth transitions in the 21st century: A synthesis of findings from the ESRC research program, Youth, Citizenship and Social Change, Trust for the Study of Adolescence.
14. Catan (1998–2003).
15. Catan (1998–2003).

INDEX

Page numbers after 258 refer to notes.